SYMBO
LANDSCAPES
The Dreamtime Earth
and Avebury's Open Secrets

SYMBOLIC LANDSCAPES

The Dreamtime Earth
and Avebury's Open Secrets

Paul Devereux

First published 1992 by
Gothic Image Publications
7 High Street, Glastonbury, Somerset BA6 9DP

Cover photograph by the author
Cover panel by Michael Foote

Text design and production by
Mentor DTP
Bruton, Somerset

A catalogue record for this book is available
from the British Library

Printed and bound in Great Britain

DEDICATION

To the memory of Aldus Huxley, who helped to open the doors of perception for my generation, and who, shortly before his death, could be bothered to correspond with me, then a mere schoolboy half the world away.

ACKNOWLEDGEMENTS

This book brings together all the many strands of research I have been engaged on during the past 20 or so years. As I have been beholden to many people for each of those strands, it is consequently hardly possible for me here to acknowledge the vast army of people who have at various times and in different contexts helped me, supported me, taught me and otherwise guided me in the component aspects that have gone into this present work of synthesis. In a single topic book, it is possible for an author to comprehensively acknowledge people, and I have done so in previous works. As I could not hope to be comprehensive in such a roll call of honour in this case, it would be invidious of me to pick out selected individuals. Rather, I extend my genuine, heartfelt gratitude to them all.

I am, of course, able to thank Frances Howard Gordon and Jamie George of Gothic Image for their faith in this specific project. Such encouragement is valued and appreciated.

Illustrations: I thank Mrs Charles Mountford for permission to use the photograph from her late husband's book, *Winbaraku and the Myth of Jarapiri*. I also thank Shirley-Ann Pager for making her late husband, Harald Pager's, drawings of San rock art available, and Professor J.D. Lewis-Williams for permission to reproduce a diagram.

LIST OF COLOUR PLATES

CONTENTS

PREFACE

This book is about worldviews. Specifically, it is about ancient worldviews, how they differed from ours, and why. This topic is taken both figuratively *and* literally - how did our ancestors *actually perceive* the landscape?

It is argued that these ancient worldviews arose out of a consciousness different to that driving our modern culture. By 'modern culture' I mean Western civilisation and its various forms, whether they occur in Europe or Australasia, in the Americas or Asia. It is the one, dominant culture now on Earth, however modified it may be by local conditions: it is the civilisation of the so-called 'New World Order'. It is that civilisation that is now inheriting the Earth - an inheritance we are, frankly, not fit to receive.

Ancient peoples are still offering us their wisdom, through their sacred sites and landscapes where they have become extinct, or through the knowledge and traditions still nurtured by their decimated descendants. This in effect amounts to a kind of transcultural, perennial manual of how to understand our minds and our planet - the two sides of the same coin, as this book argues. The wisdom is being offered, if we are prepared to pay attention. The baton is being passed on: can we take hold of it?

If we do not, then we miss our last chance, for the time of traditional and indigenous peoples is now drawing to a close. The Native Americans, the Australian Aborigines, the rain forest peoples of the tropical world - they and other similar groups are all extinct or in danger of becoming so. It is claimed, for example, that a South American Indian tribe disappears every year. It is to be hoped that wisdom and common morality prevails so that many of these traditional peoples will start being valued, respected, and their decimation halted. But even where this happens, a fundamental cultural erosion will be present. For example, when anthropologists visited the Jungle Quichua peoples of the Napo River region of eastern Ecuador in 1976, to tape-record a shamanic session (at the wishes of the shaman), they found references to aircraft and relatively recent historical events occurring in the shaman's performance. As Norman Whitten *et al* observe:

> Historically, it is false to think that the jungle peoples of Ecuador are somehow isolated from contact with western civilization. Rather, these peoples and their descendents have witnessed centuries of penetration aimed at extraction of gold,

spices and slaves, and missionary activity aimed at conversion. Over the past century the Jungle Quichua and their neighbors have experienced the severe disruptions of the Amazonian rubber boom, the growth of plantations, oil exploration, stepped-up mission activity, a Peruvian invasion during early World War II years, and a return of the petroleum exploration companies over the past two decades. Native peoples of the moist tropics of east lowland Ecuador have witnessed repeatedly and convincingly the destructive might of western civilization on the frontier territories.

[N.E. Whitten, *et al*, 'Soul Vine Shaman'; *Sacha Runa Research Foundation* Occasional Paper No.5, 1979.]

So even remote peoples who still have an active traditional life are subject to modification by Western influence. Most indigenous peoples fare even worse, as we all know. Ancient knowledge is nowhere held completely intact - it is at best fragmentary, and even revived traditions rely on the surviving information base. Even if an immediate improvement occurred in the way governments (those of Asia as well as the West) treat their indigenous peoples, a somewhat unlikely event, the situation cannot ever get better than the partial, fragmentary state we now have. Indeed, to be realistic, it can only get worse. Right now, however, there is sufficient tribal wisdom and knowledge together with what can be gleaned from sacred sites and landscapes of lost peoples, for our modern culture to correct its worldview. If we are to become fit for our inheritance, then we must hear what the former and ancient peoples of the world are telling us as they disappear from our view - as we are gradually left on our own. We must strain to hear the departing archaic whisper, for our own future ultimately depends on it.

I have attempted to write this book in a way that I trust will not too greatly offend the sensibilities of scientists and scholars on the one hand, nor, to use a catch-all term, those of 'New Agers' on the other. It has been written from a mental framework that embraces the legitimate demands for informed, intellectual accountability and the legitimate need to recognise inner reality. I stress the word *legitimate*, for in my experience people are largely divided between those who dismiss spiritual matters altogether and those who deride intellectual accountability. Both types can make illegitimate demands: the secular, rationalist scholar can insist on reductionist reason to absurd levels, while the New Ager can glory in dismissing disciplined thought - often by invoking some misbegotten notion of 'spirituality' as an excuse. Despite my many shortcomings, I do not suffer from such a 'Cartesian Split', and I have written accordingly. This book therefore addresses both polarities of modern consciousness simultaneously, and attempts to maintain a balance between them.

The subject of symbolic landscapes has made this task both possible and curiously relevant, for their study necessitates a journey from the physical world to the visionary lands of the mind - and back again. 'First there is a mountain, then there is no mountain, then there is.' Symbolic landscapes result from an intermediary state of consciousness where mind reassembles sensory (outer) data in symbolic (inner) ways. The nature of such an 'interworld' state of consciousness is the central concern of this work, and it must become, I am convinced, much more thoroughly understood by our Western-style societies if we are going to be able to fashion a worldview that will enable us to handle the inheritance to which I have referred.

The book is comprised of two essays, divided as Part One and Part Two. The first looks at several symbolic landscapes from various parts of the world, and goes on to explore certain ideas about the states of consciousness associated with such phenomena. In the process, unfamiliar aspects and implications of shamanism are highlighted, and many strands of research, some very recent and all having been somewhat diverse hitherto, are drawn together. A new context for such material is suggested, and the concept of the interworld state introduced in modern, Western terms. Part Two is more practical than theoretical, taking a specific, ancient landscape and exploring it and the process of exploring it simultaneously, in an effort to demonstrate some of the themes raised in Part One.

Paul Devereux

PART ONE

The Dreamtime Earth

THE MYTHOLOGISED LAND
AND ITS SACRED GEOGRAPHY

Most of us in modern, Western-style societies receive what little information we have of our legends, lore and myths from books and articles - and, perhaps especially nowadays, from radio, TV and film. Even our scholars glean mythological knowledge from archaic literary sources or, at best, from anthropological papers. Despite the fact that the power of myth still exists in our modern psyche, and breaks out in some surprising ways, mythology is viewed by us, culturally speaking, as something 'fixed', mere stories from the past. To tribal, non-Western societies, however, myth was (and in a few cases still is) a living reality, directly informing their beliefs, view of the universe, social arrangements, rituals - and landscapes. It is this last, special aspect of myth, its presence in the topographical surroundings of ancient or traditional societies, that is to be our concern in these pages.

The Dreaming
In seeking examples of such mythologised landscapes, an obvious starting point is with the aboriginal peoples of Australasia with their rich Dreamtime traditions. Referring to the Marind-anim(Marind people) of Papua New Guinea, for instance, Lucien Lévy-Bruhl wrote:

> The general character of the region, outstanding and remarkable features of the landscape, etc. - are for him indications, as they are for the Australians, of the presence and the activity (in the past and now) of the mythic ancestors. In short the native cannot look around him anywhere without feeling in a very vivid way that here, there and everywhere some supernatural power, some mythic being, has at some time made his presence felt, and indeed may still be present in the place. Earth and sea are to him as living books in which the myths are inscribed...
> ... a legend is captured in the very outlines of the landscape...[1]

In 1933, Olive Pink described being taken by an elder of the North Aranda tribe of central Australia to a mythic landscape. He pointed out the 'old men' (mythic ancestors) of the tribe who could be seen in the features of the terrain around them. Two pieces of bluestone were a totemic 'mother and baby blue kangaroo'; two gum trees were 'wild dogs'; several bloodwood trees were an ancestor headman commanding the 'wildcat' men formed by other gum trees to return to their 'own country' - the branch of a dead bloodwood tree was the headman's arm stretched out in command. The elder pointed out a hill to Pink whose 'spiritually blind eyes' saw at first merely a low eminence, though remarkable in that it had a limestone summit standing out starkly against the bronze-brown of the countryside. 'When one's spiritual eyes had been opened by the totemite's explanation one could quite well imagine it as the decorated heads of two *altjira* [Dreamtime] women,' Pink came to realise. 'Here they settled down, decorating their heads with lime and white rats' tails.' A mile further on, and Pink was shown the top of the head of one of the same women where she had 'gone into the ground'.

In the Dreamtime, the Earth was just a flat, featureless and uninhabited plain. Then at a certain point in this mythic past - the Dreaming or *tjukuba* - giant, semi-human totemic figures emerged from beneath the surface of the plain (or they were Sky Heroes from some vague upper region in other traditions) and started to wander across it in various directions. As they did so, they carried out everyday tasks familiar to the Aborigines of today - they camped, made fire, dug for water, defecated, performed ceremonies, and so on. In doing this they left traces which formed the topography, the flora and fauna that can be seen today. Eventually, these world-creators disappeared, in most traditions by going into the ground. Such a spot would be regarded as a sacred place - as might indeed, places where a totemic ancestor carried out a particular action. Furthermore, *the very paths the Dreamtime beings took across the land were sanctified*, and these paths, though spiritual and invisible to the physical eye, were known to the Aborigines and precisely followed during their seasonal, ceremonial journeys. James Cowan describes these Dream Journeys thus:

> ...we are not just dealing with an unending journey back and forth across tribal territory solely in pursuit of food. Instead we are looking at a sacred journey in which each stage is imbued with sacred significance...

> ...the land they cross is part of themselves. The Dream Journey on the ritual level is a way of renewing contact with themselves, since they and the land are inseparable. It is at this point that the Aborigine enters into a Dream world where the land is transformed into a metaphysical landscape saturated with significations...

> The metaphysical landscape, then, is transformed into an ideal landscape, a hagiographic history of the people's origins, their struggle to survive, how and from whom they received their cultural gifts... during that timeless moment known as the Dreaming. It is timeless because these primordial events took place both in the far distant past before even their ancestors had appeared on the earth - and are continuing to occur even as they are making their Dream Journey in the present.[2]

The water holes, rock outcrops, hills and trees define not merely a physical topography but also a real and present spiritual landscape to the Aborigine. 'In the central

Desert region inhabited by the Arunta [Aranda] people, one observer discovered a series of sacred sites linked to the Dream Journey of the red kangaroo (the First Beast of its species),' Cowan reports. 'This in turn had inspired a number of ceremonies and songs depicting the supernatural trek of the original red kangaroo, Kolakola, as it moved across the landscape.'[3]

In 1960, C.P. Mountford was led along the approximately 200 mile route of the Dream Journey of Jarapiri, the Snake Man (a version of the Great or Rainbow Snake), and his companions. Mountford's guides were members and elders of the Walbiri and Ngalia tribes of central Australia who were no longer transmitting tribal lore to their young men because they only wanted to behave like white men.

The birthplace of Jarapiri was Winbaraku (Blanche Tower), a twin-peaked hill in the western MacDonnell Ranges. From there, the totemic route stretched northwards marked by 35 sacred sites, including the rocky outcrop of Ngama, where a painting of the snake is on the wall of a cave called Jukiuta. Mountford was able to plot the precise course of the Jarapiri route, for it was *a specific way* through the landscape, and had seemingly been followed by Aborigines for unknown millennia. (All the more poignant, then, that this journey was being made with a white man so that its course would be recorded.) The kinds of sites along the route included a heap of stone where the spider Mamu-boijunda appeared; a pavement of white quartz that was once the burnt-out leaves of Wanbanbiris' fire-torch; caves that were the vulvas of the Nabanunga women; a line of rocks that marked the track of Jarapiri and his party, and

One of the many photographs of mythologised sacred sites taken by Mountford during his journey along the Jarapiri Dream Route. This rock outcrop symbolises dog-man, with paws, at Ngama. (Charles P. Mountford, from his book, Wimbaraku and the Myth of Jarapiri.)

a boulder that was the excreta of Jarapiri.[4] At each of these and the other sacred sites on the Jarapiri route, as along any other, the Aborigines would have sung the appropriate songs, conducted the correct ceremonies and decorated their bodies with the imagery belonging to the associated mythic event.

The purpose of ceremonies at the totemic places was two-fold: to renew and invigorate the fertility of the appropriate creature represented in the totemic image of the site - such sites were known as 'increase centres' - and also to kindle the mythic, inner journey the tribe and its individual members were making. They therefore journeyed through not just a physical landscape, but a sanctified inner mindscape as well.

The events of the Dreamtime imbued the landscape with a metaphysical power or 'life essence' - *kurunba, miwi* or *djang*. It would be easy but dangerous for us, with our cultural background, to think of this in simplistic terms of 'energy'. 'Numinosity' gives perhaps a better sense of *kurunba*, at least in its landscape sense. '*Kurunba*... is a metaphysical expression denoting the presence of a cultural layer within the landform itself that has been inspired by mythological contact with the Dreaming,' explains James Cowan. 'In other words, the landform has become iconic in essence, fulfilling a role of containment, not only of physical attributes... but of *meta*-physical significations. It is this quality that Aborigines term as *kurunba* - that is, the power that gives a landmark its inherent Form over and above that of its mere physical presence.'[5]

Secreted at the Aboriginal sites are sacred objects, *Churingas*, made of stone (*tjinas*) or wood (*tapundas*), which can be very old. These have various motifs marked on them that tell of that aspect of the myth associated with a particular place. They act as mnemonics, and are consulted by the elders when a site is reached on the Dream Journey. In addition, however, they also have a property analogous to that which Christians reserve for a relic such as a fragment of the True Cross, or the bone of a saint: they are particularly charged with *kurunba* in their own right. Mythically, when a Dreamtime being re-entered the Earth, it left a physical mark in the topography recognised as a sacred (or 'hot') place by the Aborigine elders, and it left its spirit behind in the *Churingas*. These sacred objects themselves yield spirits, *Kurunas*. (There is a sense, Cowan points out, in which the whole land is a vast *Churinga*.)

T.G.H. Strehlow gave a graphic account in the 1940s of a visit to a sacred site in the Ulamba region north-east of the main western MacDonnell Ranges by North Aranda tribesmen. An elder led a group of young men on a day's pilgrimage to the site. They all fell silent, and the elder pointed out landscape features which were involved in the myth surrounding the Ulamba ancestor: an opening in a rock where the ancestor first emerged; a heap of rocks marking one of the ancestor's night camps; a distinctive conical hill where the ancestor re-entered the Earth. Finally, the tribesmen came to two massive boulders, one on top of the other. The lower rock was the body of the Ulamba ancestor who collapsed there after being mortally wounded in the course of various adventures. The elder removed blocking stones in a cleft between the two boulders, and took out bundles of *Churingas* wrapped with hair string. He took each sacred object one at a time and chanted the song related to that part of the myth depicted on it. The objects were passed around the group, and were handled with awe and veneration. When the last verse had been chanted, and the *Churingas* had been cleaned, the objects were replaced and the men departed before sunset.[6]

There is probably no Aboriginal group that have a full traditional life any more, and it is a sad fact, as Mountford reported concerning the *Churingas* at sites on the Jarapiri Dream Journey route, that many of the sacred objects 'have been taken away by visitors, or sold to the tourists in Alice Springs... few of them remain in their tribal country.'[7]

Lines of songs

The Aborigines distinguish between the physical and metaphysical landscapes they inhabit, and have a clear and vivid knowledge of the physical process in nature around them. Their mythic awareness should not therefore be confused with naivety in any way. It is rather that the mythic land is interfused with the physical landscape, and they know how to relate the two aspects. Lévy-Bruhl spoke of an Aboriginal's 'participation' in 'the mystical presences which emanate from the land itself'.

The combination of the spatial and mythic properties of the land in the Aborigine's mind manifested in various ways. Mountford noted that at a certain point on the Jarapiri Dream Journey his Ngalia guides became uncertain as to the position of the next sacred site and the words of its associated chants. When he asked why this was so, he was told...

> ...that their 'line of songs' finished at Walutjara, and that those belonging to the remainder of the totemic route were the property of the Walbiri tribe to the north...
>
> This evidence suggests that the finishing place of the 'line of songs' of a mythical creator is a tribal boundary... because the mythical stories of the tribe, and the topography, art, songs, and ceremonies associated with them, which dominate all aspects of aboriginal life and thought, could also determine the boundaries of the tribe.[8]

Because the physical land embodies their spiritual life, Aborigines have a relationship with their home territories that looks like, but is utterly different to, Western concepts of patriotism or ownership. Rather, it is a life-giving participation, to use Lévy-Bruhl's term; they are possessed *by* the land, Cowan suggests, rather than the reverse. Referring to the Aborigines of the Boulia district of Queensland, Lévy-Bruhl remarked that...

> ...not only does every tribe occupy its own territory, with exclusive right of movement over it and of hunting as it wishes, but within it every family has its own particular domain. Its members know in detail how the country lies, what plants grow in it, the spots where various animals abound, and so on...[9]
>
> ... The land and the people are one...[10]

From the earliest days, Europeans were amazed at the highly developed sense of location Aborigines displayed - if they made a general encampment far afield with other tribes, for example, they would always automatically settle down in the exact compass direction of their home territory.

The Australian Aborigines knew where they were in both a physical and a metaphysical sense. But while what is known of their culture may give us the richest extant source of information on the ancient perception of the environment, the mythologised landscape can also be discerned in other, very different, ancient societies as well - ancient Greece for example.

Landscapes of the goddess

While profoundly different to Australian Aboriginal society, ancient Greece has nevertheless proved to be the best-known source of mythology for Westerners. We are greatly aided in recognising its mythologised landscape by the remarkable perceptions of Vincent Scully, a Yale University architectural historian. In 1962, he published a fascinating and important work, *The Earth, the Temple, and the Gods*,[11] in which he looked at the relationship of Greek temples to their surrounding landscapes.

The temples were not normally for containing humans, he pointed out, but instead 'they housed the image of a god, immortal and therefore separate from men, and were themselves an image, in the landscape, of his qualities'. He felt that all the sacred architecture of ancient Greece 'explores and praises the character of a god or a group of gods in a specific place'. The spirit of the gods was manifested in the physical surroundings of a temple, which acted like a signpost, a decoder even, of the local mythologised landscape. 'The landscape and temples together form the architectural whole,' Scully observed. He felt that the ancient Greeks had 'developed an eye' for 'specific combinations of landscape features as expressive of particular holiness':

> This came about because of a religious tradition in which the land was not a picture but a true force which physically embodied the powers that ruled the world, and although it may be objected that some of the landscape forms I shall define as holy are common in Greece, still the temples are many also, and their consistent appearance in relation to the sacred forms in question is never coincidental.[12]

The temple building was not just some abstract formula, however, imposed in a mechanical way on any landscape. The interrelationship between the structure and the surroundings was organic and sensitive:

> So each Greek sanctuary necessarily differs from all others because it is in a different place, and each varies from the others in certain aspects of the forms of its temples and in their relation to each other and to the landscape... This has to be so, because Apollo at Delos, for example, was not exactly Apollo at Delphi, nor Hera at Paestum Hera at Olympia. On the other hand, a deep natural pattern runs through all sites, both in the chosen shapes of their landscapes and the con-

structed form of their temples. A profound repetition, at once the echo of ancient traditions and the syntax of a new art, informs the whole and sets off the specific statements which irradiate it... So Apollo at Delos shares characteristics, in his landscapes, his temples and their arrangement, with the Apollo of Delphi in his. So too does the Hera of Paestum with her of Olympia, while Zeus there differs from, but is related to, him of Dodona.[13]

We tend to think of Greece as the font of Western civilisation, and yet the idea of the mythologised landscape seems alien to modern culture. Scully explained that the temples and sanctuaries...

...still embodied the oldest traditions of belief which had been handed down since the Stone Age. They therefore stand, like the Greek culture which imagined them, at a central point in human history: at the moment when the deepest past, with all its instinctive intuitions, fears, joys, and reverences, was brought for a while into harmony with the hard challenges of a new and liberated thought - at the moment, that is, when the self and objects outside the self were alike identified as objective realities.[14]

Scully therefore fully appreciated that the temples themselves came late - 'First, as the Greeks knew, was the earth: "well-founded Earth, mother of all, eldest of beings... Mother of the gods, wife of starry Heaven...".'

He took as his starting point the work of Karl Lehman-Hartleben, who had identified certain general combinations of mountains, springs, caves and other landscape features as characteristic of Greek holy sites, together with that of Paula Philippson, who, in 1939, had described her impressions of selected landscapes as embodying particular aspects of the Earth Mother or Great Goddess. Scully then visited a great many temple sites in Crete and on the Greek mainland and islands to see how the forms of structure and nature at those places expressed the deities to which they were dedicated. Within the constraints of an essay like this, we can look at only a few brief examples of Scully's observations, but enough to show that the ancient Greeks clearly inhabited a mythologised landscape just as surely as did the indigenous peoples of Australasia.

In studying the Minoan palaces of Crete, Scully identifed three recurring landscape elements that were used from at least 2000 BC: an enclosed valley in which the palace is set; a mounded or conical hill to the north or south of the palace and on its axis, and a higher mountain, with a cleft summit or double-peak, further away on that axis. This last was the terrestrial symbol of the Earth Mother:

The mountain may have other characteristics... but the double peaks or notched cleft seem essential to it. These features create a profile which is basically that of a pair of horns, but it may sometimes also suggest raised arms or wings, the female cleft, or even, at some sites, a pair of breasts. It forms in all cases a climactic shape which has the quality of causing the observer's eye to come to rest in its cup.

Though there are many overlaps in shape and probably many unguessed complexities in their meanings, still the cone would appear to have been seen as the earth's motherly form, the horns as the symbol of its active power.[15]

The Palaeolithic Earth Mother figurine, the 'Venus of Willendorf', Austria.

By using these landscape configurations, Scully suggested the Minoans were making conscious use of the Goddess images so clearly expressed in Palaeolithic and Neolithic 'Venus' figurines - 'carved as the child knows the mother, all breasts, hips and *mons Veneris*, full and round, with the head often inclined forward'. Erich Neumann noted the emphasis on the posterior of these early figurines (steatopygia to give it its technical name). He pointed out that the Earth Mother's 'very unwieldiness' necessitated her taking a seated posture 'in which she belongs like a hill or mountain to the earth of which she is a part and which she embodies'. The Great Goddess in this form is thus the prototype throne - echoed in the fact that a throne or chair today has 'legs', 'arms' and a 'back'. It was not accidental, Neumann remarked, that 'the greatest Mother Goddess of the early cults was named Isis, "the seat," "the throne", the symbol of which she bears on her head; and the king who "takes possession" of the earth, the Mother Goddess, does so by sitting on her in the literal sense':

> The original throne was the mountain... the mountain was the immobile, sedentary symbol that visibly rules over the land. First it was the Mountain Mother, a numinous godhead; later it became the seat and the throne of the visible or invisible numen; still later, the 'empty throne', on which the godhead 'descends'. The mountain seat as throne of the Great Goddess, of the Mountain Woman, is a later stage of development...[16]

Sign of the Goddess

There are numerous artefacts which show the 'raised arms' aspect of the goddess identified by Scully - the little Mycenaean terracotta figurines, for instance, and the Mycenaean culture of the Greek mainland was clearly related to the Minoan civilisation of Crete, though archaeologists apparently find it hard to establish what the actual links between the two were. (The evidence suggests that Mycenaean Greeks from the mainland ruled the Minoans during the latter periods of the culture.) There were, in any case, indigenous Cretan 'raised arms' figurines, and it seems Scully may have overlooked just how common the 'horned', 'saddle' or 'cleft' image was in prehistory around the Mediterranean area in general.

Tomb slabs from the Castelluccio cemetery in Sicily, for example, were carved into a crude but powerful depiction of a figure with upraised arms, breasts and head, while innumerable items of pottery from Sicily, the Lipari Islands to its north, and southern Italy, have 'horned' handles depicting a goddess figure with raised arms. Archaeologist O.G.S. Crawford had no doubt that such artefacts 'must surely be connected with the sacral horns of Crete and Anatolia'.[17] The motif was clearly of great power and can be traced back to remotest times - female figurines have been found with upraised arms in pre-dynastic Egypt, for instance, and in Palaeolithic rock carvings. Erich Neumann suggested that this universal gesture associated with the Earth Mother goddess must indicate prayer, invocation or magical conjuring of the deity.

Tomb slabs depicting head, breasts and raised arms from the Early Bronze Age cemetery of Castellucio, Sicily.

The three landscape elements identified by Scully are represented to some extent at all

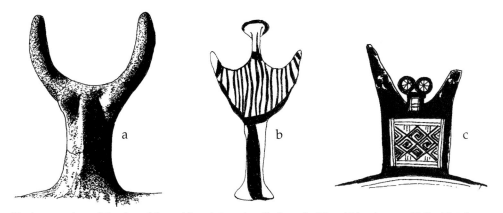

Various versions of the sign of the goddess. (a) pot-handle from the Lipari Islands, near Sicily. Note how the raised arms can be seen as horns and the breasts as eyes. (b) A typical Mycenaean terracotta goddess figurine. (c) Daunian pot-handle, southern Italy. Raised, horn-like arms and wheel-like eyes. Before the sixth century BC. (Items not to same scale.)

the Minoan palaces, and very completely at many. At Knossos, for instance, built over an important Neolithic site, the court opens to the distant, cleft-peaked Mount Jouctas (Juktas), though it is the propylaia (entrance area) which has its precise axis directed at the mountain.

Mount Jouctas (in silhouette) as viewed from the northern entrance of Knossos.

The Minoan bull ritual carried out in the Cretan palaces and well-recorded in the remains at Knossos, reveals the horns aspect of the cleft-mountain symbolism, as Cosimo Favaloro explains:

> The sacred and symbolic connection between the palaces and the mountains becomes clear when we examine the Minoan bull ritual that took place in those central courts. In it, young Minoan men and women, facing death in the bull, seized its horns and were propelled over its back. Frescoes depicting this ritual have been retrieved from the palace at Knossos. The full-bodied and vibrant charge of the horned bull immediately evokes memory of the Palaeolithic caves and beasts of the Goddess painted on their walls, all of which, except the horse, are horned...
>
> The ritual was performed in full view of the horned mountains and sacred cave sanctuaries of the Goddess [in the mountains]. The central courts offer no structural opposition to the mountains, rather they are a hollow which receives the massive powers to which the Minoans felt subordinate. Thus, the interaction of the palaces and the mountains, focused through the unilinear courtyards and the rituals performed in them, richly reorganized the symbols collected over time that express the powers of the goddess...
>
> The cleft shape of the mountain finds correspondence in much of the religious imagery we find inside the palaces. In shrine rooms and on top of many Minoan altars we find 'sacral horns', or simplified horn shapes made in stone and clay. Minoan frescoes show us that huge stone examples of sacral horns lined the central court areas, and perhaps all of the palace buildings.[18]

The so-called 'Mother of the Mountains' seal-impressions found at Knossos show sacral horns in stacks. The posture of the lions on this image, incidentally, is of course remarkably like the bas-relief on the entrance gate to Mycenae - see below. (The seal got its name from the depiction of a goddess apparently atop a mountain - see Neumann above. Here she is depicted as 'Lady of the Beasts'.) And the famous bull's head rhyton found at the Little Palace at Knossos is a very direct piece of horn imagery.

The Minoan 'Mother of the Mountains' seal impression. The goddess is shown as Lady of the Beasts. Note the pillar symbol she holds and the stacked sacral horns in background.

Goddess holding a symbolic axe, labrys, in each upraised arm. From Palaikastro, Crete.

Favaloro further notes that repeatedly inscribed on palace walls and ritual columns were depictions of the 'labrys', a highly-stylised version of the Minoan ritual double axe. This shape, like the horns, can be reduced to the basic crescent form of the cleft mountains. The illustration shows a priestess or goddess from a mould at Palaikastro, Crete, holding two labrys in a 'raised arm' posture and with exposed breasts, so the cleft motif is triply emphasised.

A common image thus seems to have run through Minoan thinking - and elsewhere in the Mediterranean area.

Favaloro points out that a further echo of the Palaeolithic caves was also present in the palaces in the form of the enclosed 'pillar crypts' set deeply inside them. The pillar provided the centrepiece for rituals and is said to have represented the stalagmites that the earlier Minoans worshipped in mountain caves. Examples of these caves occur on Mount Ida, to which the palace of Phaistos is aligned. Ida is a dramatic twin-peak mountain, and the entrance to the sacred cave of Kamares can sometimes be seen from the palaces of Ayia Triadha and Phaistos as a large black spot below the easternmost peak (the right-hand one as viewed from Phaistos). It was in this cave that the legendary Cretan shaman-figure, Epimenides, fasted, 'slept' (a euphemism for trance) and entered ecstasies. He left the cave a master of 'enthusiastic wisdom' (that is, of the techniques of entering altered states of consciousness) and travelled through many lands as a seer and proponent of health-giving arts.[19] The cave of Kamares is also the site of the finest finds of Middle Minoan pottery. This and another Idaean cave were originally the shrines of the goddess, later dedicated to Zeus, who was said to have been born in one of them.

The palace of Mallia is directed at Mount Dikte, which, like Jouctas and Ida, is a split mountain, has caves and came to be dedicated to Zeus. Favaloro writes that these type of caves in the Cretan mountains show that the landscape elements identified by Scully were held sacred from time immemorial, for...

> ...long before the palaces were constructed the Minoans held rituals and left offerings for the Goddess in the caves of Ida and, later, worshipped her in two round, stone sanctuaries that they built near its summit. Sanctuaries of the same construction have been discovered on 23 mountains around the island, including Dikte and every other mountain that would later have a palace focused upon it.
>
> Scully's argument of a connection existing between these holy mountains and the building of the palaces bears itself true archaeologically, for within the same period of years in which the Minoans were constructing sanctuaries for the Goddess high on the mountain peaks, down in the middle of their villages they were clearing whole groups of houses and then neatly paving over the vacated area. Thus were laid the central courtyards which would be in use for almost 100 years before the large and grand buildings were constructed around them that formed the palace centers.[20]

We must also consider the breast symbolism of the double peak or cleft image. At Gournia, for example, the palace aligns to two hill summits close together, which,

Scully notes, rather than giving the impression of horns, are 'so close and rounded that a more proper analogy would seem to be more directly to the female body itself, and they do closely resemble the uplifted breasts of the 'goddess of the horizon', topping her horns or crotch beneath, as she was depicted in Egyptian art'. He felt that the enclosed topography in which Gournia was located gave one the 'inescapable impression' that one was embraced by the arms of the Earth Mother.

The breasts aspect of the cleft symbolism in Minoan thought is further indicated by artefacts like the famous faience Snake Goddess found in a repository in the central shrine at Knossos. Its upraised arms and its breasts, strongly emphasised by the open bodice, both provide the cleft shape - and we have already noted similar images.

The mythic landscape of Eleusis

The cleft-peak symbolism figures in relation to sacred sites on the Greek mainland, too. An example is the temple of Demeter and Kore (Persephone) at Eleusis, about 12 miles west of Athens. This is the mythical spot where Persephone was raped and abducted by the King of the Underworld - Hades in one version, Pluto in another, and even Dionysius the wine god in a less well-known version - who took her down into his region. According to the myth, a well, a fig-tree and a cave were nearby the place where Persephone disappeared, and all are present at Eleusis. When her mother, Demeter, found out what had happened, she took the disguise of an ugly woman and walked amongst the world of humans in mourning. She sat and wept at the well (or, in older versions, a 'mirthless rock') near where her daughter disappeared. She was eventually taken into the home of a nearby king, where she nursed his baby son. Being interrupted in the process of making the boy immortal, she angrily revealed herself and demanded that a temple be constructed in her honour. She retired to this vowing to neither return to Olympus nor allow crops to grow on Earth until Persephone was given back to her. Eventually, Zeus was obliged to send Hermes to the Underworld to retrieve Persephone, but before she left, the Lord of the Underworld tricked her into eating pomegranate seeds there, thus ensuring that she would have to return annually for a third of the year to his realm. Reunited with her daughter, Demeter gave Triptolemos, second son of the king, seeds of wheat and a magical chariot in which he could roam around the world teaching the blessings of agriculture and the use of the plough. She taught humans the rites that were to be carried out at the place that became Eleusis, site of one of the ancient world's greatest Mystery Traditions.

In the Early Mycenaean period (*c*.1580-1500 BC), a settlement arose at Eleusis on the foundations of an earlier, destroyed village. The area now occupied by the ruins of the Eleusian precinct was *left empty*, indicating that an early form of the Eleusian Mysteries may have been in operation from even this date. The first stone structure known of on the site is what archaeologists call Megaron B, from the fifteenth century BC. Over the following thousand years, various structures came and went, and buildings were enlarged and added.

The Mysteries were a ten-day affair in September every year, and were open to almost anyone. The climax was the pilgrimage from Athens to Eleusis for the Mystery Night - the revelation of the Mystery itself to the *mystai* (initiatory candidates). After some initial preparation, the *mystai* were led in joyful procession along the Sacred Way linking Athens with Eleusis. As observances were made at various shrines along the Way, the procession took all day, and arrived at Eleusis by nightfall. In flickering torchlight, and after partaking of a sacred drink (which, it has been suggested, may have contained ergot, a parasite of rye with LSD-like properties), the candidates conducted rites at the various temples within the complex, including the eerie Plouton, a temple within the cave which can still be seen scooped out of the side of the hillock, the acropolis, around which the Eleusian complex was arranged. (See plate 1.) This was considered to be one of three entrances to the Underworld. Eventually, the *mystai* assembled in the Telesterion (*teleo* = 'to initiate'), a vast building unlike other Greek temple architecture in that it had a plain, undecorated exterior. Inside, there was a forest of columns and an inner enclosure known as the Anaktoron. Although the Telesterion had been rebuilt and enlarged numerous times, this central structure remained unaltered. In the great, final revelation of the Mysteries, and under the control of the Hierophant, flames erupted from the only doorway in the Anaktoron, and there was a manifestation of Persephone. Exactly what this was no one has been able to determine, for it was a secret kept at pain of death, but those who saw it, and this included many notable names of ancient and Classical Greece, felt their lives to have been changed by the experience; it was said that after it, death could hold no more fears. The flames, the 'Great Fire', could be seen issuing out of the Telesterion's roof, a signal to those outside that the revelation, the *epopteia*, had taken place. The Hierophant closed the event with an almost Zen-like act: he wordlessly showed an ear of corn to the congregation within the Telesterion.

'Eleusis' meant 'passage' or 'Gate', apparently, and it was indeed a passage between the worlds.

Today, this sacred site dedicated to the goddesses of Earth, fertility and the Afterlife, is hemmed in by the dust and squalor of cement works and the town that has grown up there. Nevertheless, the picturesque ruins of the great Mystery Centre maintain a powerful poetic atmosphere. All around, the landscape plays its part in this mythologised spot. As Scully put it: 'The site of Eleusis itself is the culmination of a whole set of symbols of the goddess which form the surrounding Attic landscape.'

The single most dramatic of these is the cleft mountain called Kerata ('Horns'). (See plate 2.) It comes suddenly into view above Eleusis as the Sacred Way winds through the pass at Daphni. Below this, a little closer to Eleusis, is a sanctuary of Aphrodite, precisely located where a horned saddle on the island of Salamis, just offshore from Eleusis, comes into view. This saddle remains in view when one is within the Eleusian temple complex itself. Indeed, the cross-axis of the Telesterion aligns towards it and another building, the so-called 'Temple of Demeter', faced in its direction. But Mount Kerata is out of sight beyond the hillock or acropolis. Its remarkable cleft peak is in view from atop the acropolis, however, and it is possible that the original 'Megaron B' was directed in the mountain's direction. Scully felt these topographic symbols 'consecrated the site'. He additionally noted that the main axis of the Telesterion aligns back towards the cleft formed by the pass at Daphni. 'The whole landscape around Eleusis is thus focused by the sanctuary,' Scully wrote.

The distinctive cleft peak of Mount Kerata rises over Eleusis. (Author)

The Horns of Hymettos

The most sacred and mythologised hill in Athens itself is the Acropolis, where an image of Gaia, the Earth Goddess, was placed by the ancient Greeks. That the dramatic hill was important from Bronze Age times, at least, is shown by the Mycenaean citadel that occupied it. The Acropolis is well-known nowadays, of course, for the Parthenon situated on it, but there were numerous other temples and structures gracing its summit. Key amongst these was the temple of Athena Polias ('of the city'). It was built on the north side of the Acropolis' summit in the sixth-century BC to house her wooden effigy, the most sacred and venerated image of Athens. Athena had many facets: she was a warlike goddess, yet was patron of the peaceful arts, and in a general sense, wisdom; she was often associated with water, but also with the land, particularly the kings of the land, which probably reveals her pre-Hellenic, possibly Mycenaean, origins. Athena at Athens seems to have been 'associated with the Aphrodite of the place' as Scully put it. Her temple atop the Acropolis almost certainly stood on the site of earlier shrines, for as William R. Biers writes, it was

...one of the most sacred places on the hill. This area contained many signs and remains of Athens' mythical past, such as the olive tree of Athena and the marks of Poseidon's trident... This place had long been sacred to the goddess, perhaps as far back as the Bronze Age.[21]

Scully discovered that this archaic temple was oriented to a distinctive horned saddle on the bulk of Hymettos to the east, an eminence which he identified as the key sacred mountain of the entire Attic region. A sacred cave lies beneath the northern horn, and an ancient cairn and a natural rock pillar all add to the sacred symbolism of the place. These 'horns of consecration' blessed the whole sacred assemblage on the Acropolis, but the patron goddess of the city was selected to have the direct link. Her temple was also dedicated to Poseidon and Erechtheus (known as a son of the Earth and in whose house Athena stayed when she returned to Athens after helping Odysseus).

A few decades after the temple to Athena Polias was built, the first Parthenon was erected on the south side of the Acropolis' summit. This was oriented slightly to the north of the horns of Hymettos, but it was angled relative to Athena's temple in such a way that the two buildings funnelled the view of anyone coming up onto the summit immediately and directly to the horns, tightly framing them.

This Parthenon, along with the temple of Athena Polias, was destroyed by the Persians in 480 BC. A second Parthenon was also destroyed by the invaders while it was still under construction. In 452 BC, the new Parthenon was started by Pericles, along with the Erechtheion, which stands alongside the site of Athena's old temple.

Later during this phase, a new entranceway or Propylia to the Acropolis was also begun. Scully noted that a natural axis forms along the ridge of the Acropolis' summit, leading to the horns of Hymettos in the east and directly along the axis of the Propylia to the horns of Salamis in the west. (See plate 3.)

Many deities were represented on and around the Acropolis, Zeus, as might be expected, amongst them. A short distance to the southeast of the Acropolis are the remains of the temple of the Olympian Zeus, commenced in the sixth century BC but most of what exists today belongs to Roman times. The siting of this temple, in a 'cup' formed by the surrounding skyline, emphasises the bowl of the sky, like most temples of Zeus, but the axis nevertheless goes towards the northern of Hymettos' horns.

The healing dream

In Greek myth, Zeus is said to have fathered Apollo, a shaman-like mythical personage who seems to have been brought into Greek mythology from a remote northern source, and whose key Greek shrines were Delos and Delphi (where he supplanted the worship of Gaia). Apollo, in turn, was the father of Asklepios, the god of medicine. The cult of Asklepios eventually became more popular than that of Apollo. His major shrine and birthplace was understood by the Greeks to be at Epidaurus, on the Peloponnese Peninsula across the Saronic Gulf from Athens, where his worship had commenced possibly as early as the sixth century BC. Asklepios resulted from the union of Apollo with Coronis, who was killed by Apollo when she was unfaithful to him, even though she was pregnant with Asklepios. Apollo, himself a god of medicine, saved the unborn child and had him suckled by a goat and guarded by a dog. He entrusted his child's upbringing to Chiron, the good Centaur. Chiron taught medicine to the child, who perfected the art. He used snakes to find healing herbs, and this, and a rod and dog, became his symbols. (In many depictions the rod has a snake or snakes wound round it, forming the symbol of the *caduceus*.)

The temple and healing centre at Epidaurus was only one of over 300 such sites in Greece. They were places where 'temple sleep' took place. This involved those seeking divination (usually concerned with an ailment) going through a series of ablutions and purifications at the temple (such sites seem always to have been associated with water sources), and going to sleep in special cells called *abatons*. This process is called 'dream incubation' (the Greeks called it *psychomanteia*), and if all went well, a person would dream of the god or one of his symbols and learn the cure to the ailment afflicting them. In this process they were helped by a temple assistant called a *therapeute*, from where we get our term 'therapist'.

Asklepios supplanted the worship of Apollo at Epidaurus, and it became a major centre of healing and worship. (See plate 4.) There were the sleeping cells (built adjacent to an ancient well), the baths, the temple of Asklepios, a mysterious round structure called the Tholos, a hotel, and, of course, as at so many Greek sacred places, there was a theatre and stadium - a centre for mind, body and spirit long before any 'New Age'!

To Scully, the landscape in which Epidaurus is set 'speaks of the power of the goddess...' and the site was 'a virtuoso performance in the use of landscape'. He analysed it in great depth, but here we may merely note that the most dramatic topographical feature obvious to the visitor is the powerful pyramidical form of Mount Velandhia towering over the temple site. This was the ancient Titthion, the 'teat' on which the baby Asklepios was suckled by the goat. Asklepios is thus mythologised into the very landscape at this place. Approaching the site from the Argolid, Titthion rises up between two rounded hills. Further back, two peaks form a gentle saddle shape. It is also apparent to the visitor that the stadium is aligned on a prominent, rounded hill.

The golden citadel

A pyramidal mountain also figures in the sacred geography of a much older site - Mycenae. This citadel, which gave its name to the pre-Hellenic Bronze Age culture, sits on a mounded hill in the 'lap' of two great peaks that soar up either side of it, Mounts Marta and Zara. Scully perceptively observed that from the appropriate angle, this arrangement echoes the Mycenaean terracotta figures with upraised arms, with the citadel taking the place of the head. The walled Mycenaean town occupies the lower portion of the mounded hill, with the king's palace overlooking it, itself at the foot of Mount Zara which appears as an almost perfect pyramid from this viewpoint. Scully felt that the cone shape was more important in Mycenae than in Crete, echoed further in the tholos tombs of the early Myceneans, which were bell-shaped stone chambers within earthen mounds.

If one stands immediately in front of the citadel's entrance gate - the famed 'Lion Gate', so called because of the two lions and the column motif so very similar to the Minoan seal impressions (see page 16) - Mount Zara is perfectly framed. Looking out the other way through the gate, Scully noticed, a notched mountain on the horizon can be seen.

Mount Zara, Mycenae's other landscape 'horn', appears in almost pyramidal form from the palace on the summit of the citadel. (Author)

Stones and lines

Moving to the other, western side of Europe now, for what will have to be our final examples of terrestrial mythology, we face even older landscapes containing mute, grey stone monuments - the great megalithic sites of prehistory. We have no knowledge of what the religions and myths of the builders of these places were, we only have the monuments they left behind and the clues they give from which to deduce their mindset. Archaeologists now recognise that there were 'ceremonial' or 'core' landscapes, in which various earthen and stone monuments were placed. Both Stonehenge and Avebury have such ritual territories around them. (In Part Two we examine Avebury in detail, revealing the 'open secrets' that my own research has only recently made apparent.)

Prehistoric landscapes in the Americas provide similar problems. Ancient Amerindians left behind curious landscape markings: effigy mounds and straight line features, such as the Chaco 'roads' in New Mexico and the pampa 'lines' at Nazca,

Peru, about which surviving Native American lore seems to say little or nothing. New research is also beginning to unlock the mysteries of these features, however, and we shall summarise this work later on.

Celtic symbolic landscapes

The pagan Celts are , fortunately, a little more readily accessible. While Hellenic Greece was emerging in the first millennium BC, the Celtic peoples of the western fringe of Europe were likewise using landscape as part of their religious life, their mythic consciousness. In an address to the *Ley Hunter* 'Moot' (conference) in September 1991,[22] Celtic scholar Anne Ross gave an account of her discovery of a remarkable survival of a pagan Celtic mythologised landscape. She began by pointing out that the earliest records we have show that the Celts had a deep feeling for the land, for the terrain. The Celtic goddesses were bound and rooted in the land, whereas the gods moved with the seasons and conditions. A Celtic king always had to have a marriage with the land. This sense of landscape was not just a generalised notion, it was tied to specific locales, to the immediacy of the landscape. Ross notes that there are Welsh and Gaelic terms for this feeling that cannot be translated directly into English - 'nostalgia' perhaps being the closest approximation. This feeling was closely linked to ancestor worship, and Celts always wanted to be buried in their home terrain. Landscape and ritual were closely bound together in the Celtic mind.

This is echoed by Celtic scholar Proinsias MacCana:

> ...it has long been recognised that all the evidence, whether literary or archaeo-logical, attests a deep concern with the land, with its sacred geography, its borders and its natural features and configurations; one important branch of Irish learned tradition is called *dindshenchas*, 'the lore of (famous) places,' and has to do with furnishing etiological tales to account for hundreds of place names, for virtually every distinguishable feature in the landscape had its mythic signifi-cance, though some were more highly charged with spiritual virtue than others... One instance of this geographical dimension of religious usage is the fact, noted by many scholars on the basis of the archaeological evidence, that Gaulish sanctuaries were often situated near territorial boundaries, and it is significant that the Irish evidence, mainly historical and literary, reveals a very similar pattern of distribution. Evidently their function was to mark the bounds of tribal unity just as other sanctuaries at the centre designated its core.[23]

Ross recalled that when she was working as a senior research fellow at the School of Scottish Studies in Edinburgh, she heard a rumour about a strange little site, a miniature 'house', at the head of Glen Lyon, beyond Loch Lyon, deep in the Grampian Hills of central Perthshire. This is wild country, and the small glen the site occupies is now uninhabited. Ross learned of a Celtic legend about the site, which told that long ago, during terrible snows on May 1 (Beltane in the Celtic calendar), a couple came over the mountains from a specific direction and into the glen. The two were a large,

1. The remains of the Plouton cave temple, Eleusis. (Author)

2. The distinctive cleft peak of Mount Kerata rises over Eleusis. (Author)

3. The 'horns' of Hymettos viewed from the Acropolis. (Author)

4. The ruins of Epidaurus with Mount Velanidhia, the ancient Titthion, beyond. (Author)

5. The St. Michael chapel on Rames Head. (Author)

6. Does the dreaming countryside around Glastonbury Tor conceal landscape symbolism of the Great Bear constellation? (Author)

powerful man with a wife twice as big - typical of Celtic mythology, the god is big, the goddess bigger. She was pregnant and they were homeless and lost in the wild terrain and blizzard. The people who lived in the glen at this time built and thatched a house for the couple's use. The woman gave birth to a daughter, and the family lived in the glen thereafter. They blessed the glen and its people, and ordered that a certain ritual be carried out each year. The people remembered this down the centuries.

Ross conducted her own fieldwork in order to investigate the location. This required a long, rugged mountain walk after travelling up the loch by boat. The site itself is a tiny earth house; in winter it has stones laid on top, and in summer (up until World War I, at least) it was thatched. The deities are represented by three anthropomorphic-looking but natural, water-worn stones from the stream in the glen. They are brought out of the house at Beltane, and put back at Samhain (November eve) and they stay inside all winter. A great quartz stone was placed on the house as a marker, so it could be readily distinguished in the wild country of the glen. The house has a Gaelic name meaning 'The Hag's House', that is, the house of the Earth Goddess; the Gaelic name for the stream is the 'Hag's Stream', and the hill behind is 'The Hag's Mountain'. Ross arrived on May 1, and found the stones had indeed been put out. It transpired that although the upper glen is now depopulated, the shepherd who tended his sheep there continued to carry out the ritual. The people in the lower glen still believed that if the rites were not performed, their crops and livestock would suffer. The stones are extraordinary, and the largest, goddess stone does actually have a face carved on top of it. The streams in that area tend to wear stones into fantastic shapes, and the waters are themselves venerated and accredited with magical powers.

As Ross and her colleague prepared to photograph the stones, the goddess stone, for no apparent reason, suddenly leaned forward, so that its rather baleful face stared at the researchers. 'It was,' Ross admitted, 'a rather frightening moment.'

Subsequently, she got to know the shepherd, being herself a Scottish Highlander and Gaelic speaker, and over many visits she has learnt much lore of the locality from him. She found it was still very much a ritual place and discovered numerous examples of very ancient ritual still being observed. She was shown stones down the glen that were seen by the locals as creatures belonging to Celtic myth, and other stones with particular shapes that were thought to have healing power. Much of what Ross learned in Glen Lyon has yet to be published.

Ross remarked that the veracity of the ancient nature of the Hag site and ritual she had documented was provided by the testimony of the associated placenames and oral tradition, because Celtic religion and superstitions

> ...are written into the landscape in the form of placenames which persist and are archaic, and the oral tradition which is a Celtic feature goes back to the oral teaching of the Druids in the Iron Age. Oral teaching was and has remained almost a sacred tradition with the Celts.[24]

While this site is small and secret, a much larger and better-known Celtic ritual landscape exists in Northern Ireland around the Iron Age site of Navan Fort, or *Emain Macha*, named after the goddess Macha, one of Ireland's three war goddesses, associated with fertility, valour and the horse. She can be equated with Epona of the Gauls and the Welsh Rhiannon. This area is giving scholars a rich insight into the ancient Celtic world, because archaeological finds are matching the testimony of the old bardic texts with remarkable precision.

Navan Fort is situated 11/2 miles south-west of Armagh, which is *Ard Macha*, because it sits on a hill dedicated to the goddess who is also remembered in name elsewhere in the region. (Armagh became a great Christian centre under St Patrick, effectively the ecclesiastical capital of Ireland). Navan Fort covers 18 acres atop a small rounded hill, enclosed by a bank and ditch earthwork. It is not a fort despite its name: it is definitely a ritual enclosure or sanctuary. The landscape around seems also to have been ritual in nature, perhaps from Neolithic times. Three hundred yards/ metres east of the circular earthwork is a small lake in which four bronze horns and a number of human skulls were found in the eighteenth century. Only one of the horns survives, and it has what archaeologists call La Tène style decoration, dating it to the last few centuries BC. A little further out from Navan, there were much older megalithic monuments - stone circles or chambered mounds - now destroyed, and an artificial pool known as 'The King's Stables', thought to date to the late Bronze Age (about 800 BC).

Within the hilltop enclosure there are the remains of a ploughed-out mound, and another, extant, mound some 20 feet high and 150 feet across. Excavations have shown that this covered a ground surface that had been repeatedly used, probably dating back to the third millennium BC, but there were also foundations of Iron Age buildings. Also found, remarkably, was the skull of a Barbary Ape, proving that this important Irish site had contact with the Mediterranean region. But the climax to the site came around 100 BC. A massive oaken post was erected - it is thought to have been about 36 feet tall. This was the centrepiece of a great circular wooden building. Rings of posts, actually, laid out radially from the centre, surrounded the central ritual post. This building was probably roofed. Ross notes that though the hill on which Navan Fort is placed is relatively low, it nevertheless commands a great sweep of country-side, and the post must have acted as 'the focal point not only of the sanctuary itself, but of the entire countryside where it must have acted as a sacred marker'.[25] There are no signs of any activity within this structure, the strange fact being that it was filled by a huge mound of limestone blocks. The decayed wooden posts trapped inside the structure left voids that allowed the post arrangements to be deduced by archaeologists. The limestone cairn came to rest inside the outer wooden wall of the building, and this was deliberately burned, perhaps barely 20 years after the building had been constructed. The cairn was then turfed over, leaving the mound that is visible today.

It is thought a ritual way connected the building with the nearby lakelet, though no one knows the rituals that took place. Navan Fort was, however, like Tara, one of

Ireland's royal sites. The early Irish vernacular literature, the oldest literature in northern Europe, tells two legends associated with the site. One states that a great warrior queen who ruled over all Ireland enslaved her enemies until they had built *Emain Macha* for her. She laid out the groundplan of the site with a brooch, and she and the kings who succeeded her ruled from there. The other legend tells of Macha's arrival at Emain, and her marriage to a local, wealthy farmer. She told him not to reveal to anyone that she was a divine personage. But when the Lughnasadh (Lammas) fair was being held at Emain, the man could not help but boast that his wife could run faster than the king's horses. He was immediately seized, and with his life under threat, Macha came and raced against the horses, and not only won but gave birth to twins on the way. (*Emain* means twins, and the motifs of horse and twins run through all Indo-European mythology.) Navan remained a centre for Lughnasadh festivities down to the present century, which corresponds to the legend, as does the fact that it was a royal site. The name for a brooch in Irish was *eomhuin*, and this may link with *Emain*. The myth is acknowledged, too, in the place name of 'The King's Stables' for the Bronze Age artificial pool. But, we can today only get glimpses of the mythic elements of this large ritual landscape and others like it.

Christian landscape myth

That Armagh should have become a major Christian centre exemplifies the way certain aspects of pagan Celtic sanctity, such as sacred sites and holy dates, were adopted by early Christianity. Some ancient churches are themselves placed in landscapes related to the Christian mythos - a trait clearly continued from earlier times. I can think of an example of this in my adopted county of Cornwall, a Celtic land at the south-western tip of England. It is the fourteenth-century chapel dedicated to St Michael on Rames Head near Plymouth. (See plate 5.) Many St Michael churches were placed on top of steep hills and craggy rocks, and the chapel at Rames Head is therefore typical in that it perches precariously atop an almost perfect cone of a hill. Records show that the chapel was dedicated to St Michael from its founding. Its axis is oriented towards the Mewstones, another conical rock outcrop that rises out of the sea five miles to the east. The Mewstones marked sunrise from the chapel position on St Michael's day, September 29, in the fourteenth century,[26] a Christian myth being silently enacted each year, linking local topography and the heavens.

More dramatic examples of this kind of thing occur in the Alps. At Elm, a ski resort 3000 feet above sea level in the Swiss canton of Glarus, the Tschingelhorner, which towers over the village to the south-east, is pierced by a natural rock tunnel, 20 yards high. Known as St Martin's Hole, legend has it that it was created by the saint's iron-tipped staff which he hurled at a giant who tried to steal his sheep. Every year on March 12 or 13, the rising sun shines through this hole and for two minutes illuminates the tower of Elm church. The clearly visible beam of sunlight is 5 km long. The same thing happens again in the autumn. Furthermore, the moon once in its 18.6-year (Metonic) cycle also shines through the hole onto the church. The church dates to the fifteenth century. It is not known if it stands on some pagan or prehistoric site, but Bronze Age remains have been found in the region.

It might be thought that such a phenomenon as this would be very rare, but Swiss researcher, Marco Bischof reports that there are in fact four more St Martin's Holes in Switzerland and Austria through which sunlight strikes a church.[27]

The virtually equinoctial sunbeam striking the church at Elm, Switzerland, through St Martin's Hole.

The mythologised land and sky

There are many cases of churches occupying prehistoric sites throughout Europe, and modern geomantic researchers think there are even more cases than are admitted to by archaeologists. In some cases, therefore, ancient churches maintain a pattern in landscapes that were there long before the Christian faith. John Michell speculates that a specialised example of this occurs in the Somerset levels surrounding Glastonbury Tor, which also has the ruins of a St Michael church on its summit. (See plate 6.) This is one of the West's great mythologised landscapes -the Lord of the Underworld, King Arthur and many other legendary personages still mythically populate this misty land. People have lived around Glastonbury for thousands of years, and one of the 'oldest roads in the world', the Sweet Track, has been unearthed - unpeated actually - in the local countryside. The Tor marks what was one island out of several rising out of a shallow sea in this region. The water levels slowly dropped, leaving marshy wastes between the islands, and this was why causeways like the Sweet Track were constructed. Michell suggests that certain of these former islands, which now stand out as green hills on the Somerset Levels, were tribal sanctuaries in prehistory and many of them 'retained their sanctity into Christian times and became the sites of churches or chapels'.[28] The first church to be founded at Glastonbury, the Isle of Avalon, is in legend if not in fact the first church in Britain, indeed the first church in Christendom. The Twelve Hides, the special-status, ecclesiastical territory surrounding the later Abbey, contains seven of these islands: Avalon itself; Beckery; Godney; Martinsea; Meare; Panborough and Nyland. Michell has noticed that they form a configuration in the landscape that approximates the pattern of the Great Bear constellation (*Ursa Major* - the Plough or Big Dipper). Michell comments:

> The relevance of this constellation of island sanctuaries to the history and mythology of Glastonbury is immediately apparent. From very early times the Great Bear has been associated with King Arthur. Welsh scholars derive Arthur's name from 'Arth Fawr', the Great Bear, and he is also associated with Arcturus, the brightest star in the northern hemisphere, whose position in the sky is indicated by the last two stars in the tail of the Great Bear. In Spanish it is named Arturo or Arthur, and old English writers... made plain its traditional connection with Arthur by calling it Arthurus...
>
> The early English... called the Great Bear the home of King Arthur. It was also called Arthur's Wain or Wagon, being seen as the vehicle in which Arthur circled the pole. Another name for the Great Bear is the Plough. By that name it is again associated with Arthur as *Arator*, the Ploughman.[29]

Michell quotes another source which breaks down the name of Arthur to Arth (bear) and Uthyr (wonderful) in the Welsh language. Thus there seems to be some strong resonance between Arthur and the Great Bear, and as Michell points out, it is a motif that ultimately goes back to the time of the hunters, the Great Hunt of the Palaeolithic period, when there was a great 'circumpolar bear cult' as Joseph Campbell has put it.[30]

Michell's hypothesised configuration of the seven island sanctuaries (*not* to be confused with the alleged 'Glastonbury Zodiac') do not reproduce the pattern of the Great Bear constellation with complete exactitude. As Michell states, 'the landscape planisphere was a symbol rather than a chart of the heavens'.

The idea that the heavens imprinted their image and influence on the landscape is of course a most ancient concept, and runs through many cultures from the ancient Chinese to the Etruscans to the Amerindians. Of the legendary first ruler of the Chinese, Fu Hsi, it was said: 'Looking upwards he contemplated the images in the heavens; looking downwards he discerned the patterns on earth'. Astrology of course emerges from this thinking. The mythologised land had a mythologised sky overhead - hence our constellations. And different peoples had different constellations. Perhaps one of the more dramatic differences between Western and non-Western concepts of sky mythology is expressed by the Andean Indians, as discovered by anthropologist Gary Urton.[31]

In their southern hemisphere sky there is no Polaris, the pole star, and the Milky

Way is the key feature instead. The Indians see the dark shapes in this (formed by interstellar dust clouds) as mythological shapes - they are 'dark constellations', in effect. The apparent swinging motion of the Milky Way in the sky over a 24-hour period creates intercardinal divisions of the sky: as its south-eastern quadrant 'rises', the north-western quadrant 'sets', and the same for the north-east and south-west. These two courses of the Milky Way cross over (conceptually) close to the south celestial pole. The Indians have 'imprinted' this orientation pattern onto the ground, and their ancient city plans, such as Inca Cuzco, and present-day villages have road systems that reflect this intercardinal system. In the Andean community of Misminay (where water canalisation also reflects this intercardinal division), the point where the intercardinal roads cross is called the *Crucero*; this corresponds to the 'crossing' point of the Milky Way in the sky overhead, the *Calvario*. The heavens are linked to the ground as if by a rod connecting these points, and this is a version of the 'cosmic axis' that we will discuss later.

The Crucero is the appointed place in Misminay from where the horizons of the four quarters can be scanned. Each direction has mythic significance and this is reflected in the names given to skyline features. The north-west/north-east quarter, for example, is associated with the ancestors, and the holy mountain on the horizon is called Apu Wanumarka - the 'Storehouse of the Dead'. These sacred mountains, apus, on the horizon not only relate to spatial and mythic orientation, but are also *'transitional between terrestrial and celestial space'* as Urton emphasises, and provide markers for sun, moon and star watching.

These sort of linkages were common amongst ancient cultures. We can pick it up in Europe by using the hint of placenames, which, as we recall Anne Ross stated, are mnemonics of ancient religious thinking 'written into the landscape'. Placenames 'persist and are archaic'.

No mythic image is more embedded in archaic landscapes than that of the Earth Mother. The island of Jura off Scotland's western coast, for instance, has a range of mountains called the Paps, the very breasts of the goddess. These, too, would seem to be 'transitional' between sky and land, for the late Professor Alexander Thom, who conducted decades of meticulous surveying at megalithic monuments, found two sites that gave accurate solar observations using the Paps of Jura as foresights. One of these is Ballochroy, a row of three standing stones on the western coast of the Kintyre peninsula. The middle stone is a thin slab with one of its faces apparently smoothed. Looking westwards along this to Jura, 19 miles distant, the most northerly peak of the Paps, Beinn Corra, is indicated. This would have been the point of midsummer sunset in prehistory.

Roughly 40 miles north of Ballochroy is a now damaged prehistoric site at Kintraw. This consists of a standing stone and a stone mound or cairn. A possible viewing platform behind these features has also been uncovered. Viewing over the mound to the southwest, the Paps of Jura are visible 27 miles away. The midwinter setting sun in prehistory would have set in the 'V' formed by two of the Paps, Beinn Shiantaidh and Beinn a Chaolais.

The mountain range known as the Paps of Jura (in silhouette) as viewed from the standing stones of Ballochroy. The rounded symmetry of the central peaks makes it clear why the mountains acquired their name.

The 'Sleeping Beauty' range in Pairc, southeast Lewis, as viewed from Callanish. The 'face' is on the right-hand side and the slightly drawn-up 'knees' on the left. Every 18½ years, at the southern extreme of the so-called 'major standstill' point of the lunar cycle, the moon rises out of the Sleeping Beauty and skims the horizon - a dramatic sight from most of the Callanish sites.

The 'Breasts of Anu' in Ireland.

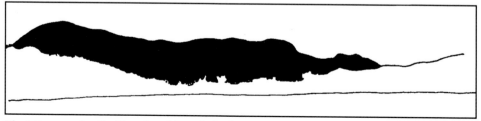

The 'Woman on her Back' as viewed from the harbour at Poros, Greece. Her head is on the right, and her neck, breasts, torso and knees are realistically imaged.

On the Scottish island of Lewis there are a cluster of stone circles and settings known collectively as the Stones of Callanish - the 'Stonehenge of the North'. These have some remarkable astronomical properties in themselves, especially associated with the moon, but their landscape also seems to be implicated. At this latitude the most southerly rising moon in its complex 18.6-year cycle appears to skim along the horizon, and this was one effect the builders of Callanish (and other Scottish megalithic sites) seemed particularly interested in. Most of the Callanish sites are grouped together in a diamond-shaped area that is formed by drawing 'viewing lines' to two ranges of mountains - the Pairc Hills on southeast Lewis and the Clisham range on North Harris. At the southern extreme of what is known as the major standstill, the moon viewed from the Callanish stones appears to rise out of the Pairc Hills and skim along the horizon before setting behind the Clisham range. Locally, the Pairc Hills are known as 'The Sleeping Beauty' because they form the profile of a woman on her back. It is as if the Sleeping Beauty, another name for the Earth Mother, gives birth to the moon at this key time in its cycle.

The sleeping goddess

But placenames give away the presence of the embedded goddess even where no astronomical findings have yet been noted. Two symmetrical, rounded hills near Killarney, Ireland, are called in Gaelic 'The Two Breasts of Anu'. Anu was the mythical mother of the last generation of gods that ruled the Earth, the Tuatha De Danaan. The hills 'personify the powers of the goddess embedded in the land,' says Anne Ross. 'She is still regarded as the local fairy queen, and people still gather there at Lughnasa and climb the heights nearby.'[32]

Similarly, Scully learned that a mountain range viewable from Poros in Greece is perceived locally as a woman lying on her back. 'The resemblance is indeed persuasive,' he observed; 'the head low on the north, a long neck, high breasts, arched stomach, long legs with the knees drawn up.'[33] He felt that it might not be accidental that the legend involving the 'frantic lust' of Phaedra was connected with an area defined by these formations. There is also a shrine to Aphrodite in the area.

Even Sir Arthur Evans, the famed figure of Cretan archaeology, recorded that from the direction of Tylissos the peak of Mount Jouctas looked like a man's head facing skywards, and that it is indeed known as 'the head of Zeus' to locals. While this does not prove that it was so regarded in prehistory, Evans was prepared to accept that it did indeed stretch back that far.

Such anthropomorphic configurations exist in many mythologised landscapes worldwide; some are still known, while others are now doubtlessly invisible to us. It takes the mythically-sensitive eye to discern them and to focus on their symbolism. It is to the processes of consciousness that might be involved in this that we must now begin to turn our attention.

2

DREAMING THE EARTH

It seems difficult to arrive at a clear understanding of the nature of myth, for it is a particularly mercurial aspect of humanity. Scholars still fail to agree on a precise definition.

It was because C.G. Jung saw basic mythological motifs (mythologems) occurring in the dreams of his modern patients that he came to the conclusion that there had to be such a thing as a Collective Unconscious. He postulated the existence of transpersonal processes he called archetypes deep in the Collective Unconscious that can produce related thematic imagery in any society or person of any period. These images can vary dramatically according to the cultural context they occur in, but their underlying function remains true to the archetype that originated them. Because it exists in the unconscious realms of mind, the archetype itself can never be directly known or understood but merely interpreted by the imagery it occasions in a dream or vision - or in a myth. Jung warned that modern society in cutting itself off from such mythological roots ran the risk of neurosis and 'psychic epidemics', as it had a literally rootless consciousness. According to Jung, this modern condition has come about because of the pronounced development of differentiated, conscious mentality in civilised peoples, which leads to a one-sidedness and a deviation from the roots of our being. *Archetypal material does not come from our rationally-conscious minds.*

The recurrence of certain mythological themes at widely separated times and places around the world gives great credence to some kind of Collective Unconscious. The mythologem of the ladder to heaven, for instance, occurred virtually everywhere. There is of course the Biblical story of Jacob's visionary dream of angels on a ladder leading to heaven, but versions of the theme, which I suggest *derives from shamanic trance experience*, as we shall see below, can also be found in the myths of Arctic Europe, Siberia, Tibet, the Americas and Oceania.[1] Depictions of figures in a shamanic context teetering atop ladders is even found in the rock art of southern Africa.[2] French anthropologist Claude Lévi-Strauss has studied the myths of related tribes in Brazil and Paraguay as recorded by missionaries over hundreds of years, and found that though particular personages and events in them changed over time, the fundamental structure of a story remained constant.

Clearly, there seems to be something in the human mind, or at least in the common neurological structure and functioning of the human central nervous system, that is outside the timescale of individual persons or societies.

Since Jung's time, it has been suggested that archetypal images can provoke automatic responses analogous to the way that certain sensory cues can cause an animal to react in a predetermined manner. (For example, a newly-hatched chick will cower if shown the shape of a hawk, yet will not react to other bird forms.) 'Each society gives its own particular form to such "archetypal images" or stimuli,' says Sheila Savill, 'for myths and legends are expressions of communal feelings and intuitions.'[3] Joseph Campbell warned that even though our culture no longer lives by myths, they are active and dynamic parts of the psyche, however we might ignore or forget them. Myths derive their source from 'an immemorial imagination', and can be driving us in ways our conscious, civilised minds do not perceive.

Alan Watts defined myth as 'a complex of stories... which, for various reasons, human beings regard as demonstrations of the inner meaning of the universe and human life'.[4] He saw myth as quite distinct from philosophy, as it was 'always concrete - consisting of vivid, sensually intelligible, narratives, images, rites, ceremonies and symbols'. The processes that give a story a mythic dimension are 'very largely unconscious', which, if Jung was right, they would have to be. Watts further noted that if the appearance of archetype-derived transpersonal images in a person's dreams indicated a healing process, as Jung maintained, then those societies that lived by myth were also healthy - healthier, indeed, than our own peculiar culture. He remarked that A. Coomaraswamy saw myths as one of the ways the 'perennial philosophy' was communicated, the perpetual spiritual reality underlying all religious forms and yearnings, the reality that allowed those who could partake of it to 'wake up' to 'a vision of the world startlingly different from that of the average socially conditioned man... because of the discovery that time - as ordinarily understood - is an illusion'.[5]

Great time

Greek scholar G.S. Kirk has warned that myths are so varied that it is unwise to seek one single definition of them. He finds some of the theories to be questionable, while others work for certain bodies of myth in the world but not for all of them. But while he is cautious about accepting Jung's ideas *in toto*, he admits that myths can have a dream-like quality, with the dislocations of sequence and location common to dreams. He notes, too, that it 'is a commonplace among several tribal societies... that myths and dreams evince a similar insight into reality. Many of the Indian tribes of the American South-west agree in spite of other cultural differences that myths are dreamed, and are created in that way. They are of great importance, being closely connected with the complex of rituals on which the life of the Pueblo Indians, in particular, is centred'.[6]

Like Watts, Kirk notes that true myths tend to be 'set...in the timeless past' while their lesser cousins, folktales, are realistic, placed in specific if anonymous time and place, with characters having generic names. The anthropologist V.W. Turner simi-larly mentions the unusual time quality associated with myths, and points out that in tribal societies where myths form the basis of ceremonies, the activities are performed in 'liminal' situations, between the mundane and supernormal worlds, at sacred sites in remote locations, at night, naked or in strange garb. Myths could also be 'told at a time or in a site that is "betwixt and between"'. He felt that myths were 'high and deep mysteries' which put a tribal person into a temporary rapport 'with the primary or primordial generative power of the cosmos'.[7]

Various anthropologists have created phrases to describe this mythic dimension of time: Preuss referred to it as *die Urzeit* ('pre-time'); Lévy-Bruhl as 'pre-temporal time', noting that the mythic events of the San or Bushmen of southern Africa take place in a time that 'is not time at all in any rational sense; it is a special kind of time, itself as mythical as the events it embraces...'[8]

People from any culture, modern or traditional, who experience altered states of consciousness can encounter this mythic time, Great Time, in which a sense of unutterable antiquity is linked to a quality of timelessness which allows mythic events to have happened in some remote past and yet to be somehow eternally occurring. Tribal shamans who use hallucinogenic plants as a sacramental part of their trance rituals report that they can 'look back to the very beginning' and go 'where the world *is* born' (my emphasis). They meet mythic beings such as tribal ancestors or deities and are shown the secrets of creation.

Taking a loose, general consensus, then, we can view myths as having dream-like qualities, their own dimension of time - at once ancient and present - and deriving from other sources of consciousness than the rational-type of waking awareness we moderns possess. They may also reveal neurological functions common to all humanity. High or serious myths represent deep realities of mind and nature.

Myth and mind

This is our clue. Dreams are private myths, as someone put it, and myths are tribal dreams. They both clothe processes going on deep within the human psyche. Looking at the examples of mythologised landscapes given in the first section of this essay, it is indeed difficult to avoid the feeling that we are dealing with some kind of dream world, a dream world that was allowed to develop a resonance with the physical world. I can vouch for the fact that this can happen directly in dream consciousness, for I am one of those weird people who sometimes sleeps with his eyes a little open. I have on numerous occasions experienced a dream in which some object my sleeping eyes happened to be fixed on in the bedroom became something else in my dream - an ornate doorknob becoming an eagle, for instance. Conversely, when I have awoken from such dreams, the dream image slowly dissolves and I am left staring at the physical object in my surroundings that gave rise to it. As I awake, the physical object becomes divested of its dream or 'mythic' aspect.

Even those who do not possess my curious sleeping quirk, must have experienced an external sound or touch working its way into the matter of their dreams.

Dreaming is, of course, the one type of altered state of consciousness familiar to us all. Even those who are most vehement about the horrors of hallucinogenic drugs (which they unfortunately mix up with dangerous 'hard drugs' and chemicals which can be 'sniffed' from certain commercial products) have dreams, and dreams, it now seems, are produced by hormonal hallucinogens secreted by our own brains.[9,10]

In my heady youth, when I was an art student in London during the 'Swinging Sixties', I took some LSD (it was still technically legal then). I took, unknowingly, a very large dose and I had a wild cosmic ride. One of the multitude of experiences I underwent has a bearing on our discussion here: as the session finally began to subside from its overpowering, transcendental heights, someone with me took out a handkerchief. It was what in those days was a rather fashionable khaki colour. He held it at one corner, and as he had taken a teaspoonful out of the tall glass I had drunk containing the LSD, he paused to look at it, empowered   with the enhanced observational abilities released by the hallucinogen. I did likewise. The limp, hanging cloth fell into folds from the held corner. As one might catch a semblance of a face or a castle or whatever in a cloud, I saw the lineaments of a dove. A dirty, mud-covered dead dove, an impression literally due to the colouring given by the khaki material of the handkerchief. In the twinkling of a mythologising eye, the piece of cloth and its folds 'hardened' into a very perfect, realistic representation of a dead dove being held by its beak. I knew it was a handkerchief, but I was looking at a dead dove. As I was 'returning' from transcendental heights back into the world of mortals, of fallen humanity, I found the symbolism of the dead dove to be powerfully relevant. I marvelled at the fluid ambiguity of perception and of symbolism, and the symbiosis existing between them.

It is this type of 'loosened' perception, this mixing of sensory and symbolic data, I feel we have to acknowledge when we look at mythologised landscapes. We are not dealing with the enforced, brittle, intellectual consciousness we tend to employ in trying to 'read' a reclining woman 'into' a range of hills, or a Dreamtime hero 'into' a boulder. The Dreamtime is literally that, and we must envisage a people who could see in the fashion I have described above. They can *see* the 'lineaments of legend' in the land. They do not have to translate it as some simulacrum as we have to do.

Writing in 1935, Lévy-Bruhl acknowledged that to Aborigines 'the mythic world and dreams have some important principle in common'.[11] The Kalahari Bushmen told Laurens van der Post that 'there is a dream dreaming us'. They felt themselves to actually be part of the dreaming of the world.

The term 'Dreamtime' is not an Aboriginal word. It was, in fact, coined by B. Spencer and F.J. Gillen, the explorer-anthropologists who trekked through the Australian Outback in the latter part of the nineteenth century, observing the ceremonies of, and speaking with the Aborigines they encountered. To Aborigines the term is *altjira, dzjugur, bugari, lalan,* depending on the tribe. Mountford noted Gillen's and Spencer's invention was a 'particularly apt word' for the Aboriginal term, a feeling obviously shared by the Aborigines themselves who adopted it when trying to explain *altjira* to Europeans. Anthropologist A.P. Elkin learned that the Aboriginal terms had a number of meanings for the Aborigine

> ...all of which, however, are summed up in the long-past time when the culture-heroes and ancestors introduced the tribal culture and instituted its rites and laws... *The same term also means 'dream'* (noun or verb). But to the Aborigines this does not signify mere phantasy, but spiritual reality. A man's 'dreaming' is his share of the secret myths and rites, of the historical traditions, of the old or 'eternal dreamtime'.[12] (My emphasis.)

James Cowan is at pains to emphasise the altered states of consciousness quality of this Aboriginal Dreaming. Contact with the Dreaming is the primary objective for participants in ceremonies at sacred sites along Dream Journey routes, he states. 'It is not a divine *place* that they are endeavouring to enter by way of ritual gesture, but a state of mind - a return to the source.'[13] Aboriginal holy men, 'Men of High Degree' or *karadjis*, have direct contact with the Dreaming and the spirit figures that populate that realm of mind. As a consequence of this direct contact, a *karadji* is the only person who can create new dances, songs and stories. In Jungian terms, it would be said that because he has access to the Unconscious, he is able to extract authentic mythic material - transpersonal, timeless. Jung was confident that '"myth-forming" structural elements must be present in the unconscious psyche'.[14] Cowan points out that the Dream Journey is at once an exoteric activity, a social activity, and an esoteric or inward journey:

> In both cases, however, there is a certain amount of ritual activity designed to encourage a new awareness of environment and the way personal 'country' can inspire a greater understanding of nature itself... both journeys overlap in their significance because many of the stories, myth cycles, sacred environments... and cave paintings are common to both.[15]

By using the Dreaming, Cowan argues, the Aborigines were able to find in topo-graphical features a 'profoundly symbolic language'. Their Bible, Bhagavad-Gita, Torah or Koran was written on the face of the Earth. The landscape became 'a rich source of information on the sacred... the land *had a story to tell* to mankind... a topographic story elicited from a given landscape by a tribal member is not a 'just-so' tale but a demonstration of mythic data'.[16]

The mythologised land emerged, then, from the interaction between the physical environment and a particular state of mind experienced by its human inhabitants. The land came to be haunted - by human consciousness. Ideas of 'sacred places' do not emerge from the land, they can only be sacred if human consciousness is present. Symbolism and sanctity are what *we invest the landscape with* - they are not factors that exist separately in the environment.

The nub of the matter revolves around the state of consciousness in which this process took place. We do not mythologise the land nowadays; not, at least, at any sort of cultural level. Why not? Surely because our modern, urbanised (literally 'civilised') Western-style consciousness is much more differentiated than that of traditional or early peoples. Our minds have hard edges. We do not melt into the landscape, we sit aloof on it, dig into it, use it as a material resource. It is 'separate'. In the way that we put up walls and fences, and hedge in blocks of land, so too does our modern consciousness have its defined boundaries. From an originally diffuse sense of self, we have developed iron-clad egos, that is, personal mental vehicles. But early and traditional peoples were not so 'locked into' our present-day form of waking consciousness. Indeed, the question arises as to whether they were in continual, or at least readily-accessible, altered states of consciousness. Did earlier, prehistoric, peoples wander the Earth in an actual dream or entranced state? I have elsewhere[17] suggested that the great division of time we moderns with our 'hardened conscious-ness' make between 'history' and 'prehistory' - documented and undocumented time - can be seen as analogous to the division between waking consciousness and the unconscious psyche. In such an analogy, the waking mind floats like a small cork on the unknown depths of the Unconscious, as history bobs along on the ocean of prehistory. To try to interpret ancient sacred sites or mythologised landscapes is, therefore, a little like attempting to peer into the depths of our unconscious minds.

Landscape as a gateway to the mind

Whatever the state of mind earlier peoples may have had, we have to accept, I think, that they were more easily able to enter trance conditions than we are, generally speaking, today. We see this still with the !Kung of the Kalahari (the exclamation mark denotes a glottal, click sound). They engage in trance dances that can project them into a profoundly altered state of consciousness (they call it *kia*)[18] that most modern Westerners in normal conditions would require a drug as potent as LSD to experience. Ancient and traditional peoples were or are more at home in extended states of mind, and needed less of a stimulus to enter into them. The very landscape could act as such a stimulus. Elkin said that the country of the Aborigine 'is the symbol of, *and gateway to*, the great unseen world...'[19] (My emphasis.) Working with the Marind-anim of New Guinea, anthropologist Paul Wirz observed that holy spots, the places of *Dema* or spirits, had hallucinogenic properties in themselves:

> In most cases such spots have a striking outward appearance in consequence of some strange or unexpected aspect. In them occur unusual land formations, chasms, uplands, swamps with sandbanks or gravel deposits fresh or salt. Curious noises may be heard in them... Occasionally people catch sight of strange apparitions, the *Dema* themselves, rising out of the earth, though mostly such visions are but fleeting and uncertain...[20]

Given the right preparation, a spiritual or poetic interaction with the external environ-ment can still occur with modern people, of course, though without the framework of tribal myth. An intriguing instance of this was given by Philip O'Connor, an articulate vagrant. He felt that the study of the mental effects of walking were akin to the effects of certain drugs, and has been insufficiently researched. He found that in walking endlessly the roads of England that he could sometimes obtain an 'incomparable feeling...as though one were a prayer winding along a road; the feeling is definitely religious...'[21] He found that during prolonged periods of tramping a deep mental rhythm, 'poetic in its effects', began to dominate all his perceptions. 'All hard nodules of concepts are softly coaxed into disbursing their cherished contents...' he observed. 'Maybe mental fireworks will gloriously light the mind - but quickly *the world will attach the inner light to outer phenomena*... The speed of transit between inner state and outer appearance is a feature of tramping.' (My emphasis.) One's 'identity-sense' becomes 'diffused into the landscape'. On one occasion O'Connor passed an uprooted tree by the roadside. He thought, or heard within his head, the curious words 'She has left me'. O'Connor noted that a pressure at the back of his head accompanied 'this perversion of thought, or insight of poetry'. Furthermore, '*Time* stops in such perceptions'. A cessation of mechanical, linear time-sense was somehow caused by 'a high sky, a statically spread landscape'. The different experience of time when alone in the landscape was markedly shown up whenever he came in contact with townspeople. They would appear 'terribly quick, jerky, and doll-like, with chatter to suit'.

In normal modern, urban consciousness, with its mechanical rather than elemental, cyclical kind of time, we are prevented from entering into a poetic dialogue with the land.

The bicameral brain

Julian Jaynes, a professor of psychology at Princeton University, has put forward a contentious but well-argued and attested theory that ancient peoples did actually have a differently-functioning consciousness to ours today.[22] It is worth spending a little time to consider this idea.

The human brain is divided into two 'halves' or hemispheres, separated by a band of over two million fibres called the corpus callosum. In each hemisphere is an area known as the temporal lobe, which seems to be related to dreaming, hallucinations or visions, language and other functions. These two are connected across the corpus callosum by a thin bundle of nerve fibres called the anterior commissure. In very crude terms (it is more complicated than this), the left brain handles speech, logic, analytical thought, stage-by-stage cognition, while the right hemisphere handles *gestalt*, patterns, connections, intuition, emotion and poetic matters. (O'Connor's reaction to the uprooted tree, above, was a right-brain response.)

Many of our sensory functions cross over, so that what is seen by the left eye is processed by the right hemisphere of the brain. When a person has undergone a complete commissurotomy, that is, the cutting of the midline connections between the hemispheres, nothing is generally seen or felt to be different. But when sensory input is closely monitored, defects are found. For instance, on a page of writing everything to the left of the middle of a line of writing is 'seen' by the right hemisphere, and *vice versa*. The 'you' in your left hemisphere, which has articulated speech, would cognise the words on the right-hand side of the line as normal, but those on the left-hand side could not be 'told' to the 'you' in the right hemisphere, because that hemisphere does not have speech. Similarly, a person with 'split brain' cannot describe the contents of a slide shown to the left eye (and thus the right brain), *but the left hand could point to a matching picture*. It is as if there were two persons inside the brain. As only the left brain has articulate speech (though both hemispheres under-stand language) it is the one that dominates cognition in a culture like ours.

Voices of the gods

Jaynes argues that the ancients had each hemisphere of their brains operating on separate tracks as it were, and 'heard' voices that originated in their right brain or hemisphere and for which, Jaynes suggests, the anterior commissure acted as a bridge. Like the voices 'heard' by schizophrenics today, these auditory hallucina-tions, which were taken to be the voices of the ancestors or the gods, had an inescapable authority, and gave instruction to ancient peoples' left hemisphere or waking, daily consciousness. Jaynes calls this condition 'the bicameral mind', and has argued in the sort of detail that cannot be given here how this structure of conscious-ness gave rise to great bicameral civilisations of the past. Early tribal peoples 'heard' their ancestors, but as societies grew more complex and cities formed, the ancestors' voices became those of the gods, and it was the king who spoke to and was guided by the hallucinatory commandments of the main gods of the culture. The instructions of the gods were carried out through extremely hierarchically-organised societies. Although individual people could consult 'household deities', their voices were culturally accepted as subordinate to the institutionalised voices of the great gods transmitted through the king or governing theocratic elite. The consciousness of these bicameral peoples was pitched so differently to ours that even the stress of an unfamiliar situation could be enough to trigger auditory hallucinations in them.

As with people who hear voices today, the inner speech could seem to come from some point in the environment. A schizophrenic may hear a piece of furniture, or a wall, issue sounds at him, for instance. In the bicameral world, if Jaynes is right, *auditory hallucination was highly organised* and was conducted mainly through the use of statues and idols. These were consulted and they spoke in reply. Indeed, there were ancient ceremonies involving the mouth-washing of idols, to keep their speech clear, and the Spanish conquerors of the Maya were told by the Indians that their statues spoke. The earliest forms of writing also give the speech of the gods as if dictated, and some, such as a Mesopotamian cuneiform tablet of the first millennium BC, specifies that it was 'the royal image' (statue) that spoke. (I knew one mental patient who organised his auditory hallucinations in something of a similar fashion, so he could cope with his condition in daily life: when he heard a voice 'coming on', he would make for the nearest telephone booth and lift the receiver. In this way, he could converse with his voices in a socially acceptable way!)

Such idols were often depicted with large eyes, as eye-to-eye contact is an important factor in communication - when a mother speaks to an infant, for example, it looks at her eyes, not her lips. Ancient idols the world over often had huge eye orbs, or had gems inserted for eyes, and sometimes their lips were half open as if in speech. These powerful images held their human makers in their thrall.

An 'eye goddess' idol from the temple of Ishtar at Tell Brak, Syria, circa 3000BC.

Talking heads

The use of idols as organised sources of hallucinated speech may have derived from much older traditions of ancestor worship, if Jaynes' ideas are correct. The whole groundplan of some early communities was so designed as to place the tomb of a dead chieftain in a position still at the centre of living activity. With a range of evidence that cannot be entered into here, Jaynes suggests that the voice of the dead king could still be 'heard', if not by the community in general, then by the chief's or king's successor. The arrangement of the ancestor's bones, particularly the skull, and the type of grave goods, as if for a living person, together with the veneration and even dread obviously bestowed upon the graves of the ancestors, all suggest that the dead leader was thought of as in some way still alive. The dead king became a living god.

Temples eventually replaced tombs, and as the ancestors became the gods, their skeletons were supplanted by idols. As Scully noted, the temples were houses for the gods, not for people. Jaynes has identified particular types of street and building layouts in ancient communities that he feels indicate bicameral consciousness.

The hallucinatory associations with the ancestors' bones could explain the various head cults of early societies, Jaynes suggests. It is certainly a fact that the head was seen by many people as the seat of the soul, and in Stone Age temple-tombs skulls are often found placed in separate compartments to other bones. This was noticeably the case at the Neolithic chambered mound of Isbister, the so-called 'Tomb of the Eagles' on Orkney, and we will encounter something similar in the Avebury complex in Part Two.

An example of a speaking head being mythically associated with a particular topographical feature occurs in ancient Celtic literature. The tale of Branwen in the old Bardic stories collected in the *Mabinogion* tells that Bran the Blessed ('The Blessed Raven', possibly originally a major Celtic god) was mortally wounded during a raid in Ireland. His followers cut off his head and took it back to Wales with them. The head continued to speak and instructed the group to take it to the White (meaning sacred) Mount in London (now site of the Tower of London). On the way, the Assembly of the Wondrous Head was delayed for years in an enchanted condition, but eventually reached the White Mount and there buried Bran's head, to protect the sovereignty of Britain. The origin of this story is, of course, the Celtic head cult, and hundreds of pagan Celtic heads fashioned from stone have been found, and countless more made out of wood must have been lost.

In and out of style

We have to try to envisage a style of consciousness in the bicameral world in which the sense of 'I' is greatly diminished, and with no sense of space within the head. (We all think of ourselves as a little person inside our head , which is, of course, a sustained, culturally-sanctioned hallucination. We feel a sense of mental space, in which the little inner person sits looking out at the world as if in a room with five sensory 'windows'. Our little person can also wander around in our thoughts, like a clerk sifting through a filing cabinet, and we can glimpse ourselves, our little person, in our memories and fantasies. We can create mental space. All this is likewise a sustained hallucination. There is no 'person' nor any empty space inside our head, which is solid tissue, liquids and bone. A characteristic of altered mental states is that the location of the 'person' can wander to other parts of the body, or even out of it; the seat of consciousness becomes mobile.) This state of mind was not because of some different physical structure of the brain, but due to a differently jigged range of neuronal patterns and connections. To use computerese - a software difference rather than one of hardware. Bicameral awareness would feel a little like our mental state when doing a task such as driving a car, things were done almost 'unconsciously'. When a novel situation was encountered, the bicameral person would be instructed by their god or gods, that is, their right brain, how to handle it: there were thousands of portable idols and household statues to focus any daily instructions by the lesser 'gods'.

Jaynes points out that our present-day style of consciousness is probably quite recent (no more than 2000-3000 years old in his opinion) and not necessarily permanent. We produce a culture based on our state of consciousness, and that in turn gives us feedback helping to sustain that state. But for all sorts of reasons, changes in worldview can change dramatically, and long-term, cultural-scale changes of worldview require actual alterations in the way consciousness works, how perceptions are made, what priorities govern thinking. Our present cultural state of consciousness could transform into something that would be unrecognisable to us today. (This could happen on a scale hitherto impossible because of the worldwide telecommunications that now exist and which are themselves approaching the global equivalent of the human cortex in information connections.)

The speaking environment

Although the use of idols was the great organiser of hallucinated 'god'-voices during what Jaynes would call bicameral times, actual topographical features could also take on the aspect of deity in themselves. He records the Hittite mountain shrine of Yazilikaya in central Turkey:

That the mountains themselves were hallucinatory to the Hittites is indicated by relief sculptures still clearly visible on the rocks within the sanctuary, showing the usual stereotyped drawings of mountains topped with the heads and headdresses used for the gods. As the Psalmist sings, 'I will lift up mine eyes unto the hills whence cometh my help.'

On one of the faces of this mountain temple, the robed king is carved in profile. Just behind him in the stone relief towers a god with a much loftier crown; the god's arm is outstretched, showing the king the way, whilst the god's left arm is hugged around the king's neck and grasps the king's right fist firmly. It is testament to an emblem of the bicameral mind.[23]

So the topography *could actually speak* to earlier peoples, if Jaynes is correct.

Schizophrenia is considered by Jaynes to be a vestige of bicameral consciousness, and he notes that many patients 'heard... voices as emanating from strange and unknown places'. Amongst several examples he gives is of a 26-year-old woman whose topographical 'stimulation point' was a river bank where she would hear a man and a woman calling to her. Also the sounds in the world around a schizophrenic can provide the matrix in which voices can form. One patient described hearing voices...

> ...sometimes sounding from the wind, sometimes from footsteps, sometimes rattling dishes, from the rustling trees... I hear the voices only if I attend to them... The voices are words that tell me one story or another... The whole day through they keep on telling truly my daily history of head and heart.[24]

Researcher John Steele quotes the case of 'The Talking Stone' in Seneca Indian tradition, which long ago told a Seneca boy the history of his people, a history which itself became enshrined in the story of the speaking rock. 'Thus our earliest ancestors,' writes Steele, 'lived in what can be described as a conscious interactive environment.'[25]

The bicameral fate of cities

In Jaynes' view, hallucinated voices may have been responsible both for the foundation of city sites and their desertion during the bicameral period. Jayne's cites the mysterious case of the lost Mayan cities:

> ... the curious inhospitable sites on which Mayan cities were often built and their sudden appearance and disappearance can best be explained on the basis that such sites and movements were commanded by hallucinations which in certain periods could be not only irrational but downright punishing - as was Jahweh sometimes to his people, or Apollo (through the Delphic Oracle) to his, by siding with the invaders of Greece.[26]

(In this regard, it is worth noting that Istanbul was effectively founded by Byzas in 657 BC as a result of a somewhat oblique pronouncement by the Delphic Oracle.)

The actual bicameral act may be recorded on stone reliefs from Santa Lucia Cotz umalhaupa, a non-Mayan site in Guatemala: a man is depicted laying face down on the ground listening to two spiritual beings speaking over him. To this day, seers in the region adopt this posture in order to hear prophetic voices, though they now use the hallucinogenic cactus peyote. (Jaynes considers the use of hallucinogens to have developed as natural, spontaneous bicameral ability began to decline. Personally, I doubt that this is true. However, proto-historic peoples like the Etruscans did develop the use of *divination* techniques to found cities, and it is possible, as we shall note, that this began to emerge as bicamerality broke down.)

The sacred sun

Auditory and other hallucinations can originate from parts of the cortex that imbue them with a religious aura - there are apparently brain structures that accommodate this function. Jaynes notes that the sun, 'as the world's brightest light', takes on a special religious significance in many unmedicated schizophrenic patients, just as it did in the theocracies of bicameral civilisations. One modern schizophrenic has written:

> The sun came to have an extraordinary effect on me. It seemed to be charged with all power; not merely to symbolize God but actually to be God. Phrases like: 'Light of the World,' 'The Sun of Righteousness that Setteth Nevermore,' etc., ran through my head without ceasing, and the mere sight of the sun was sufficient greatly to intensify this manic excitement under which I was laboring. I was impelled to address the sun as a personal god, and to evolve from it a ritual sun worship.[27]

Fairly recent research, probably unknown to Jaynes, at the great temple complex of Karnak, at Luxor (the ancient Thebes), on the east side of the Nile some 370 miles south of Cairo, gives some support to the bicameral theory. (See plate 7.) It has been suggested by researchers since the beginning of this century that the axis of this temple complex, which was respected throughout the many centuries of structural changes and additions in the second millennium BC and possibly earlier, was oriented on the setting midsummer sun. But Gerald Hawkins, an astronomer with the Smithsonian Institution, discovered that the orientation was, in fact, in the other direction, eastwards, giving midwinter sunrise during the second millennium BC. Hawkins found that in the main building housing the sanctuary there was an upper chamber, the 'High Room of the Sun', from where the event could have been observed:

> There was a square altar of alabaster in front of a rectangular aperture in the wall. This roof temple was dedicated to Ra-Hor-Akhty, the sun-god rising on the horizon. The wall carried a picture of the pharaoh, facing the aperture, one knee to the ground, making a gesture of greeting to the risen sun...

> The platform was elevated, the view clear of obstruction. Here the priest-astronomer could make his observations to check the sun was on course.[28]

Eastwards beyond this building are two small temples, one dedicated to Ra-Hor-Akhty, the other 'The Temple of the Hearing Ear', an intriguing and - in the light of the bicameral theory - significant dedication. It contains hymns of praise to the god that appears at dawn. It may relate to auditory phenomena 'heard' as the sun rose on the special day - if the ancients could 'hear' mountains, why not the sun? It is perhaps worth recalling that William Blake, the poet, painter and mystic, indicated that he was able to *hear* the sun rising like a host of angels singing. It would be unwise, especially in the case of Blake, to assume this to be mere poetic license.

Across the Nile from Luxor is the Valley of the Kings, itself defined by a horned skyline on one side, according to Scully, and a conical mountain, an extraordinary natural pyramid, with a 'teat' - a pre-dynastic mound - on the other. Two giant sandstone statues, 60 feet tall, stand near the Nile in isolation. They represent Amenhotep III and flanked the entrance to his mortuary temple which was also dedicated to Ra-Hor-Akhty but has now disappeared. Their stoney eyes stare eastwards, and Hawkins has been able to confirm an earlier suspicion of Sir Norman Lockyer's that they are in fact also oriented to the midwinter sunrise. During an earthquake in 27 BC, one of these great statues was cracked, and began to make sounds at dawn. In proto-historic Graeco-Roman times they became known as the Colossi of Memnon, and were consulted as an oracle because of the dawn sounds which issued forth.

The age of oracles

According to Jaynes' view, the 'age of oracles' in the proto-historic period (the period between undocumented pre-history and fully-documented historical times) was a symptom of the breakdown of the archaic bicameral mind as modern mentality with its sense of 'I' and illusion of interior, mental space began its ascendancy. He considers this process began to occur in the Old World during the third and second millennia BC, but accelerated dramatically in the final thousand years BC due to vast natural disasters (such as the eruption of Thera - Santorini - in the Mediterranean, which sent out a tidal wave 700 feet high that drowned key areas of Mediterranean civilisation) and the subsequent chaos caused by refugees and disruption of the carefully-balanced bicameral social structures. In fact, the size of cities had begun to threaten these structures in any case. The emergence of writing, too, can be seen as increasing left-brain dominance.

Slowly the gods became dumb and retreated, mythically, into the sky. Heaven was created. (Although the sun, planets and stars had become gods, and there were important sky deities, most of the gods *had physical locations in the landscape*.) Mesopotamian cuneiform tablets of the late second millennium BC bemoan the disappearance of the gods. 'One who has no god, as he walks along the street, headache envelopes him like a garment' says one, perhaps referring to a physical sensation caused by the neurological re-patterning. 'My god has forsaken me and disappeared' wails another tablet. And around 1230 BC, Tukulti-Ninurta I, an Assyrian tyrant, had a stone altar made that showed him, sequentially, emphatically gesturing towards and kneeling before *an empty throne*. The empty throne became a feature of declining Mesopotamian bicameral civilisations.

Carving from the Tukulti Altar. The Meso-potamian king, Tukulti, stands, kneels and gestures towards an empty throne. The god has gone. As drawn by Susan Hockaday in The Orgins of Consciousness in the Breakdown of the Bicameral Mind.

Oracles were a carry-over of the earlier mentality, Jaynes claims. They occurred, he notes, in locations where 'because of some awesomeness of the surroundings, or some important incident or some hallucinogenic sound, waves, waters, or wind, suppli-ants, any suppliants, could still "hear" a bicameral voice directly'.[29] Over time, the bicameral ability diminished in the general population even under such stimuli, and selected people with surviving bicameral traits - prophets, priestesses (women are more 'lateralised' in brain function than men, their psychological functions being less tied to one or other hemisphere) - took over the role until eventually even they could not 'hear' and actual right-brain consciousness was overtaken by rote procedures or divination.

One of the greatest oracles of the ancient world was at Delphi, on the southern slopes of Mount Parnassos, Greece. Originally dedicated to Gaia, the Earth Goddess, the site was appropriated by the cult of Apollo. (See plate 8.) A temple complex developed. A female prophetess, the 'Pythia', gave responses to questions from commoners and the high born. She drank the waters of the local holy springs before giving audience. Even today this place is still redolent with numinosity, and seems wedded to the elements. It is prone to earthquakes (the ancient Greeks built the temple of Apollo on an anti-seismic wall of ingenious design), and fierce electrical storms that blaze and roar within the confines of the steep valley on the side of which the temple complex clings vertiginously. Zeus and his thunderbolts are very close, and in its heyday the oracle site must have seemed profoundly awesome. Even archaeologists acknowledge that the 'brooding physical power of the site must be considered in any account of its history'.[30] Jaynes suggests that due to the stresses of the pilgrimage to the site, plus preparation and powerfully-endorsed social expectation, a suppliant would be in a primed psychological state.

> To this causative expectancy should be added something about the natural scene itself. Oracles begin in localities with a specific awesomeness, natural formations of mountain gorge, of hallucinogenic wind or waves, of symbolic gleamings and vistas, which I suggest are more conducive to occasioning right hemisphere activity than the analytic planes of everyday life. Perhaps we can say that the geography of the bicameral mind in the first part of the first millennium BC was shrinking down into sites of awe and beauty where the voices of the gods could still be heard.
> Certainly the vast cliffs of Delphi move into such a suggestion and fill it fully: a towering caldron of blasted rock over which the sea winds howl and the salt mists cling, as if dreaming nature were twisting herself awake at awkward angles, falling away into a blue surf of shimmering olive leaves and the gray immortal sea.[31]

The voice of Zeus could be heard at Dodona, and was consulted by Odysseus. At that time the site was probably just a great sacred oak, and Jaynes suggests that the voice was stimulated hallucinogenically from 'the wind trembling in its leaves' and wonders if the oaks of the Druids may have acted as similar stimuli. In the fifth century BC, Zeus could no longer be heard directly, and there had to be a priestess who spoke for the god while in trance. As the direct voice connection at oracle sites diminished, more elaboration had to take place at them.

At Lebadea, 20 miles east of Delphi, was another oracle site and one of the last 'direct voice' oracles where suppliants heard the gods for themselves without temple intermediaries. Jaynes finds that Lebadea 'even today bears some remnants of its ancient awesomeness'. It is at the junction of three steep precipices, where 'murmuring springs' emerge and fall away into the ravines. The suppliant, after extraordinarily complex preparations, retired to a carved-out cell in the rock where one ravine winds into the heart of the mountain, and is situated over an underground flume.

Dreams became a source of omens, a contact with the ancient processes of the bicameral mind, as they still are. Dream omens were collected in Assyrian society in the first millennium BC and recorded in dream books such as the *Ziqiqu*. 'Temple sleep' was commonplace in Greece, as noted in the previous section of this essay, and throughout the Mediterranean world. In fact, all forms of divination proliferated, from the relatively simple, such as the casting of sticks, soil and stones, to the more sophisticated, such as reading bird flight, the heavens or using cards and charts, because *mancy* is another way of circumventing the tyranny of the left brain.

And there was singing and chanting. Although the left brain has speech, the right brain has song. This is shown by the so-called Wada Test, in which a person has one brain hemisphere sedated. With only the right side active, a person cannot speak, but can sing. When the right hemisphere is sedated, the person is unable to sing but can speak. Electrical stimulation around the temporal lobe in the right hemisphere often produces hallucinations of singing and music. The right brain is dominant, also, in our attention to music and song. Knowing this, we can see the significance of the fact that the first poets *sang* their verse. The wandering Celtic Bards, the Greek Aoidoi, and others, sang the ancient myths, the stories of the gods, the history of the people. We might also recall from the previous section that the Aborigines chanted at their sacred sites. Each piece of mythically significant topography had its song; the Dream Journeys were lines of songs, and tribal boundaries were noted by song. At sites, the elders would scan the imagery on the *Churingas* and chant what they told.

The words of the gods and songs of the Muses (what 'music' is) only became imaginary to a left-brain-dominated consciousness. We moderns have lost the soundtrack of prehistory.

Gateways to the Dreamtime

We cannot be sure, of course, if Jaynes is right in his theorising, but it has to be admitted that when all his evidence is considered, his case is persuasive. Whether he is right or wrong, or, more likely, partially correct, however, we can be certain that the ancient worldview was arrived at through a different filter of consciousness than that prevailing today.

One of the ways we do know for sure that consciousness was modified in the ancient world - and often today also where traditional societies survive relatively intact - was by the use of hallucinogens. Botanical sources gave access to the Dreamtime Earth - the spirit version of the material world, what Lévy-Bruhl called 'supernature'. (Interestingly, this is also the term the Irish nature mystic, G.W. Russell - 'AE' - gave to his perception of the visionary environment: see the final section of this essay.) Certain plants, trees, bark, vines and fungi provided 'doorways' into the Earth's Otherworld. All Eurasia had its botanical drugs for religious and shamanic use: hemp (cannabis; hashish) - samples of which have been dug up in Iron Age burials in Germany; Fly Agaric (*Amanita muscaria*) and psilocybin mushrooms; henbane; mandrake; belladonna; ergot; opium... The list is almost endless. Africans, too, used plants to give access to the Otherworld: marijuana; khat (murungu, otyibota); *kwashi* bulbs and who-knows-what herbs and roots. The Australian Aborigines made use of pituri. The Americas are vastly rich in hallucinogens, and the shamanic Amerindian peoples made great use of the fact: in North and Central America there was wide use of hallucinogenic mushrooms; *Datura*-type hallucinogens such as Jimson Weed (a pre-Columbian wall painting in a Zuni kiva in New Mexico shows a medicine-man holding Jimson Weed); the

The Amanita muscaria, or Fly Agaric mushroom. It has a distinctive red cap with white spots and was the favoured hallucinogen of Siberian and Arctic European tribes.

mescaline-containing peyote cactus, and mescal bean amongst many others - even toads which secreted hallucinogenic bufotenin and hallucinogenic fish! In South America there were a variety of narcotic snuffs; coca; hallucinogenic fungi; San Pedro cactus and many preparations of the vine, *Banisteriopsis*, such as *ayahuasca*. Such substances taken in a ritual setting were viewed as sacramental to ancient and traditional peoples, and enhanced their social integration: we have to be careful not to project our own, modern drug prejudices.

I also suspect that there were other 'gateways' into the Dreamtime Earth that have been largely overlooked by archaeologists and many alternative researchers alike, namely, the actual materials of the landscape itself. That ancient peoples were good geologists cannot be in doubt - otherwise, where did the Bronze Age come from? They knew how to find and work copper seams and iron deposits. Before that, they knew where the very best sources of quality flint were to be mined. They would not have thought in geophysical language like we do today,

The wooden effigy of a psychoactive mushroom, found in what is believed to be the burial mound of a Hopewell Indian shaman in Chillicothe, Ohio. The effigy is over a foot long and was sheathed in copper. It may have been the shaman's rod or wand of power.

naturally, but the knowledge was there. It is surprising that we have tended to overlook the geophysical characteristics of prehistoric sacred sites, for both folklore and anecdotal experience tell of unusual 'energy effects' at sites, such as curious light phenomena, stones that give electrostatic shocks, and sites where effects on mind and body can be had.

Power places

The Dragon Project Trust[32] has done extensive if poorly-resourced work on this aspect, and I have written at length on what is currently known about various energy effects at sites in books such as *Earth Lights Revelation*[33] and *Places of Power*[34], where the interested reader can obtain detailed information. Here it is enough to state just in caption form some things we have found.

We have discovered naturally-magnetic stones at stone circles (usually just one at a site and in a key position) and at natural holy spots - such as a rock outcrop, an Indian power place, on Mount Tamalpais, near San Francisco, and a mountain peak called Carn Ingli ('Hill of Angels') on the Preseli range of south-west Wales, where a Celtic saint had visions and where modern people have reported physiological and mental effects. (See plate 9.) (It is known that magnetic fields can affect the temporal lobes and the pineal gland, both areas of the brain that seem involved in the production of dreams, memories and visions or hallucinations.) Compass needles spin and magnetometers record unusual magnetic variations at such places.

The Dragon Project has confirmed that certain types of sacred sites the world over occur in close proximity to fault lines - fissures or breaks in the Earth's crust (like the San Andreas Fault) which tend to be the scene of tectonic stress, magnetic and gravitic anomalies, and enhanced mineralisation (which can cause variable electromagnetic fields).

Such geological zones also tend to be high-incidence areas of 'earth light' phenomena - exotic and currently unexplained lightforms apparently emerging from processes within the earth and which hover at the extreme limits of known geophysics. They sometimes act as if they have mass, at other times as if weightless. They have electromagnetic properties, yet also possess other characteristics that go beyond known physics. There is even a strong hint in the available evidence that these lights possess some rudimentary intelligence of their own. Energy fields associated with the lights may also have hallucinogenic properties in close-encounter witnesses.

I think it possible that this last factor was put to use by some ancient shamans. Certainly, such 'earth lights' were known by many ancient and traditional peoples. *Min min* lights were sorcerers or ancestor spirits to some Aborigines, and *eskuda'hit*, 'fire creatures' to the Penobscot Indians of Maine, were shamans in flight, as they were to the Lapps. The Snohomish Indians of the American north-west saw the lights as gateways to the Otherworld, and some Yakima Indians to this day use the lights for divination, much as the old Etruscans used birds. Hawaiian Islanders saw their *akualele* lights as spirits. Folk living in the Himalayan foothills around Darjeeling were warned not to approach the lanterns of the *chota admis*, 'little men'. Similarly, the Wintu Indians of California called such lights 'spirit eaters'. West Africans called the lights *aku*, and saw them as devilish. In the Celtic world until recently, and still in some remote, rural parts, lights would readily be identified as fairies - literally 'fairy lights' - or 'corpse candles', denoting an imminent death.

Sacred monuments where lights are seen from time to time range from temples in India and China to stone circles in Britain. Indeed, Asian temples could be built precisely because of the appearance of lights at a spot, and even in the Alps there is a chapel dedicated to 'St Mary of the Lights'. Also, sacred peaks often have reputations for unusual light phenomena. Sorte Mountain in Venezuela, for instance, produces lights near its peak at sunset. They are thought by contemporary shamans to be spirits, and to see them is a good sign that healing there will be effective.[35] Mount Shasta in northern California is said to produce curious lights and fleeting apparitions. (See plate 10.) Identical reports abound about Pendle Hill in Lancashire, where George Fox, founder of the Quaker movement, had a mystical vision and where the Pendle Witches, the shamans of their day, congregated. In May 1869, for instance, a 'firey goose' was seen flitting a hundred feet above the hill slopes. This happened at the time of a local earthquake. In modern times, of course, such lights seen over the hill are interpreted as 'UFOs' - the sci-fi mechanistic myth of our times. The holy mountain of Athos in Greece displays light phenomena from time to time which are interpreted as appearances of the Virgin. The legendary Welsh mountain of Cader Idris is said to harbour the entrance to the Underworld and to produce lights at the Celtic new year. In fact, it was midsummer eve of 1982 when I personally witnessed (with others) a ball of blue-white light erupt from the north side of the mountain. It flashed overhead, and I was later able to estimate its speed at over 600 mph. The mountain is of volcanic origin and stands on the Bala Fault.

I suspect that these lights are nature's most direct intermediary between mind and land.

By accident, the Dragon Project has stumbled on another aspect of natural energy: it has found that areas of heightened natural radiation seem capable of precipitating spontaneous but fleeting altered states of consciousness of a very vivid nature in certain people. Granite is a particularly radioactive rock, and the Dragon Project has identified stone circles containing granite megaliths that have exceptionally active spots on them which emit constant streams of gamma radiation. Could this have been used by the old shamans of the megaliths? Possibly. Alberto Villoldo has reported how the contemporary Peruvian shaman, Don Eduardo Calderon, teaches his students to place their spine or foreheads against certain sacred stones at Machu Picchu.[36] These stones are granitic (and the site is situated on a fault).

Enhanced natural radiation zones are created in enclosed ceremonial monuments (such as Neolithic dolmens) built from granite. Egypt's Great Pyramid is a vast limestone structure, yet granite was shipped 600 miles from Aswan to clad the interior of the King's Chamber. To the Egyptians, granite was the stone of spirit, *Maat*. I have measured the interior of the King's Chamber and found its radon levels to be virtually identical with those so far measured in prehistoric granite monuments in western Europe.

Subterranean ritual sites such as the kivas of the Pueblo peoples of the American Southwest and the Iron Age souterrains or underground stone passages of the Celtic fringe of Europe, all seem to occur in areas of high natural radiation, such as granite regions or zones with relatively high uranium levels in the ground. The role of enhanced natural radiation in mind-change effects awaits a serious study. (See plate 11.)

The use of a fire in ceremonial practices increases the ionisation of the atmosphere generally, and, particularly, negative ions, as well as inducing trance-friendly alpha brain rhythms by the flicker effect of the flames. But there are more powerful negative ionised environments. Harner comments that the Jivaro Indians of South America might retire to 'a cave, the top of a mountain, or a tall waterfall' in their quest for a guardian spirit.[37] Mircea Eliade records how the Aranda shamanic initiate of Central Australia goes to sleep in the mouth of a remote cave. The spirits come and carry him into the cavern's interior, where the Aranda's paradisal land is situated. And we have already noted the Greek legend of Epimenides who 'slept' and fasted for a long time in the cave of Zeus on Mount Ida in Crete and emerged as a master of trance consciousness.

Now, caves, mountain peaks and waterfalls are all notable places where natural ionisation occurs. The moving water of a waterfall charges the surrounding air, and mountain peaks can sometimes be seen with ionised glows around them (well-known in the Andes as the 'Andes Glow'). Light phenomena have even been seen around the apex of the Great Pyramid. Cave mouths are notorious for being subject to a high incidence of lightning strikes due to ionisation. (Indeed, earlier this century, one of the explorers of the Henne-Morte caverns in France was struck by lightning 200 feet beneath ground!) The reason for intense ionisation in caves seems to be the accumulation of radioactivity from subterranean rocks by the action of groundwater. The radiation builds up within the enclosed space of a cavern. This is sometimes expelled during hot, summery weather, and can cause a stream of ionisation skywards, providing a path for lightning.

Ionised air is known to have an effect on certain hormone levels in mammals, and hormones in turn regulate brain function and hence affect consciousness. It is now thought that emissions from rock can affect serotonin levels in mammals,[38] for instance, and serotonin is associated with the production by the pineal gland of hallucinogenic beta-carbolines, which, it is thought, aid in producing dream imagery.[39,40]

Caves are also very dark places, of course. The training for a 'Mama' ('Enlightened One') or shaman in the Kogi Indian society of Colombia involves his being incarcerated in a cave from infancy or childhood, and not seeing the light of day for several years. Even when brought out at night, he wears a broad-rimmed hat so he cannot see moon or stars directly.[41] This must have an enormous effect on the hormonal workings of the pineal gland, which is regulated by light-dark cycles. When he finally emerges, the young Mama can 'see' the Spirit or Dreamtime Earth, which the Kogis call *aluna*, interfused with the physical terrain. He can see supernature.

As we have noted, cave environments contain heightened levels of radiation. We associate radon - the naturally radioactive gas that is produced by uranium decay in the ground - with cancer, because a house sealed for air-conditioning or heating situated over a radon emission point (a 'radon chimney') will accumulate radon. A person breathing this in over many years is subject to greater risk from lung cancer. However, there is some evidence that in limited doses, or in aerated environments, radon might well have a beneficial effect. At the turn of the century, people resorted to radon-filled caves in Colorado much as their European counterparts took the waters at fashionable spas for the betterment of their health. Yet in at least some cases, those European waters also contained mildly enhanced radiation. The famous hot springs of Bath in Britain, for instance, used for seven thousand years from Neolithic times through the Celtic and Roman periods into recent centuries, are radioactive. The waters of Chalice Well at Glastonbury are likewise said to be radioactive. Even now, old gold and uranium mines in Montana are used by people suffering ailments such as arthritis and diabetes. Sufferers are placed in the old mine workings for timed periods, and cures over a given course of such 'treatments' have been claimed. Further, Dr Bernard Cohen of the University of Pittsburgh has taken measurements in 415 US counties and found that in those where the level of radon would have been expected to produce a 25 per cent increase in female lung cancer, cancer incidence was actually down 30 per cent. Similar unexpected inverse relationships have been found in Finland, the UK, and elsewhere.

Geophysical conditions were probably not used on their own for producing mind-change, and are perhaps best seen as factors augmenting other techniques such as trance dancing, drumming, breathing methods, hallucinogens, and so on. Further, relevant geophysical conditions do not exist uniformly throughout the world, any more than do plant hallucinogens, so they could only have been made use of where they occurred.

Entranced

In overview, then, it seems that ancient peoples sought altered states of consciousness - trance conditions - by many routes, botanical, geophysical and physiological, used both separately and in conjunction with one another. Myth is the reflex of other realms of mind, from dreams to trance states. The very word 'trance' derives from a Latin term meaning 'a passage' or 'a crossing over', as in en*trance*. The landscape therefore provided literal entrances to the *Other* world. The ancients' neurological software may have been 'rigged' differently to our own, if Jaynes is right, at some point in the past; they may have sought other techniques when this began to change. All we know for sure is that states of consciousness other than that consensus one we nowadays claim as 'normal' were used. When studying ancient sacred sites and mythologised landscapes, this factor has to be taken most powerfully into account. We have to learn to view them with different eyes.

We also have to understand that when in trance states, it was possible, is possible, *to move around in a spirit version of the physical landscape*, and the figure in ancient and traditional societies who best exemplifies this ability is the shaman.

3

THE SHAMANIC LANDSCAPE

The shaman linked mind and land. He or she was an intermediary between the spirit world and the tribe. Through the sort of methods indicated in the previous section - various combinations of hallucinogens, drumming, dancing, physiological and psychological conditioning and the use of special places - the shaman would enter trance and travel to the spirit worlds in order to seek information required by the tribe, to reclaim the wandering or abducted souls of sick tribal members, to guide the soul of a dying person to the Otherworld, to engage the aid of spirit helpers, to ward off the attacks of shamans of other tribes or perpetrate his own. The shaman could see backwards and forwards in time, and was thus the repository of the tribal history and a prophet.

The shamanic role emerged out of animism and totemism, out of the generalised sense of spirituality that early peoples felt permeated all nature. It was the first conscious religious role, and underpins major religions of post-tribal societies. Joan Halifax writes that shamanism is 'nearly as old as human consciousness itself... Through the ages, the practice of shamanism has remained vital, adapting itself to the ways of all the world's cultures... The shaman lies at the very heart of some cultures, while living in the shadowy fringe of others... Shamanism's origins in the Palaeolithic period inevitably link it with the animal world of the hunt. The shaman became identified metaphysically with the untamed creatures which provided food, clothing, and even shelter.'[1]

Shamans were 'technicians of the Sacred, the specialists of the Beyond'[2], the 'technicians of the supernatural'.[3] Mircea Eliade, the religious historian who was a great scholar of shamanism, defined the shaman as one who 'specializes in a trance during which his soul is believed to leave his body and ascend to the sky or descend to the underworld.'[4] This is the key element in shamanism, as we shall discover - the ability to apparently travel in mind to the Otherworlds or through the environment, observing distant events, meeting ancestors or other spirits, or seeking the ways into the Underworld. This was accomplished in what we would call an out-of-body experience, in which the shaman's spirit would enter or take the form of an animal or bird, or simply 'exteriorise' as a disembodied locus of consciousness travelling by means of 'magical flight'. This is, in fact, the essential meaning of 'ecstasy' - 'out of the senses'.

Eliade emphasised that the basics of shamanism occurred in many parts of the world; *it was a primary experience of human consciousness*, not a learned affectation or belief system (though specific tribal beliefs strongly coloured the phenomenon). However, he considered that shamanism 'has had its most complete manifestation in North and Central Asia'.[5]

The person who survived shamanic initiation and apprenticeship learned how to control and integrate altered states of consciousness, and it is that element of control which makes the shamanic ability distinct from mediumship. The shaman had the ability to survive death and rebirth. Shamans were active in the spirit world.

A shaman would have spirit helpers, either in animal form - the prototypes of the 'familiars' of European witchcraft - or as invisible entities, often residing inside his or her body.

The actual form of shamanism varied amongst different societies. Usually, the shaman was the solitary religious focus for a tribe, but in some cultures there would be defined ceremonial sessions where everyone had direct experience of the supernatural realms. In yet other societies, there would be varying grades of shamans.

The fundamental cosmology of shamanism consisted of three worlds, the 'middle Earth' of human reality, the upper world of spiritual beings, and the underworld of the shades. (This basic model, which of course left its mark in Christian cosmology as in many others, has had many variants around the world, particularly schemes based on it using nine or seven worlds.) Access to these Otherworlds was by means of a conceptual axis that linked them - a World Tree, a Cosmic Mountain, or actual features that symbolised such an axis, such as a tent pole, smoke rising through a tent's smokehole, a beam of sunlight, a rope or a ladder. By symbolically travelling in trance states along this axis, the Shaman could ascend to heaven or enter deeply into the body of the Earth, the Underworld. A mythological expression of this occurs in the Norse legend of the sovereign-shaman, Odin, who hung on Yggdrasil, the World Tree. Again, Christ was crucified on a cross or tree.

The sacred centre

It is this concept of the world axis that formally links mind and land in shamanism. In classical terminology, the world axis, the *axis mundi*, is the *omphalos*, the centre, the point from which the sacred circle, the temenos, is struck, and from where the Four Directions, the cardinal points, are marked, quartering the horizon. It is a spatial extension of the human body's 'directions' of front, back and sides. Marking the omphalos is the first great act of geomancy, or sacred geography, remembered today in the laying of a foundation stone for a building. The omphalos is the centre of a circle whose circumference is nowhere and everywhere. It is the navel or umbilicus of the world, the point of sustenance, and the point of cognition. At its deepest level of correspondence, *it represents mind in the landscape*.

The omphalos stone at Delphi is the classic world navel: Zeus sent out two eagles from the extremities of the Earth; where their flight paths crossed was the central

7. *The great sun-oriented axis of the temple complex of Karnak, Egypt. (Author)*

8. The moody atmosphere of Delphi had hallucinogenic powers, Julian Jaynes has suggested. (Author)

9. Carn Ingli, the Hill of Angels, in Wales. A place of visions and magnetic anomalies. (Author)

10. Mount Shasta, California. (Author)

11. Now roofless kivas in Chaco Canyon, the Anasazi ritual centre in New Mexico. (Author)

12. A German Maibaum. In some designs there are more than one circular garland, which symbolise the various planes of existence or worlds on the cosmic axis. (Author)

13. A heavily-eroded ceremonial staircase, carved out of the north wall of Chaco Canyon, where a straight Anasazi 'road' comes in from the surrounding desert. (Author)

point where the stone was to be erected. Probably the greatest religious omphalos is Jerusalam, sacred to Judaism, Christendom, and Islam alike. Also in the Holy Land, Mount Tabor possibly means 'navel', and Mount Gerizim was, Eliade assures, 'undoubtedly invested with the prestige of the Center, for it is called "navel of the earth".'

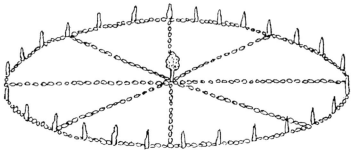

Stone circle at Sola, Nerike, Sweden. It is divided into eight equal divisions, with a holy tree at the centre. (John Palmer after N.H. Sjöberga, 1824)

The omphalos stone, Delphi. (Author)

But everywhere, in all cultures and at many types of sites, an omphalos stone, a pole or tree or some other marker was employed as part of ceremonial groundplans. In the Celtic world at sites as far apart as Navan in Ireland (as we noted in the first section of this essay) and Goloring near Koblenz, massive poles were erected within earthen enclosures to represent the World Tree. They acted as dramatic landscape markers and ceremonial focal points. The first Zuni Indians of the American south-west were shown the directions of north, south, east and west by *K'yan asdebi*, Water Skate, using his long legs spread out. Where his body touched the ground he told the Zuni that there was 'the midmost place of the Earth-Mother, even the navel'. He instructed them to build the first Zuni town on the spot. When the diviners or *haruspices* of the ancient Etruscans of northern Italy constructed an omphalos, they dug a pit, a *mundus*, and put offerings of the first fruits into it, then capped it with a stone. From this point a city's street grid would be laid out. At special times, the central stone would be removed to let out the spirits from the Underworld to mix with the world of humans. The Yakuts of Siberia believed that 'at the golden navel of the Earth' stands a tree with eight branches. For the Semangs of the Malay Peninsula, the omphalos is a huge rock, Batu-Ribn, which emerges at the centre of the world.

And so on - the omphalos or world axis point is a major element in the mythologised landscape. It is truly archetypal, occurring in completely unconnected cultures around the world. In the way that we are always *here* wherever we happen to be - that is, our point of cognition is always at the centre of our environment - the omphalos or world axis is *here*, a point placed in the physical landscape, at the mythical centre of the world, where access to the Otherworlds could take place.

The mythical centre of the world was the human mind - *a mental, non-material reality symbolically given a physical location.*

The Cosmic Axis
The shaman, then, entered the Otherworlds by ascending or descending the World Tree, the Cosmic Mountain or other representation of the omphalos, the *axis mundi*. The omphalos was the shaman's point of entry to the spirit world in trance. In classic Eurasian shamanism, the use of the drum was the prime means of entering trance, perhaps aided and abetted by ingestion of the hallucinogenic Fly Agaric mushroom. The drum would be covered with protective symbols, and by tradition, the wooden frame was fashioned from a branch of the World Tree. When the shaman fell down in trance - 'away' on the shamanic journey to the Otherworlds via the World Tree - his drum would be placed on his back to warn others against disturbing him, as that would be dangerous for the shaman. The drum was the shaman's 'steed' or 'canoe', the vehicle for the shamanic journey. In certain Siberian traditions, the shaman would ride during his seance to the World Tree astride a hobbyhorse device consisting of a stick with a horse's head attached - literally a steed, and a forerunner of the witch's broomstick.

A seventeenth-century engraving showing a Lapp shaman in trance with his drum on his back. The drum was both the v ehicle for the shaman to travel to the world tree on his out-of-body journey, and was also a warning against anyone touching the entranced shaman, which might have fatal consequences for him.

The Tungus shaman's ritual robe had a depiction of the World Tree emblazoned on it, and in other Siberian shamanic seances a birch pole would be raised outside the shaman's tent to symbolise the world tree. (The interesting point here is that the birch tree has a symbiotic relationship with the Fly Agaric mushroom.) Several Siberian tribes felt that the souls of children awaiting birth perched like birds in the branches of the World Tree, for it was living and gave life. The World Tree is symbolised in its fertility aspect also by the European tradition of the maypole or *maibaum*; the garlands suspended around the central pole originally symbolised the various planes or worlds of existence as envisaged in the shamanic cosmology. (See plate 12.) In Siberian myth, shamans have nests in the branches of the giant fir tree at the centre of the Earth (the Northern European tradition of the Christmas Tree is of course another symbol of the World Tree). In several traditions around the world, the shaman, during a seance, would symbolically climb notches in a pole or up a ladder placed against a pole or tree. At the top he might flap his arms like a bird's wings. In Chile, where a range of sacramental hallucinogens were used, the female shaman or

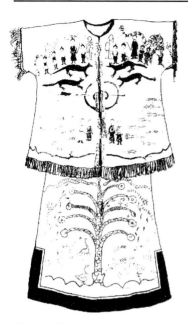

The World Tree as depicted on the ritual garment of a Tungus shaman.

machi climbed to the top of such a notched pole and span around to symbolically journey to the heavenly realms. The Lakota Indians erect a Sun Pole on the third day of their Sun Dance, and a bundle of sweet grass, sage and buffalo hair is placed in a fork of the pole. A song is sung: 'At the centre of the Earth, Stand looking around you...' In the Wiradjuri and other Aboriginal myths, the first men reached the sky by climbing a tree. The climbing of a prepared tree was undertaken in some initiatory rites - in others, an elder would rise to the top of the tree magically on a 'cord' extended from his body.

The range of such symbolic versions of the World Tree are legion. Eliade sums it up:

> Tree- or pole-climbing rites, myths of ascent or magical flight, ecstatic experiences of levitation, of flight, of mystical journeys to the heavens, and so on - all these elements have a determinative function in shamanic vocations or consecrations. Sometimes this complex of religious practices and ideas appears to be related to the myth of an ancient time when communication between sky and earth was much easier. Regarded from this point of view, the shamanic experience is equivalent to a restoration of that primordial mythical time and the shaman figures as a privileged being who individually returns to the fortunate condition of humanity at the dawn of time. Many myths... illustrate this paradisal state of a beatific *illud tempus*, to which shamans intermittently return during their ecstasies.[6]

In a sense, the omphalos was a feature 'left behind' in the mythologised landscape by the shaman, to be embellished by later cultures. In *The Myth of the Eternal Return*, Eliade writes: 'Every temple or palace - and by extension, every sacred city or royal residence - is a sacred Mountain, thus becoming a Center... being an *axis mundi*, the sacred city or temple is regarded as a meeting point of heaven, earth and hell.' It is now sublimated into a rote foundation stone ceremony or forgotten about entirely.

However, it is just now being realised by various researchers that the ages-long practice of shamanism has left us with some other relics - rock art, mysterious effigy mounds and straight linear features in certain ceremonial landscapes. They are *the marks of the shaman*, and are all curiously related to one another through the common denominator of shamanic trance, the 'journey' to the *axis mundi*, the way between the worlds. I have gone into this matter in considerable depth and with extensive references in *Shamanism and the Mystery Lines*?[7] (which is being published shortly after, and could profitably be read as a companion volume to, this work, despite being written earlier), but here there is only need, and space, to present an overview - albeit one that is already an updated and refined version despite the recent nature of the work.

The signatures of trance

Cave walls in Europe, such as those at Lascaux or Les Trois Frères in France, contain marvellous Palaeolithic paintings of animals. Rock paintings and carvings in the Americas and by Australian Aborigines are no less remarkable, but it is with the San (Bushman) rock art of southern Africa that archaeologists have made their break-through in understanding the nature of these ancient and mysterious markings. The key to this lies in the fact that in addition to the animal and human depictions in such rock art, there are also semi-human creatures and, particularly, grids, dots, zig-zags, spirals and other semi-geometrical images. These latter are, overall, the most common ingredient in all ancient rock art worldwide, though seldom reproduced in photographs. Long disregarded, they have been assumed to be either crude representations of animal enclosures and hunting nets, or symbols the meaning of which were forever beyond our ken. However, the San told the archaeologists that these particular rock depictions were produced by shamans in trance. Certain of these archaeologists, in particular J. D. Lewis-Williams of the University of the Witwatersrand, Johannesburg, realised that these markings were similar to neurological patterns being studied by neurophysiologists examining hallucinations occurring in trance.

These brain researchers found that the parts of the cortex that process vision can produce spontaneous patterns during trance, patterns which can also occur during migraine attacks (typically the so-called 'fortification pattern' consisting of a complex white-edged zig-zag form that blots out part of the visual field). The range of these *entoptic* ('within vision') patterns break down into what the scientists call 'form constants', chief amongst them being lattices (grids, nets, filigree, honeycomb); tunnels or funnels (alleys, cones); spirals, and webs (really amalgams of grids and funnels).[8] The categories are more extensive than this, though this list encompasses the broad range of forms. Such patterns appear before the eyes in early stages of trance when induced by any method, though they are particularly strong, it seems, when hallucinogens are used.

Anthropologist, Geraldo Reichel-Dolmatoff has found that the South American Tukano peoples actually use these patterns as the basis for their decorative art. These Indians see the patterns in *ayahuasca* trance, and certain patterns are 'owned' by certain kinship groups. Moreover, the Tukano have developed techniques that allow them to enhance and manipulate such patterns.[9]

Szuman, an early investigator into entoptic imagery who personally experimented with hallucinogens, found 'these vivid visual pictures completely covered real objects...', they were 'projected onto the surfaces of the floor, the ceiling, or the wall, or they appear in space, covering the objects that lie behind them'. Two later

Entoptic phenomena in the three stages of trance imagery as depicted in San, Coso and Palaeolithic rock art. (J.D. Lewis-Williams and T.A. Dowson, after various researchers in their 1988 paper, 'The Signs of All Times'.)

researchers, Ronald K. Siegel and Murray E. Jarvik, conducted extensive sessions with volunteer subjects who were placed in darkened environments and saw entoptic imagery suspended in front of their eyes as if about two feet away.[10] The rock art painter-shamans similarly saw these patterns as if they were slides projected onto the rock walls during trance, assuming them to have been produced by the spirits. They 'fixed' them with paints or carving. (Over time, such neurologically-produced images may have taken on rote ceremonial symbolism, their forms being standardised in the traditions of the cave artists, and so trance need not necessarily have always been involved in their production.)

It has already been noted that these entoptic visual forms occur early in trance. As this deepens, however, they can take on partial representational aspects, so, for example, a zig-zag line might acquire additional visual details giving it a vague serpent-like appearance. These semi-representational images are sometimes called 'construal' forms. Later, in what can be seen as a third stage of trance, the entoptic images turn into actual pictorial or 'iconic' trance hallucinations when composites of memory material is merged with them. The entoptic forms underlie the structure or texture of these trance visions like dots underlie a newspaper photograph. One subject under *yagé*, a preparation of *Banisteriopsis*, described this well:

> I saw tiny dots, like those on a TV screen, transparent dots that agitated and turned... around a cone forming a sort of funnel... [which] opened upwards from the floor I was gazing at... In this swirl of particles lies all my visual experience.[11]

Sometimes there are mixtures of imagery in trance hallucinations or visions, so two different mental images of animals, or a man and an animal, can become combined. In rock art, people are sometimes depicted who are clearly wearing masks, but others show fully merged human-animal forms. The technical term for these is 'therianthropes'. Such imagery would clearly have had totemic significance for tribal peoples, and the use of animal masks and costumes would have developed from this.

Shamanic markings

But there are other, much larger markings than cave art which have been left on the landscape itself by ancient shamanic peoples and which are only just now beginning to be seen as also resulting from shamanic trance. These markings are geometric and effigy earthworks and curious linear features - alignments, straight tracks or 'roads', earthen avenues - in ceremonial landscapes.

Such terrestrial markings survive in various parts of the world, and particularly well in the Americas. This is because the Amerindian peoples were mainly shamanic in outlook, and had at some point in the remote past entered the Americas over a land bridge across what is now the Bering Strait, bringing with them the elements of Palaeo-Siberian shamanism. While shamanism in Eurasia became subject to a multitude of cultural influences, and itself affected and was in turn modified by later religious and social developments, in America the ancient shamanism was isolated

from such turmoil up until relatively recent centuries. The rich diversity of hallucinogenic botany available in the Americas further nurtured the continuance of shamanic
practices. Amerindian shamanism developed its own characteristics, of course, but it
retained the stamp of ancient shamanism for a longer period than was possible in
Eurasia, and its effects on the landscape have thus survived in better order, though
now even these are rapidly disappearing.

Modern-day USA has a great many Adena and Hopewell effigy earthworks
roughly two thousand years old. Though a large number were destroyed by the
settlers through agriculture and the building of cities, hundreds or even thousands
still remain. The mounds, best seen from the air, are found in Mid-West states such
as Wisconsin, Iowa and Illinois, and are in the shapes of bears, birds, human beings
and winged human beings. The Hopewell culture, a shamanic sphere of influence
centred in the Ohio region, built huge earthworks in the form of geometric shapes
with linear avenues and a range of mound shapes. Much further south, in Mexico, the
Olmec peoples built a vast terrestrial effigy at San Lorenzo on the Gulf Coast. The
Olmec site there is situated on ridges so massive that they were assumed to be natural
features, but archaeologists have subsequently discovered that they are, in fact, part
of a huge earthwork depicting a flying bird three-quarters of a mile long and
comprehensible only from the air. In desert areas in North and South America, figures
or 'biomorphs' were depicted on a grand scale.

As enigmatic as such features are, and we shall refer to them again later, the
landscape lines are even more mysterious. They occur in many forms in different parts
of the world.

'Leys'

In Europe, possibly surviving hints of linear patterns in the form of alignments of
ancient sites, many of them evolved from even earlier sites, have been noted by a
variety of antiquarians and researchers from the eighteenth century onwards. The
most famous of these researchers was doubtlessly the English inventor and business-
man Alfred Watkins, who some 70 years ago perceived alignment arrangements in
his native Herefordshire and Welsh border country. He thought they were the
remnants of Neolithic traders' routes, 'old straight tracks' laid out by line-of-sight,
which had evolved over subsequent millenia acquiring sanctified shrines along them,
some of these in turn being preserved by old churches replacing them. He gave an old
Saxon term, 'leys' (meaning 'a cleared stretch of ground'), to these alignments and
started a popular interest in them that has grown extensively in recent decades. His
ideas caused much controversy, though, and mainstrean scholarship scorned or
ignored them.

Alfred Watkins, the controversial discoverer of 'leys', seen here taking a photograph on one of his alignments. (F.C.Tyler/Northern Earth Mysteries)

Earth lines

Undoubted linear markings in England dating from 4000 or more years ago do exist, however, though Watkins (and his detractors, it would seem) appear not to have known of them, or, at least, not to have seen their significance to the whole issue. They are called 'cursuses' and were earthen avenues of ditches and banks linking long barrows and other Neolithic mounds. The eighteenth-century antiquarian William Stukeley was the first to draw attention to a cursus, a linear earthwork nearly two miles long close to Stonehenge. It can still be visited today, though its banks are very low or missing entirely. It links a 'pseudo long barrow' at its western end with an authentic one at its eastern terminus. Ironically, it was an archaeologist rather than a 'ley hunter' who noted that the axis of its northern, virtually straight ditch can be extended another mile through a standing stone and a Neolithic ritual site known as 'Woodhenge'. This line, which is in all respects a 'ley', can be extended some miles further to a ridge infested with prehistoric mounds called Beacon Hill - and beacon hills were considered by Watkins as key features on his 'leys' as they had the excellent line-of-sight advantages made use of for rapid communication by the Elizabethans (as they were elsewhere in Europe).

Between Stukeley's time and 1944, another nine cursuses were noted. Since World War II, because of the advent of aerial photography, the total has leapt to around 50. Very few of these show up at all at ground level, appearing now only as fleeting markings in vegetation seen from the air.

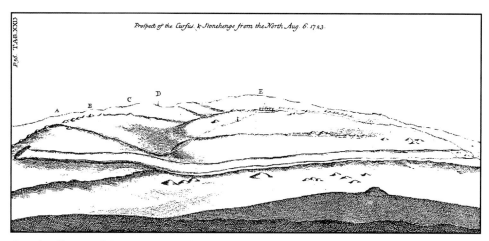

One of William Stukeley's drawings of the Stonehenge Cursus, viewed from the north.

Stukeley had given the name 'cursuses' (Latin for 'racecourse') to them because he thought they were Romano-British running tracks. We now know that they are much older than this, dating from Neolithic times, and were likely to have been ritual avenues of the dead, or, as I would prefer to put it, ceremonial linear enclosures for the spirits of the ancestors.

These cursuses are for the most part straight, or are in straight segments set to different orientations (perhaps dating from different periods). A very straight cursus at Aston-upon-Trent in Derbyshire had one ditch aligned for a mile towards a (now eroded) mound, and another at Scorton in Yorkshire similarly aligned to a hilltop site. At Godmanchester near Cambridge, a cursus three kilometres in length has recently been discovered running in a straight line to a Neolithic enclosure which investigation shows to have been an astronomical temple of great precision. This cursus contained burial mounds along its central line, and was built after the enclosure had been ceremonially burned. A two-mile-long, dead-straight segment of a crop-mark cursus was found by air survey to the west of Heathrow Airport, London, dwarfing the runways designed to handle Jumbo jets! So straight was it, in fact, that archaeologists thought the crop mark must indicate a Roman road, until excavation proved otherwise.

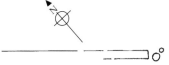

The patchy crop markings of a typical cursus at Scorton, North Yorkshire. Its surviving length is just over two kilometres. Its south-east end is against a set of ring ditch features (also now just crop marks), but the other terminus has not been found. The hole of a possible siting post associated with the cursus was found by archaeologists, along with evidence of an internal row of central mounds. (Simplified after Peter Topping.)

Sometimes, straight segments are linked clumsily, with misaligned or curvilinear sections intervening. Examples of this are to be found on two cursuses butted end-to-end, stretching for over six miles across Dorset, and known inaccurately as The Dorset Cursus. The south-western end of this composite feature, on Thickthorn Down, is still marked by substantial earthworks, from where the two lines of the ditches and banks (now invisible) went straight up a ridge, Gussage Hill, aligning on a pre-existing long barrow there. Eastwards from this point, the cursus wanders and terminates in a valley. Another cursus starts at that point and continuing eastwards goes up to a ridge on Bottlebush Down, where the alignment again wanders for a short distance, then proceeds directly through and along the axis of another long barrow *en route* to its north-eastern terminus. Close by this terminus, and pointing towards it, is what seems to be a deliberately lenthened long barrow (we will encounter this phenomenon of a 'stetched' barrow again in the Avebury complex, Part Two). Indeed, at the other, south-western, end, long barrows also point to that terminus. The whole feature is thus clearly related to the long barrows in the region (and some of these seem to have been built when the cursus was under construction).

Archaeologist Richard Bradley has made an extensive study of the Dorset Cursus, and finds that 'it is the alignment that matters' relative to the distribution of the various long barrows. Excavations have revealed that mounds close to the cursus had straight avenues of poles linking with the cursus. Bradley discovered that when looking westwards along the cursus from inside its banks, its orientation towards the long barrow atop Gussage Hill gives the midwinter sunset: the sun appears to sink into the venerable burial mound. Thus the cursus, Bradley concludes, 'links the positions of the ancestors with the movement of the heavenly bodies'. It is, he feels, 'a British Avenue of the Dead'.[12]

I have made a study of about half of the known cursuses, and have found that over 60 per cent of those point to either a prehistoric site or an ancient church (presumably on an earlier site) a few miles beyond one of their termini.[13] This confirms the type of pattern noted at the Stonehenge Cursus (above), and it is remarkable that it can be recovered so distinctly considering the damaged state of the cursuses and the changes that have occurred in their environments.

Other prehistoric linear features in Britain include stone rows and boundary systems. These and the cursuses show that ancient Britons did lay out straight landscape lines, despite Watkins' detractors, and that they often linked sacred sites with them.

Native American landscape lines

Ancient and mysterious straight line features of various kinds exist in many parts of the ancient world, but none are more remarkable than those in the Americas. Forty-mile-long straight tracks, 'airline in their directness'[14], were left in the California sierras by the now extinct Miwok Indians, and the lost Anasazi ('Ancient Ones') who lived a thousand years ago in the New Mexico area, set out great lines which radiated

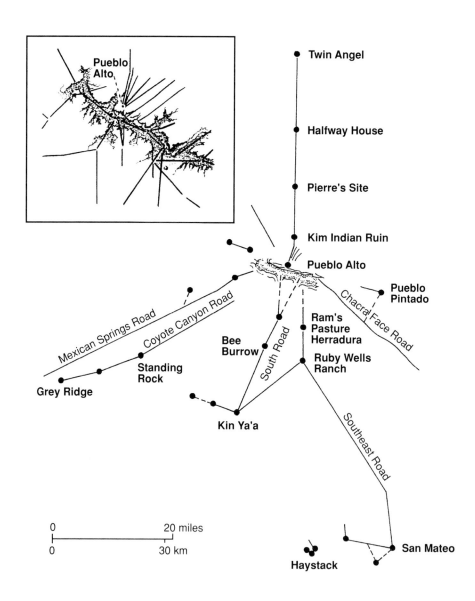

The system of Anasazi 'roads' so far discovered in the mesa landscape around Chaco Canyon, New Mexico, and some of the great houses and other sites along them. Inset: detail of the roads (bold lines) in and immediately around Chaco Canyon.

for tens, perhaps hundreds, of miles around their cult centre of Chaco Canyon. These straight, 30-feet-wide features are called the 'Chaco Roads'. Although noted occasionally in the early years of this century, serious research on these amazing mesa lines began only in the 1970s. Using hundreds of air photos plus judicious ground survey and excavation, archaeologists have now mapped some 400 miles of Chacoan roads. On the ground they are, like cursuses, usually difficult to see. They are very straight and change direction only occasionally, at some marked topographical feature or at a 'Great House' (pueblo complex). Subtle intervisibility between these Great Houses and between them and curious 'shrine sites' out in the desert have led researchers to realise that there was a sophisticated line-of-sight signalling system used in connection with the 'roads'. A cluster of several roads meet at Pueblo Alto, on the northern rim of Chaco Canyon. (See plate 13.) Where the roads come to the edge of the canyon rimrock, what appear to be ceremonial staircases up to 25 feet wide were carved out of the living rock of the canyon walls.

But why did a people without the horse or the wheel need such strange 'roads'? The mystery has been compounded by recent infra-red air surveys by NASA which reveal multiple parallel sections to the roads which are no longer visible to the eye or the normal airborne camera.[15] Most researchers now think these roads were not so much for mundane travel, but were, rather, ceremonial or sacred ways, linking the Great Houses which archaeologists assume were ritual centres, where people would gather periodically and have great feasts. There were rooms at these sites which opened out *only* onto the roads. A researcher was told by a Navajo elder in the 1920s that though the landscape lines looked like roads, they 'were not roads'.[16] (The Navajos came to the area after the Anasazi had disappeared, presumably by dispersing into adjacent pueblo tribes.)

Various other Amerindian societies - all of them shamanic, and all of them using hallucinogens for religious purposes - built straight landscape lines of various kinds throughout the Americas. Pre-Hispanic Indians built straight road systems around La Quemada in Mexico; the Mayans of Central America had their *sacbeob*, wonderfully-engineered straight ways linking ceremonial centres; the Taironas of Colombia had paved paths across their mountain retreats; the Nasca culture of Peru engraved dead straight lines on the pampa, and the Indians of the altiplano of Bolivia built even longer straight tracks linking shrines, and on which the Spaniards built their churches (in similar vein to what old Watkins had suggested had happened on his 'leys').

Nazca

The most famous of these lines are, of course, those at Nazca. Much research work has been done on them over recent decades, but the most intensive work was conducted during the 1980s by an inter-disciplinary tream co-ordinated by Anthony F. Aveni of Colgate University.[17] The Nazca lines, formed by removal of the darkened, oxidised desert surface revealing a lighter subsoil, are of various widths, ranging from large trapezoid areas to fine track-width features. They criss-cross in bewildering array.

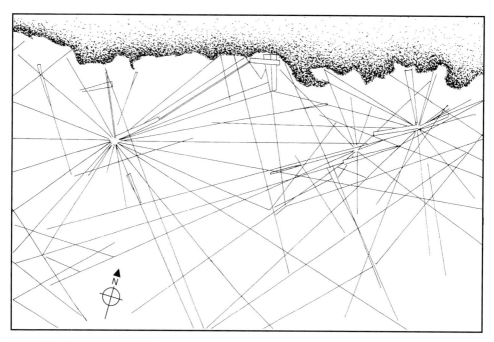

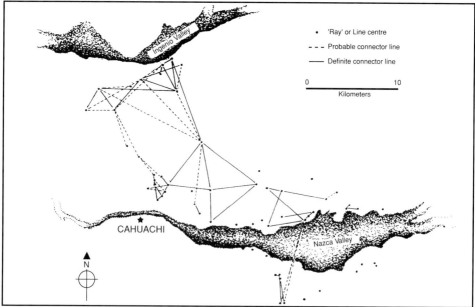

The Nazca lines. Top: detail of lines and 'ray centres' on the northern edge of the Nazca pampa, above the Ingenio valley. Bottom: simplified plan of 'ray centres' and connecting lines on the Nazca pampa. (Based on the work of A.F. Aveni et al.)

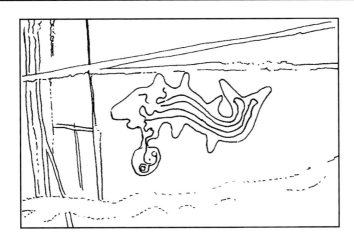

One of the Nazca pampa's continuous line 'biomorphs'. This killer whale, hemmed in by Nazca lines and a dried river bed, is 85-feet long and is believed to be carrying a human trophy head from a lower fin. Mummified skulls with ropes have been found in Nazca tombs.

They are interspersed with a variety of 'geoglyphs' - unicursal ground drawings of animals, geometric forms and apparently abstract shapes.

Aveni and colleagues found a number of factors that had either been overlooked or given insufficient emphasis in previous work on the features, which I can only briefly summarise here:

i. There had been a ritual centre called Cahuachi at the edge of the pampa. The name indicated a magical, prophetic connection in the local Indian language, and some lines were directed at it.

ii. It was clear from detailed ground survey that some of the Nazca lines had been walked - deep paths weave along within the confines of the pure geometry of the linear markings. It was assumed this was due to ritualised walking ceremonies, as the lines do not lead to or from obviously significant spots.

iii. Stone settings were also discovered on the pampa amongst the lines: people had evidently spent time out in this inhospitable terrain.

iv. There was evidence that the lines had, long in the past, been *ritually swept*. (Anthropologist, Gary Urton made a significant connection in this respect when he observed a ceremony in an Andean community where the church plaza was swept in strips - each strip assigned to a kinship group in the community - in order to symbolically create 'sacred space' before a saint's statue was brought out of the church and paraded.)

v. Pottery deposits were found along the edge of some lines and ground drawings, as if left as votive offerings. (In recent work by Helaine Silverman and David Browne at a hitherto unexplored set of lines with undisturbed pottery deposits, it has been possible to date the lines with some confidence to a period spanning 100 BC - 500 AD.)

vi. Above all, Aveni and team found that there was a certain order in the lines - many of them interlinked 'ray centres', natural prominences or artifical mounds. Over 60 such line centres were found to be involved in the array of pampa lines. *vii.*There were only a very few possibly significant astronomical orientations among the lines.

Lines of the Inca

The much later Inca, who ruled a vast empire stretching from Colombia to Chile, built thousands of miles of roads in straight sections, some of which at least incorporated older Andean straight tracks.[18] These roads crossed at the Inca capital, Cuzco, which means 'navel' in the Inca language and supposedly had an overall groundplan the shape of a puma. Cuzco was a sacred city as well as an administrative centre, and from there the Inca, the Son of the Sun, ruled the 'Land of the Four Quarters', as the Inca empire was known. The main ritual centre was the Coricancha, known as the Temple of the Sun but in actuality more a temple of the ancestors. From this location 41 mysterious lines or *ceques* radiated out into the surrounding countryside. These invisible lines, like Watkins' 'leys', can be traced nowadays only as alignments of sacred sites or *huacas*, which can be a standing stone or natural rock, a temple or shrine, a bend in a river or a waterfall, a sacred cave or holy hill, a special tree, or even a battle site or bridge. There are, or were, 328 of these in the landscape surrounding Cuzco, the number of days in the Inca year (which was lunar-based).

Remarkable long-term research by Dr Tom Zuidema has revealed much about this *ceque* system. Only about ten of these mystery lines had astronomical significance, mainly for sun watching using special towers (now destroyed). Other uses are less clearly understood, though one was to provide ritual passage of sacrificial victims to their place of ceremonial execution. Zuidema discovered that the lines were significantly associated with water, and in turn with the ancestors. This apparently bizarre linkage came about because water came from undergound, and that was where the ancestors dwelt. Different kinship groups were responsible for the upkeep of specified *ceques*, and this was because their ancestors dwelt beneath the particular sector of ground the designated lines crossed.

Zuidema also found evidence for ritual straight walking. Huanacauri, a sacred peak on a *ceque* was the starting point for a straight-line pilgrimage, continuing the course of the *ceque*, that contained 21 *huacas* along its route. It went upstream along the Vilcanota River to a place known to the Spanish as La Raya, or 'dividing line'. This ritual walk or pilgrimage took place in June, the midwinter month in that part of the world, and its orientation was south-east, the direction of the December (midsummer) solstice. Zuidema tantalisingly noted that 'this straight line emanating from Huanacauri may have continued... all the way to the Island of the Sun in Lake Titicaca...'[19] A distance of some 200 miles!

Most interestingly, British researcher Tony Morrison succeeded some years ago in photographing some *ceques* using specially-filtered infra-red film. Not only were they alignments of sites, the *ceques* were clearly old straight tracks too, for though now invisible to the naked eye, the infra-red false-colour photographs picked up tell-tale variations in vegetation colouring revealing dark straight lines radiating out from Cuzco to the surrounding mountains.

The landscape around Cuzco was, in Inca times, clearly a deeply mythologised one, having religious, sociological, astronomical, hydrological, sacred geographical, and symbolic significance all mediated by the lines or *ceques*, which emerged from a navel or omphalos (the Coricancha). The complex significance landscape lines could have for the ancient mind thus becomes increasingly apparent.

Can these large land markings - the effigies and the lines - also be explained, like the rock art, as the results of shamanic trance? I have come to think so. I think they indicate that the mythologised landscape was one that could, effectively, be *moved around in* at the level of mythic consciousness.

Flight of the shaman

Unknown to me, I came to this conclusion years after it had been at least partially suggested by Marlene Dobkin de Rios, an anthropologist at California State University. She realised that the landscape markings belonged to peoples who were known to have taken hallucinogens as part of their religious cults. (In Peru, for instance, there is a 3000-year-old stone carving at the site of Chavín de Huántar of a deity or demon holding a San Pedro cactus.) In a 1977 research paper, Dobkin de Rios suggested that the landscape markings may have been associated with the out-of-body 'aerial journey' experienced by the shaman during trance.[20] The effigy mounds described earlier certainly show forms such as birds and winged human beings which are shamanic images. Dobkin de Rios feels these terrestrial effigies, best seen from an aerial perspective, may have been territorial markers by a shaman and his people warning against intrusion by other shamans on 'spirit flights', for in most shamanic societies there was intense rivalry between the shamans of different tribes.

Dobkin de Rios suggests that the lines may have an entoptic origin. While I think she has accurately perceived the nature of the effigy earthworks, I think this explanation for the lines is not *quite* right or, at least, complete. I suggest that they also have to do with the supposed out-of-body, magical flight that takes place in shamanic trance.

We have noted that when the shaman went out-of-body, he did so either in the form of an animal or as a free, disembodied spirit *in flight*. Looking a little more closely at this magical flight, as it is so central to the core shamanic experience, and, indeed, as we shall see, to the landscape lines themselves, it is useful to start by going back briefly to rock art. The San rock art, we discovered, contained shamanic elements as admitted to by the San themselves, and as recent ethnological evidence is suggesting for certain Amerindian peoples such as the Coso.[20] Aside from the entoptic markings in the southern African rock depictions, there is another vital indicator of trance -the *ales* or 'flying buck'. The archaeologists now concentrating on the shamanic aspects of San rock art tend to refer to this feature nowadays as a 'trance buck'. It appears time and again in the rock imagery, sometimes in association with depictions such as antelope-headed men, figures teetering atop ladders (that universal motif of shamanic trance), or figures apparently engaged in trance dancing. This flying buck is an odd figure - essentially an antelope or eland with its legs raised and flying through the air, usually trailing curious long lines behind it. There are many versions of this flying figure, some of them barely recognisable as deer.

Some of the beautiful depictions of 'trance bucks' from San rock art, southern Africa. The top row shows images from various rock shelters apparently showing various stages in the transformation of a human being into an antelope - therianthropic images. It is common for a shaman entering an out-of-body trance state to experience turning into an animal (usually one of special tribal symbolic significance), and even the medieval witches of Europe reported that when they took their hallucinogenic 'flying ointments' they sometimes felt themselves seemingly turn into wolves and other creatures. The lower image shows a fully-fledged San 'flying buck' - the very image of shamanic flight. (Harald Pager.)

Joan Halifax notes that the flying deer occurs in the mythology of shamanic peoples as widely separated as the Samoyeds of Siberia and the Huichol Indians of Mexico, and points out that it is 'associated with magical flight, transfiguration, and spiritualization'.[21] The late Joseph Campbell, referring to the San flying buck, re-marked that it represented 'the released soul of the trance dancers as well as of the dead'. In Bushman myth, he noted, the dead are transformed into elands, and 'also...

the "half-dead" visionaries in trance fly forth and about in the forms of antelope men'. Campbell further emphasised that the invisible threshold between the physical world and the Otherworld 'was being actually crossed in shamanic flights of ecstatic trance'.[22] The Kalahari !Kung have specifically described to anthropologists the sensation of leaving their bodies during the state of *kia* caused by their trance dancing.[23]

Another symbol of the disembodied spirit in trance is that of the eye. To the Selk'nam of Tierra del Fuego, the shaman leaves the body like a disembodied eye, travelling in a straight line to a given destination in the surrounding countryside. The Eskimos have a rich vein of shamanic lore associated with magical flight, and one of their songs says: 'My body is all eyes... I look in all directions!' This was echoed by Gordon Wasson, a great mycologist (researcher into mushrooms). He was one of the first modern Westerners to experience trance induced by hallucinogenic mushrooms in the context of a Mexican Indian ceremony. He lay in his sleeping bag listening to the shaman's chants and felt his spirit soar out of his body: '...the bemushroomed person is poised in space, a disembodied eye...'[24]

Even modern societies retain acculturated images of shamanic spirit flight derived from long-past traditions of shamanism. Rogan Taylor, for example, has pointed out that the image of Santa Claus flying across the sky in his sleigh pulled by reindeer is in fact a relic of Siberian and Arctic European shamanism, in which shamans, who all belonged to reindeer-herder societies, took Fly Agaric mushrooms to help them to conduct their out-of-body journeys to the spirit worlds. Taylor also points out that the red and white colouring of Father Christmas' costume echoes the strong red and white colouring of the Fly Agaric mushroom.[25]

Another example is the witch flying on her broomstick. This image has a basis in fact, for we know from church records during the medieval witch persecutions that there were greenish 'flying ointments' witches rubbed on their bodies or applied to their genitals by means of a broomstick. These salves were made from hallucinogenic herbs such as belladonna, henbane and mandrake. These contain the powerful hallucinogen hyoscyamine in a form which can penetrate intact skin. Weston La Barre, an anthropologist who has specialised in the study of native use of hallucinogens, remarked that hyoscyamine 'gives the sensation of flying through the air'.[26]

He also notes that the hallucinogenic bufotenin, excreted by certain toads that were used by peoples such as the Maya, 'seems specifically to promote a feeling of flying through the air'.[27] The South American *Banisteriopsis* preparations likewise produce this sensation. There are many accounts of this, and I select just two as examples. A nineteenth-century geographer ingested *ayahuasaca* when staying with Indians and felt himself 'being lifted up into the air' and undergoing 'an aerial journey in which I recall perceiving the most gorgeous views'. In 1953, another researcher had sensations 'of being suspended in the air'. San Pedro cactus similarly gives the effect of spirit flight, according to the contemporary Peruvian shaman, Don Eduardo Calderon.

Bird symbolism, however, is that most universally associated with magical flight, as might be expected. *The Upanishads* refer to the out-of-body spirit or soul as 'the lone wild gander', and geese are a recurring image in shamanic lore worldwide. They figure prominently in Eskimo shamanic tales of magical flight, and carved effigies of geese were even found in an Eskimo shaman's grave many centuries old. In a number of widespread traditions, the shaman is said to return from the land of the dead (or the spirit world, the two images are quite interchangeable) riding on a gander.

We have already referred to Amerindian mounds depicting birds and winged humans, and this was typical of Amerindian symbolism. The eagle feather, especially attached to a stick, was a sign of magical flight. The Mississippian people (c. 900 - 1500 AD) left many examples of pottery decorated with human-bird figures classed by scholars as the 'flying shaman' motif, and a stone tablet found in the vast Monks Mound at Cahokia, their great ceremonial centre near present-day East St Louis, depicts a man in a bird mask and winged costume. A similar image has been found carved on a rock in Nebraska. The Carib Indians of the West Indies rubbed a shamanic initiate's body with gum and covered it with feathers 'to make him able to fly and go to the house of the *zemeen* (spirits)'.[28]

The antiquity of this bird imagery in shamanism is shown in the Palaeolithic depiction of an entranced man on the cave walls at Lascaux, France, who wears a bird-mask like the Mississippian shaman. Near him is a bird-headed stick, and this was also a symbol of shamanic flight in Siberia up until recent times. In addition, the Siberian shaman might wear bird-claw shoes and a metal representation of a bird's skeleton on his ritual garb, in a similar fashion to the way a Hopewell Indian shaman would hang bird claw shapes cut out of mica on his robes.

In Norse tradition, the goddess Freya was the mythical founder of *seidhr*, a shamanic practice carried out in rural Scandinavia in which a prophetess would enter trance and divine the future. She sat on a pillow of feathers symbolising magical flight. These *seidhonkas* wore ritual garb which included embellishments and gloves made of catskins, and Freya was depicted flying in the air on the back of a cat. Freya also had a magical feather garment that enabled her to fly, and she taught Odin the secrets of magical flight by use of a coat of falcon feathers. (This is just one of several traditions, incidentally, stretching as far as China and India, in which it is a woman who teaches a man the secrets of shamanic trance.)

Chinese Taoist priests were known as 'feather scholars', denoting their shamanic origins, and at the other end of the Eurasian landmass, Druidism, too, was associated with the ability of magical flight. In the legend, 'The Siege of Druim Damhghaire', the powerful Druid Mog Ruith is described as wearing an *enchennach*, 'bird dress', and rising up 'into the air and the heavens'.[29]

And so on - bird symbolism meant magical, shamanic, spirit flight virtually everywhere in the ancient world.

Shaman-sovereigns

In many societies at different periods and places, the shaman developed into a priest, a transitional process that anthropologists think is still taking place in the Campa Indian society of South America.[30] As tribal societies developed into proto-states, shaman-priests gave way to various kinds of theocracies in some cases, or became shaman-chieftains or kings in others.

That the thread of shamanism persisted into monarchy is attested in the traditions which abound from all parts of the ancient world telling of flying kings and emperors. 'The "magical flight" of sovereigns manifests the same autonomy and the same victory over death' as the shamanic journey, Eliade wrote.[31] He further commented that: 'a perfect sovereign must have the powers of a "magician". "Ecstasy" was no less necessary to the founder of a state than his political virtues... And so we find that many emperors, sages, alchemists, and sorcerers "went up to heaven".'[32] 'Flying up to heaven' is expressed in Chinese as 'by means of feathers he was transformed and ascended as an immortal'.

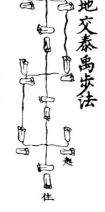

A plan of the dance steps for the 'pace of Yu', practised by T'ang Dynasty Taoist adepts. It was designed to carry the Taoist 'star-treader' through the stars of the Great Bear (Ursa Major) constellation. It derived from shamanic trance dances for magical flight, versions of which were ceremonially carried out by Chinese emperors. (Edward H. Schafer, after a twelfth century source.)

The first man in Chinese myth to be credited with the power to fly was the third-millenium Emperor Shun, and it became the tradition for Emperors at inauguration to ritually perform the steps of a special dance designed to achieve ecstasy. In India, likewise, Eliade affirms that there are 'numerous legends of flying kings and magicians'.[33] In Britain, too, the legendary king Bladud was reputed to have a stone on which he was able to fly. This is similar to the tales concerning various Celtic Christian saints who were also said to have magical stones they could use for flight.

All these legends doubtlessly reflect the traditions of Druidic flight (above), and it would be an error to take the stories literally - they are unquestionably myth-relics of shamanic flight. (This is not to necessarily dismiss the possibility of physical levitation, but that is outside my brief here.) Another Celtic example of this is the legend of Conaire, a High King of Ireland, whose father was a supernatural birdman, and was bound by a taboo (*geis*) against hunting birds, which had to be privileged creatures.[34]

Shaman-kings were divine, and had to marry the land, the Earth Goddess, in order to have the right to rule. In Celtic Ireland this was called *banais rigi*, and the land goddess was Sovereignty. The Irish marriage to the land involved curious horse ceremonies, as elsewhere in the Indo-European world, and the making of the 'king and the land as one' was often symbolised by the king at his inauguration standing on footprints carved in a sacred rock. (An echo of this occurs in Arthurian legend where only the true king can pull the sword from the stone.) Even in the full state societies that emerged from these earlier proto-states, relics of this persist. The British monarch, as a prime example, is crowned in Westminster Abbey on an ancient chair which has a special compartment that holds a sacred kingstone known as the Stone of Scone.

The Zasliai sacred stone in Lithuania, with engraved footprint. (John Palmer)

The magician-chieftains of Ireland, the flying Indian kings and the Norse mythical sovereign-shaman, Odin, and many more such instances, are from the traditions of the linguistic group we call Indo-European, which emerged about 6000 years ago out of the Black Sea area and spread across Eurasia between Iran-India in the east and Ireland in the west. Little is known about the first, proto-Indo-European society, but linguists have been able to trace back some word roots to the original, ancestor language, and also have used mythology to pick up a hint of the actual ordering of the proto-Indo-European society (a society's structure has been found to be often reflected in its myths).

It is clear that at the earliest times in the Indo-European world there was indeed a shadowy chieftain role that combined both secular and shamanic elements. Eliade has suggested that vestiges of shamanic tradition in early Indo-European society 'were principally grouped about the mythical figure of the terrifying Sovereign, whose archetype seems to have been Varuna, the master of magic'.[35] Scholars have traced an Indo-European tradition back to at least the second millenium BC where Varuna was paired with Mitra, who relates to government and judicial aspects. This Mitra-Varuna figure, then, is the mythic analogue of the proto-Indo-European shaman-sovereign, priest-king or magician-chieftain, however one wants to describe the role.

The Indo-European name of the shaman-sovereign

The ancestor language of the Indo-European peoples contains a curious word, **reg*, which seems to relate to this shaman-sovereign stage of development, and also relates in an obscure way to straight lines. It and its variants like *rec* are found in European languages in words relating to spatial descriptions, moral and social order, and into words associated with kingship. So in English we have, for example, words like region, regulation, regime, regiment, rectitude, correct, regal, reign, and so on. The word for king in Latin is *rex*, and *regina* for queen, while *regula* meant a straight piece of wood and *regio* meant a straight boundary. In German and Dutch, *recht* means 'right' in English which is similarly derived from **reg*. 'Right', in several languages, can mean correct, a right as in human rights, or a direction. The word 'direction' itself contains the same root word, and can mean spatial information, or a command. *Droit* in French also means right, but the word for king, *roi* is lodged within it. *Tout droit* means straight on, and the English phrase 'keep right on' likewise means to continue straight.

There are a great many more examples in many languages of Indo-European origin. So it is that the English word 'ruler' can mean both a straight-edge and a king or leader.

Language scholar, Eric Partridge finds that the basic meaning of **reg* is: '... to set straight, to lead or guide straight, hence, as a noun, a true guide, hence a powerful one, hence a chief, a king; perhaps the basic sense of **reg* is 'a straight line' or, better, 'a movement straight from one point to another, hence a movement along a straight line.'[36] More recently, other scholars have found a meaning for **reg* in the Indo-European language of Sanskrit that can best be translated as *mana* or supernatural power, and, possibly, 'protector'.[37] So we have the image of a shaman-chieftain, a protector figure, with charisma or special power. This generates the idea of the king 'ruling the land' with his special charismatic power, his will. 'His [the king's] person is considered, if we may express it so, as the dynamical centre of the universe, from which lines of force radiate to all quarters...' as Sir James Frazer put it in his book *The Golden Bough*.

Straightness and kingship were associated in societies from Asia to the Americas: the Inca ritually ruled from the Coricancha in Cuzco, the focus of 41 straight alignments of sacred sites radiating out far beyond the city, as we noted earlier, while the Chinese emperor sat in state on a golden throne placed on a straight marbled meridian that was the axis of the Forbidden City. Even in recent centuries, Western societies have unconsciously kept the association of straightness and kingship/ government: at Louis XIV's Palace of Versailles, with its radiating patterns of straight rides and paths, for example, or the ceremonial way of The Mall running out in a straight line from Buckingham Palace in London, and even The White House in Washington DC sits at the centre of a Masonic plan of radiating straight avenues.

But why should *straightness* have been a part of the meaning of *reg*, in addition to associations with kingship and government? We can obviously envisage a king or chieftain as someone 'guiding straight' in ceremonial processions, ritual walking and pilgrimages; boundary-setting, and the marking of the sacred precincts of a temple, but I suggest that all these expressions symbolised a deeper, inner fact of spirit, of mind, that went all the way back to the shamanic legacy inherent in kingship. I suggest that it was *spirit* that was the common denominator in the link with straightness, and that the term *spirit lines* would be the most appropriate one to encapsulate the conceptual context we are uncovering.

It is now possible to explore how and why this should be so. In the case of kingship, it was the image of king's *mana* or supernatural power radiating in lines out to all parts of the kingdom that provided the spirit-straightness element. But the conceptual complex this image derived from created actual landscape features. For example, a straight, mile-long 'cult road' has been uncovered at Rösaring, Sweden, along which a Viking chieftain was ceremonially drawn in a wagon to a burial cairn. In this case, straightness could be associated with spirit in two senses: the chieftain's *mana* and his departing spirit.

Below, we look at other examples of landscape lines emerging out of the archaic spirit-straightness-line conceptual complex. As at Rösaring, many of them associated the spirit-straightness connection with spirits of the dead, because in the ancient mind there was little distinction between species of spirits, and all were associated with shamanism. As Eliade pointed out, the shaman's ability to have contact with the souls of the dead 'signifies *being dead oneself*'. Hence the shaman 'died' during trance and was 'reborn' when he came out of it. During trance *he was in spirit*. In Australian Aboriginal traditions, too, Eliade found that 'the role of the dead often overlaps that of "pure spirits"'[38]

Ghost roads

An unambigious association of death and straightness is found in the medieval *doodwegen* (deathroads) of Holland. Examples on Westerheide between Laren and Hilversum have been brought to researchers' attention by John Palmer.[39] These roads pass over country riddled with prehistoric burial mounds and converge on medieval cemeteries which may, possibly, be on older sites. Palmer has found hat the roads were also known as *lykwegen* (corpse roads) and *spokenwegen* (ghost roads). Documentary research by Palmer has further revealed the existence of a medieval, legally-binding oath which guaranteed the carriage of the dead in straight lines only, along the deathroads.

Alerted by Palmer's work, Ulrich Magin conducted research in his home country of Germany. He found archive references to a feature called a *Geisterweg* (ghost path).[40] He found this old definition:

> Ghost paths are always the same, on them one meets with ghosts quite often. The paths, with no exception, always run in a straight line over mountains and valleys and through marshes... in the towns they pass the houses closely or go right through them. The paths end or originate at a cemetery. This idea may stem from the ancient custom of driving a corpse along a special dead man's road, therefore, this way or road was believed to have the same characteristics as a cemetery, it is a place where the spirits of the deceased thrive.[41]

This definition was written well before Alfred Watkins' discovery of 'leys'. If such ghost paths and death roads existed in Germany and Holland, it is likely that they also existed in Britain. It is surely a strong possibility that what Watkins was uncovering was the vestigial traces in the landscape of such spirit ways. This would also explain the old churches he found on his alignments better than simplistic 'site evolution' ideas.

With these crucially important archive discoveries by Palmer and Magin, it is now clear that up until the medieval period, at least, conscious planning in parts of western Europe accommodated straight landscape lines that were for the usage of the dead; for spirits.

The precursors of the *doodwegen* and *geisterwegen* were surely the Neolithic cursuses, mentioned earlier. We have seen that these have now been clearly associated by archaeologists with long barrows and other features in Neolithic ceremonial landscapes, and seem to have been 'British Avenues of the Dead'. Spirit paths, in other words.

Spirit ways

This also points up other linear features - stone rows. Their highest concentration is in Brittany, around Carnac-Ville, but they also occur in places as far from there as Malaysia. They occur in several places in the British Isles, but most, over 60, are to be found on Dartmoor, Devon, in southwest England. Only one archaeological excavation has taken place (incredibly), and nothing informative was unearthed. Because they present such an intractable problem of interpretation, there has been an archaeological tendency to ignore them. But one thing has been noticed, and it is the most important: at the end of a row or rows (most are multiple), the end stone is set at right angles to the line of stones. No one knows their function, but they are normally referred to in the literature, perhaps instinctively, as 'blocking stones'. I suggest that these rows, which usually have a large standing stone, burial mound or cairn situated at one end or along their length, are spirit lines, and the stones set across their courses were to block the passage of the spirits of the dead associated with the cairns or monoliths.

Much the same principle is expressed in the low walls inside the gates of

Stone rows at Merrivale, Dartmour. The 'blocking stone' is the nearest to the camera. (Author)

Indonesian temples, which are said to prevent straight-moving spirits from entering. In Indonesian mythology spirits which move in straight lines are harmful, a concept picked up from Chinese *feng shui*, a geomantic system first recorded in the West by Victorian missionaries to China. It is a subtle and complex system designed to harmonise the forces of heaven and earth, with some landscape engineering if necessary, to provide the optimum location for homes and tombs. According to *feng shui* traditions, straight features in the landscape, be they roads, river courses, ridges, lines of trees or fences, allow the passage of malevolent spirits. Straight lines in the landscape are therefore to be guarded against. *Feng shui* developed out of ancestor worship, which came, in turn, out of shamanism. Innumerable additions have been made to the system over any centuries which has come to be almost ridiculously cerebral. Many of the rules relate to conditions in medieval China, though they are still taken as standard geomantic practice by many occidental and modern oriental practitioners today.

There are marked similarities between Asian beliefs in straight-moving spirits and Celtic traditions of 'fairy paths'. This Fairy Faith is probably best preserved now in rural parts of Ireland. The fairy paths run invisibly between 'raths', or prehistoric earthworks. To build one's house on them is to invite disaster.[42] Fairy paths, too, must have close kinship with the *geisterwege*.

The Amerindian sweat lodge has a hollow scooped inside for the spirits of the dead. A straight ridge of earth runs towards the entrance of the sweatlodge from the pit where the fire burns to heat the stones to be used for the ceremony. This straight earthen line is for the spirits to use in entering the lodge. Similarly, a straight 'path' is created for peyote ceremonies. The Navajo, the inheritors of the Anasazi lands, have a sand-painting motif of a 'tree of life', which contains a straight 'pollen path' or 'blessing way' running along its centre; above is the image of a bird, symbol of flight. These kinds of examples surely give a clue to Amerindian thinking when we have to consider their straight landscape lines.

Other versions of the spirit line

As all these kinds of observations indicated above have come together, it has become apparent that in addition to pathways and other landscape features, the association of spirits with straight linearity has in some instances become attached to traditions concerning threads, cords, ropes and the like. These 'lines', too, act as spirit ways in physical space.

In some Aboriginal traditions, a healer would run a filament secreted by a certain insect from the head of a patient to a nearby tree, where the sick person's spirit was perceived to be lodged. The filament provided a path for the spirit to return to the patient and thus end the illness. The Aborigines have various other beliefs about a thread issuing from the penis or the mouth linking body and spirit during *miriru*, the out-of-body state. Also, there are traditions that a particular class of spirits, the Rai, travel on ropes in the air. James Cowan was told by one Aborigine informant:

> They (the Rai) followed the 'aerial rope', that's the one they followed. They are spirits-of-the-dead, they don't walk on the ground. The world is big. They travel in the air following the 'aerial rope' all the time. Only magicians can see it. *He is a magician who follows the aerial rope all the time.*[43] (Cowan's emphasis.)

These 'magicians' are the *karadji*, or men of high degree. An Aborigine informant tells me that there are few of these men left now, but they can sometimes be identified because they wear feathers on their ankles, symbolic of their ability to fly.

The Kalahari !Kung 'climb threads' when they go out-of-body in *kia* during trance dancing, and climb up to where god is. The Rigo of Papua New Guinea claim that in the out-of-body state a 'fishing line' is attached to the spirit and remains taut, extending indefinitely, and by implication, therefore, in a straight line, as it flies.[44] The Spiritualists had a similar idea, of course, with their claim of a 'silver cord' linking the physical and 'astral' bodies during 'astral projection'.

In Siberia, the Tungus shaman would poke poles through the smoke hole of the wigwam where he or she was to hold a seance. A cord would run from these to sacred objects outside the tent to provide a 'road' for the spirits. The Tungus of Manchuria had further traditions associated with threads. When a shamanic initiate had been identified, three *turö*, trees with their crowns preserved but with branches lopped off, were erected outside the candidate's dwelling. A rope or thong made of red Chinese silk or sinews coloured red connected two of these trees. At intervals along it, bunches of ribbons or feathers were tied. 'This is the "road",' Eliade informed, 'along which the spirits will move.'[45] The candidate sat and drummed between two of the turö. In a ceremony lasting many days, and supervised by an old shaman, spirits emerged from the trees and travelled down the rope 'road' to the candidate who had to reveal all they told him about themselves. Elaborate precautions were taken to prevent the spirits from possessing the initiate. At nights during the procedure, the old shaman climbed up into one of the tree crowns.

Still in Siberia, the Tunguska tribes believed that an invisible thread linked them in a straight line with the god of fate. When healing a sick person, the Buryat shaman would place an arrow (itself a symbol of out-of-body flight, see below) on the ground alongside the person's head and lay a red thread in a straight line from its point out through the entrance of the tent to a birch pole erected outside (the 'World Tree' and association with Fly Agaric, remember). This provided the sick person's soul with a route to return to the body, almost identical to the Aborigine tradition referred to above.

In Maori traditions, a spirit 'road' is often represented by the stem of a plant. When summoned to a sickbed, the shaman or *tohunga* places the stem on the patient's head and exhorts the evil spirit causing the illness to depart by way of the 'road'.

In Tibet, ascending to the sky by means of a rope (or ladder) is a common motif in Bon-po tradition, and is an ability particularly associated with kingship.

Spirit baffles

If straight threads facilitate spirit travel, we could reasonably expect the opposite to apply, and so it seems. In magical traditions of Northern Europe, which Nigel Pennick has admirably summarised, spirit traps were made with, interestingly, *red* threads as in the Eurasian shamanic examples mentioned above, stretched across a copper hoop and placed on a staff 'on the pathway or spirit track... which the sprites will take to cause their disruption, for example, between a cemetery and a house'.[46] These types of devices must surely have originated in tandem with the idea of *geisterwege*. 'Witch bottles' likewise contained tangled threads to hamper the progress of a spirit. In Russian lore, a bride-to-be had a fishing net cast over her to prevent malevolent spiritual interference. Some medieval witches wore knotted string shawls so their spirits could not be taken, and there was a whole tradition of magical knots.

This idea of hampering spirit movement with tangled or curvilinear lines is also found in ground markings in the form of the extremely ancient stone and turf labyrinths of Europe. They occur in Iceland, Britain and throughout Europe, particularly in the Baltic countries, where hundreds of stone labyrinths are scattered around the Baltic Sea. Some of them are thought to date back to the Bronze Age. The last witnessed folk usage of them was by fishermen, who, presumably in keeping with the traditions of their forefathers, would run round a labyrinth in order to ensnare any mischievous spirits or trolls attached to them, then jump out and rush to the fishing boat. The trolls inside the labyrinth were unable to extricate themselves in time to board the boat! It is doubtlessly significant, too, that such a labyrinth occurs amidst the burial cairns at Rösaring (below), perhaps, like the blocking stones on the British stone rows, to stop the spirits of the buried dead from straying.

The stone labyrinth at Kuggören, northern Sweden. This was used traditionally by an old fisherman up to the 1950s. Unfortunately, he died without anyone bothering to find out from him the details of the old traditions. (John Kraft)

The straight way over the land

The burning question, of course, is why spirits and straightness should have become associated in the first place. I suggest that the origins of this are extremely archaic, and that the entire straightness-line-spirit complex, whether in thread lore, landscape lines, or as a now forgotten shamanic legacy inherent in kingship and revealed by the *reg* language vestige, ultimately reaches back to that central experience of shamanic trance - the shaman's 'journey'. This was, remember, the out-of-body flight of the shaman, whose 'exteriorised' spirit passed over the tribal landscape on its journey to the *axis mundi,* or to the entrance to the underworld, or to visit some location in the landscape in order to gain information, meet a nature deity, or to confront an evil spirit or rival shaman. *Flight is the straight way over the land.* The phrase 'as the crow flies' carries precisely that meaning. Another phrase with a similar meaning is 'as straight as an arrow', and arrow symbolism, too, was strongly associated with shamanic flight: in Greek myth, Abaris flew on a golden arrow dispensing healing and divination; the Koryak shaman left his body along a path traced by an arrow; the Samoyed shaman held two arrows points upwards during his seance, and so on. Just as aircraft routes are plotted as straight lines on maps today, the ancients came to mark the *lines of spirit flight* onto their ceremonial landscapes. This may seem a bizarre idea to Western minds, but, then, we are not dealing with our kind of consciousness.

Spirit ways through the land, initially the envisaged courses taken by the shaman's 'exteriorised' soul but eventually extending to the spirits of the dead - an early association with the shaman's exteriorised spirit, as we have noted - and then to various ideas of spirits, became ritualised and seen as sacred. After all, what is meant by a special 'Sacred Way', familiar even to our way of thinking, if not some specialised, sanctified route across the land? We saw this kind of thinking in the first part of this essay, where for untold generations Aborigines undertook their Dream Journeys following the route across the terrain taken by the mythic Dreamtime beings, the *altjirangamitjina*. Where the spirits had been became inherently holy. In some cultures, these spirit ways became conceptual lines - fairy paths, or courses of malevolent spirits as in *feng shui* - while in others they were physically marked as landscape lines, linear earthworks, straight tracks. These would have in effect been *traces* of the passage of spirits or the spirit of some shaman or entity. If the Dreamtime Earth was envisaged as somehow co-existing or being interfused with the physical Earth, then such landscape features would be the analogs of spirit routes in the Spirit Earth.

In some cases the landscape lines would themselves have become holy. We have already noted what appears to be votive pottery scattered along the lines on the Nazca pampa and around Chaco Canyon, and Nigel Pennick has pointed out a seventeenth-century French source which refers to the 'pagan trackway which they name *Yries*, marked with odds and ends of cloth or with shoes'.[47] In addition, the practice of placing shrines along Inca roads and all the Amerindian roads, like the Roman roads of Europe, carries the same implication.

The making of such religious trackways in many cultures would inevitably have sociological dimensions. Scholars studying Peruvian societies have already suggested that the making of the Nazca lines would have helped develop community organisation and co-operatiton, and this is still seen in action in present-day Andean Indian communities. In such societies there is a complex kinship group organisation, and shared labour on communal projects is called *mit'a*. (This certainly applied to the ritual sweeping of strips or *chhiutas* of the church plaza referred to earlier.) Landscape lines, the traces of spirit ways, would quickly have become socio-religious features. We have seen with Zuidema's work on the *ceques* around Cuzco just how intricate ideas could become in association with the lines. The physical expression of the shamanic lines would also have provided a tangible, concrete reflection of a ruling shamanic theocracy's power.

Over a long period of time in certain societies, as they moved from tribal, through proto-state and finally into state complexity, the initial impetus behind the lines would have been forgotten, and only vague associations and superstitions of sanctity would survive in connection with the Straight Way. As kingship also shared the same development, also emerging out of shamanism, it is only to be expected that it would retain the symbolism of the Straight Way. As the actual origins of the connection became forgotten - which were, after all, usually the experiences of individual shamans in 'exquisite solitude' as the *Mandukya Upanishad* puts it, only rarely undergone by larger numbers of people - and with them the actual experiential knowledge of out-of-body travel, the lines became rote ceremonial ways, boundaries, royal roads, imperial avenues, and so on. Every level of such evolution taking them further from the the original meaning of the lines. Only the inarticulate sense that somehow such features were 'special' and part of the aura of rulership, survived. Ultimately, in modern societies, even that vestige has all but disappeared.

From the Heart of the World

But is the suggested basis of these ideas correct: could the landscape lines, the whole lines-straightness-spirit complex, really have originated in shamanic out-of-body experience? Fortunately, circumstances allowed me to confirm the theory, at least to the extent that one might reasonably expect to be possible nowadays. I saw Alan Ereira's BBC TV documentary, *From the Heart of the World* [48] which dealt with the Kogi Indians of Colombia. These people live on an exceedingly isolated mountain complex that rises rapidly from the tropical Colombian coast to perpetual snows: it contains virtually every type of climate and ecological niche to be found on Earth. The Kogi think of themselves as the Elder Brother and the rest of us as the Younger Brother. They see ecological problems emerging in their Eden, and blame the behaviour of Westernised culture for them. Because of this crisis, they allowed Ereira to film them so they could get their message across to the Younger Brother. They had never been filmed before.

The Kogi, survivors of the Tairona culture, preserve their pre-Columbian roots better than any other surviving Native American society. They have an active

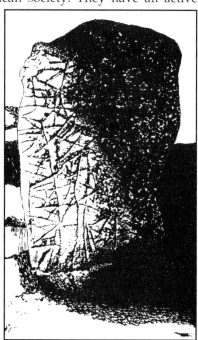

The Map Stone of the Kogi Indians, Columbia. The lines depict the out-of-body spirit paths of the Kogi shamanic priests or Mamas, and partially relate to the physical stone path system used by the Kogi. (From a photograph by Alan Ereira.)

shamanic theocracy, the shamans being known as Mamas, Enlightened Ones. These are subjected to extreme training as children, being brought up in the darkness of a cave, as mentioned earlier. When they emerge, they are able to see *aluna*, the Spirit Earth, interfused with the physical landscape. They can travel in *aluna*, and talk to the ancestors and the deities. Further, the Kogi have mysterious pathways that criss-cross the sierra, linking very ancient Tairona megalithic towns, most now abandoned and lost in the mountainous forest (lost to non-Kogis, at any rate). In addition, Ereira saw and filmed a 'map stone' during his privileged stay with the Kogi. This is a standing stone with a network of lines incised on its surface. These, the commentary to the film stated, related to the Mamas' journeys 'in a space we do not understand' and partly related to the physical path system which had been laid down by the ancestors.

Could it be that here was a still-living shamanic usage of landscape lines? I held my breath and wrote to Ereira asking him if the Kogi paths 'relate to the Mamas' out-of-body journeys - spirit travels in a spirit version of the physical world'. He replied promptly, saying that that phrase would be understood by the Mamas themselves, and was indeed what they had told him. He drew my attention to a sequence in his film which showed the ordinary tribal folk, the 'vassals', cleaning one of the paved pathways in a Kogi town under the guidance of a number of Mamas. The pathway ran up from a river in a straight line and disappeared beneath a building in the Kogi town, which the Indians claimed was pre-Tairona. The Mamas had carefully explained to Ereira that the pathway was the physical trace of a spirit path which continued on beyond the building in *aluna* only, extending the same straight line to another river. Ereira admitted that it had required some adjustment on his part to see road cleaning as an aspect of the out-of-body experience! Spirit *flight* was not specified by the Mamas, but we have seen that it is central to the shamanic out-of-body journey.

Ritual sweeping

Of course, we know now that the idea of ritually sweeping or cleaning a line or area was a symbolic way of creating sacred space. The Kogi procedure is entirely in keeping with what anthropologists had seen in Peru, and what they suspected about the Nazca lines. And the idea of ritual sweeping is widespread. In Britain, for instance, there are numerous folk assemblies where Morris Men conduct ancient dances, such as the annual 'Plough Stots' in Yorkshire, in which ritual sweeping takes place - often by a man dressed as a woman, a 'she-male', itself a throw-back to certain tribal shamanism, in which 'soft men' and transvestite behaviour could be involved (associated with the transcendence of dualities). Again, in northern European folk-lore, a special spirit flail made from branches and tied with willow bark was used to sweep pathways which had not been walked for a long time in order to remove any unwanted entities that might be there (surely another echo of the *geisterwege*).[49]

Common origin

As with rock art, we can consider a common origin to landscape lines from all over the world, because the out-of-body experience is a universal product of the human central nervous system and transcends cultures. So while there are no cultural links between, say, the makers of the British cursuses or the Peruvian pampa lines, the human experience that lies behind them is the same. The actual, physical or conceptual form of the lines, the beliefs that gave rise to them, and the socio-religious practices that grew up around them, are as varied as there are cultures, but the initiating shamanic impetus is common to all.

I am not claiming that all shamanic trance out-of-body journeys took a straight line course, especially if the shaman 'went out' as, say, a black panther or an anaconda, but when *flight* of the soul was involved - which was the most usual form and the one most clearly stamped in shamanic lore worldwide, as we have seen - straightness was one of the leading characteristics.

What we can be sure of now is that on any ancient landscape where we have effigy mounds or ground drawings, where apparently inexplicable linear features exist, and in most ancient landscapes that bear the imprint of myth, we are looking at a *shamanic landscape*. This is an important new perception for us to have.

Shamanic reality versus modern fantasy

Almost all the pieces of information were available all the time for this understanding of the landscape lines to be assembled, but for various reasons this has not come about until this present time. There are, perhaps, two chief reasons why this has been the case.

On the one hand, the orthodox scholars, archaeologists, anthropologists and others who might be expected to perceive the pattern in the evidence put forward here and in the forthcoming *Shamanism and the Mystery Lines*, have failed to do so because they are trained and inculcated in a worldview in which such things as out-of-body experiences simply do not happen and are automatically relegated to the domain of superstition. (Marlene Dobkin de Rios is of course amongst the exceptions to this rule.) As a consequence, the association of such vitally important strands of human experience with other areas of inquiry remains unrecognised.

On the other hand, the only other group of people likely to study landscape lines at any depth, the 'ley hunters' or 'alternative' students of ancient landscapes, sites and peoples, the modern geomants, have until now also failed. This is because for the last 20 years there has been an overpowering, conceptually-smothering belief that 'leylines' are 'lines of energy' - dowsable phenomena, detectable by divining rod. Fantastic worldwide 'grid systems', 'etheric networks', 2000-mile-long energy leylines, yang lines of energy six-to-eight feet wide, interplanetary (even intergalactic!) leylines, energy lines with 64 band widths or having hourglass-shaped cross-sections, and dozens more notions, have swamped the alternative approach and distracted thinking. A relatively small number of 'energy dowsers' have had their notions amplified by the media, books and the New Age lecture circuits, creating ever-increasing circles of confused fantasy.

For years this material has, at least publically, hi-jacked the field of study, yet its basis is merely that white, primarily middle-aged and middle-class men (I know the tribe all too well), hailing in the main from Britain, America and Germany, have been indulging in their various pet notions on no other grounds than their unquestioned say-so, backed by the spurious authority of a dowsing rod. (I have, incidentally, every confidence that there is an authentic basis to some claimed dowsing work, but that does not mean that this particular 'energy line' brand of the subject is *bona fide*.) The whole 'energy leyline' business has been an orgy of spiritual juvenility and intellectual ineptitude that has either attracted devout armies of well-meaning but unthinking and crucially-uninformed followers, or caused others to reject the whole area of inquiry out of hand, baby and bathwater. It has inhibited the perception of the deeper implications contained within the subject area.

The dubious (though curiously instructive) history of these dowsing fantasies, and the inherent fallacies within them, have been presented by myself and others elsewhere,[50] so I will not re-iterate that material here. Suffice it to say that what these energy ideas represent is the spectral projection of ingrained twentieth-century images reflecting power grids, circuits and hard-wiring onto the landscape, which has been turned into a kind of pseudo-spiritual circuit board. It is one of several modern manifestations of the electro-mechanical motifs that have been created within the twentieth-century soul, and is, with the cruellest of ironies, the very antithesis of the 'spiritual' activity it claims itself, in New Age circles, to be. It has been a minor 'psychic epidemic', to use Jung's phrase, that has taken us ever further from the true spiritual realities and potential of the human psyche.

The 'energy line' is simply the latest conceptual accretion to obscure the original impetus behind shamanic markings on ancient landscapes.

The all-important shamanic journey that lies at the heart of those markings brings us to the question as to whether the human mind or spirit actually can move about in the environment. This matter is deceptively complex and far-reaching, ultimately determining how we are to view the world. The final part of this essay can do no more than touch on some of the issues involved.

4

INTERWORLD

The paradise myth is probably the most widespread there is: it is a fundamental concept of the human mind. No other mythic theme better reinforces Joseph Campbell's contention that the myths of the world 'resemble each other as dialects of a single language'.

Westerners are particularly familiar with the Judaeo-Christian idea of the Garden of Eden, but this was possibly adapted by Hebrew scholars from earlier Mesopotamian ideas - perhaps dating back to around 5000 BC. The ancient Greeks recalled a Golden Age 'in the time of Cronus', when a golden race of happy and perfect people lived in ease and peace. The Hindus have a cyclic system of great ages or Yugas, of which this present time is the densest, most material. The cycle started long, long ago with the Krita Yuga, the Perfect Age. The Irish had their magic island, Hy Brasil, far to the west, in the Atlantic. The Chinese, Amerindians and Africans all have or had their lost paradises. But as Richard Heinberg, who has made a wide-ranging study of the paradise theme[1], points out, the motif of paradise has a 'once and future' quality to it. A New Age will finally come into place as we run down to the limits of our Fall from the original paradise. Furthermore, this has a correspondence on the scale of the individual as well as the race, and we find the theme merging seamlessly into concepts of an Afterlife state that shares similar attributes to the original paradise. Thus the Greeks looked forward to the Elysian Fields after death, with Hermes as psychopomp to lead their souls there. Christians look to the celestial New Jerusalem, or, at least, a generalised idea of Heaven. The Iron Age Celts had Tir-na-nog, the 'Land of Youth', also known by numerous other names. The Tibetans had Shambhala, the Polynesians had Pulotu, and so on.

There was a fairly universal belief that Heaven and Earth were once much closer, and that it was physically possible to communicate between the two, but now we are Fallen - either because of some transgression which was punished by a deity, by a cataclysm such as an earthquake, or by the intervention of some evil cosmic force - it is only through some form of enchantment, trance or death that access can now be made.

There is considerable agreement, too, about the characteristics of paradise, the Otherworld. The *people* who lived there had certain attributes that are common to many paradise myths. They could fly; they were able to speak with the animals, and may have been telepathic; they lived in happiness, peace and ease. They glowed with inner light, as did the heavenly lands and buildings. The *time* in paradise was/is mythic time, Great Time. In folktales of those taken to Fairyland, for instance, we have the common theme that those returning to normality cannot touch the ground for fear of dissolving into dust, because ages of human time have passed in what seemed to them only days or months in Fairyland.

The *geography* of paradise is rather similar in many versions of the myth. There is a central tree or group of sacred trees, like the Trees of Life and Knowledge in Eden; a cosmic mountain or set of sacred peaks centrally placed. There are (usually four) sacred rivers emerging from a rock, fountain or spring - almost always flowing in the cardinal directions. The Scandinavian *Edda* describes four rivulets in the Otherworld emerging from the spring of Hvergelmir within the roots of Yggdrasil; the paradise of Brahma has a well from which streams flow to the compass points, according to the *Vishnu Purana*; the Chinese paradise mountain of Kwen-lun issues the 'four great rivers of the world'; in Navajo myth, the paradisal Earth on which the First Man and First Woman lived had a spring from which rivers flowed to the Four Directions.

Why should there be such a universal mythic motif of the Otherworld with so many common elements attached to it? Presumably because it developed at some incalculably remote time before the human race divided over the Earth, or because of the diffusion of ideas over the globe by means of trade, migrations and war, or because paradise has no time or place but is, rather, the mark of a paradisal *state of consciousness* perennially producable on the common canvas of the human nervous sytem. While there may be some possibility of mythic themes surviving from exceedingly remote antiquity, and cultural diffusionism in various parts of the world may account for some spread of ideas, neither can satisfactorily explain the universality of the paradise myth. It *has* to be a level of consciousness that is its main source.

What is the actual nature and significance of that state of consciousness? The common inheritance of our human neurological make-up, or an access point to a non-material dimension of our physical world? As we tease out this conundrum in the following pages, we will perhaps see that, to some extent, elements from both interpretations need not be mutually exclusive. In any case, whether or not paradise is a mind phenomenon as such, or a mind-accessed Otherworld, it makes little difference to the potential it has for showing us the way to a renewed worldview for our times.

But let us take a step at a time - and where better to start out from than that mythic centre of the landscape, the omphalos.

Return to the Garden
The mythic geography of paradise - the central mountain, tree, spring and so on, and the four cardinal rivers - tells us that the idea of paradise, of the Otherworld, is intimately linked with that of the *axis mundi*. It has already been suggested that the

omphalos is a mythic apparatus to place mind in the landscape. We are all at the centre of our universes - over our heads the dome of the sky, around us the horizon, eye-level, centering on us. The world is a circuit around us - ahead, behind, to the sides. The centre is our point of cognition, our minds. Translated into the landscape, that becomes the sacred centre from where space is divided, which allows the marking of natural (astronomical) time, and where access to the Otherworlds can be achieved. The omphalos is the mythic point where the figuratively *vertical* axis of mind intersects the figuratively horizontal plane of the material world, contained within the round of mundane time. This psychogram is the mandala of space, time and consciousness. Who travels to the *axis mundi* to enter the Otherworlds? The shaman. How does he achieve this? By leaving his body; by going on a trance 'journey'.

Eliade wrote that this 'myth of a paradisal period brutally abolished by the "fall" of man... is in one way or another bound up with certain shamanic conceptions... the shaman is able to... abolish time and re-establish the primordial condition of which the myths tell... Both metamorphosis into the animal ancestor and the shaman's ascensional ecstasy [magical flight] represent different but homological expressions of one and the same experience - transcendence of the profane condition, re-establishment of a "paradisal" existence lost in the depths of mythic time.'[2] The shaman enters paradise on a temporary basis. The shamanic experience, in Eliade's phrase, expresses a 'nostalgia for paradise', and contains the report of Inner Light found in most post-shamanic mystical traditions.

The human being at the *axis mundi* - the sacred site or symbolic feature, the outward sign of mind in the landscape, the projection of consciousness onto the physical Earth - negotiates the Way between this world and the Otherworlds; between, if you like, the physical Earth and the Spirit Earth. This condition is a kind of *Interworld*. There are, wrote Eliade, '"pure lands" of a mystical space' that have 'at once the nature of a "paradise" and of an "interior space" accessible only to initiates'.[3] Campbell, paraphrasing Harald Pager, says of the San rock art that it depicts the Bushmen's...

> ...everlasting scenery to which the great *ntum* masters in their half-death states [the trance dancers] pay visits three or four times a month. Prominent in such visionary scenes brought back from the 'world behind this one we see with our eyes,' are 'antelope men,' partly eland, partly human, frequently flying.
>
> ... the paintings had the power of a medium uniting the two worlds, of the outer eyes of the body and the inward eye of the mind.[4]

It is crucial for us, for our culture today, to try to understand this 'Interworld condition', because it was the experience of that intermediate state that caused the ancients to mythologise the physical landscape and to leave shamanic markings on it, and which gave rise to ancient worldviews in some important respects superior to our own.

Visionary geography

These worldviews, by which I literally mean views of the world, can still be detected in Aboriginal perceptions, as Cowan remarks: 'The earth becomes the manifestation of a vision, of a visionary geography, in which the soul can meet and converse with its maker by way of symbolic and ritual expression.'[5] *We*, however, no longer operate through this kind of interface - it is culturally absent. And we are only now beginning to see the problems that arise by not having a *living, culturally expressed*, inner model of paradise. Alas, a dynamic version of such a model can come about only if people *directly experience* the mythic realm of a paradisal state, or, at least, unless culturally-recognised figures repeatedly enter it.

Our present-day model of the world, our mindset, will have to be significantly modified in certain areas if we are to continue for any appreciable number of future generations. We will need to *learn* from ancient, wiser models - *not to copy them*, for that would be pastiche wisdom, and in any case inapplicable to our present conditions, but to decipher what their underlying principles relate to.

One such model that we can use here as an example in order to attempt to decipher at least some underlying principles, has been made accessible to Western readers largely through the scholarship of Henry Corbin: it is a core of ancient Iranian traditions in which paradise, the omphalos, the mind and the doctrine of an Interworld are brought together in a particularly complete way. These traditions emerged out of the Zoroastrian Mazdaism of Persia. And Zoroastrianism, as Eliade affirmed, itself originally derived from shamanism.

The very word 'paradise' comes from ancient Iran - *pairidaeza*, a walled garden. Mythically, it goes back to the paradisal enclosure, the *Var*, of Yima, a god-figure of at least early Indo-European antiquity. The Iranian paradise-garden symbolises the Earth, in all its degrees from physical to spiritual ('celestial'), and in its purest form involves a quincunx arrangement of trees (one at each corner of a square or rectangular layout with the fifth in the centre) around a central body of water. 'Their height decreases progressively from the horizon, which they outline,' explained Corbin.[6] There was also a Mazdean system of flower symbolism, in which flowers corresponded to given spiritual entities stationed on the spectrum of manifestation between the ultimate godhead, the Light of Lights, and the material world. A garden could be a sacred text.

The Earth as an angel

In the spiritual traditions of old Iran, a fourfold-body was envisaged for each person - a perishable physical body and a subtle elemental body that is imperishable, and is specifically the denizen of the interworld, plus two spiritual bodies of which one is eternal. The physical body has the physical Earth as its environment, while what we might call for simplicity the soul (in Corbin's terminology, the *Imago Animae*) had a spirit, soul or visionary Earth as its environment (Corbin's *Imago Terrae*). To put this more subtly and accurately, each body *projected* its Earth, rather than passively experiencing an environment as such. To the Shi'ite adept, for example, his 'spiritual body' is 'the Earth of his Paradise'. This philosophy means that the distinction between subject and object is removed, and is, of course, an unfamilar pattern of thinking for the modern Western mind. We could say that in the way that Adam (the physical body) was 'made' from the clay of the physical Earth, so the soul is 'made' from the substance of the 'Earth of Visions'.

This visionary Earth can be glimpsed 'through' the physical Earth as an Angel; in the ritual canon of the *Avesta* we can read, for the twenty-eighth day of the month, the homily: 'We are celebrating this liturgy in Honour of the Earth which is an Angel'. Corbin used the modern example of the spontaneous mystical vision of G.T. Fechner, who, witnessing a rural scene illuminated by an evocative cast of light, suddenly and helplessly perceived the Earth as being - literally - an Angel, an emanation of its angelic or celestial Otherworldliness. The Earth 'is an Angel, such a gorgeously real Angel...!' he exclaimed.

Thinking in this Mazdean sense of the Earth as an Angel, Corbin rightly pointed out that we do not need to ask *what* the Earth is, but *who* it is. In the Zoroastrian system, there are seven archangelic Powers of Light, the Immortals, who are mysterious emanations of the Lord of Wisdom, Ohrmazd, the Avestan Ahura Mazda. One of these Powers, the feminine *Spenta Armaiti* (later Spendarmat, and then Isfandarmuz), is the Archangel of Earth. The Archangels are aided in turn by Yazatas, Angels, the next order of differentiation out from the godhead. The Angel of Earth is Zamyat, also feminine. In the Zoroastrian system, these figures are not mere poetic symbols, they are actual powers, and the Earth (in all its forms of subtlety or density) they preside over is in a sense their soul, and our human souls partake of these greater souls (or 'Earths') in so far as they are able at each stage of manifestation.

The Sacrament of the Earth

Plutarch translated *Spenta Armaiti* as Sophia, Wisdom. There is a Mazdean Sacrament of the Earth, Corbin states, which 'in its essence, and from the very name Spenta Armaiti Sophia... can be described as a *geosophy*, that is to say as being the *Sophianic* mystery of the Earth'.[7] The enactment or consummation of this mystery, Corbin maintained, necessitated the idea of a *visionary geography*, because there is an interaction, or more accurately, an inter-relationship - inter-dependence even - of outer, physically-visual Earth, and inner, symbolic or subtle, supramundane Earth.

The mythical paradise, the *Var* of Yima, is the omphalos, Eran-Vej, of the Mazdean visionary geography (see Figure overleaf) which involved eight keshvars or 'climates', better understood by us as zones. Eran-Vej was the centre, where the primordial river is divided into four branches, and point of origin - the navel, in other words. Effectively, it was the Earth of the 'Eighth Climate', the Interworld, the Spirit Earth, the Earth of Visions, the Transfigured Earth (I shall use all these, and similar, terms interchangeably, as they all apply to the same 'zone'). Surrounding Eran-Vej is Xvaniratha, the totality of geographical space now accessible to man, and equal in area to the other keshvars. These are mythic spaces interfused with the physical geography, symbolic divisions of the actual material landscape, and are given their boundaries by reference to annual solar positions relative to the central keshvar which 'has the quality of *situating* space, before itself being *situated in* that space' as Corbin put it. 'In other words, it is not a matter of pre-existing, homogeneous, and *quantitative* space *in* which regions are distributed but the typical structure of a *qualitative* space.'[8]

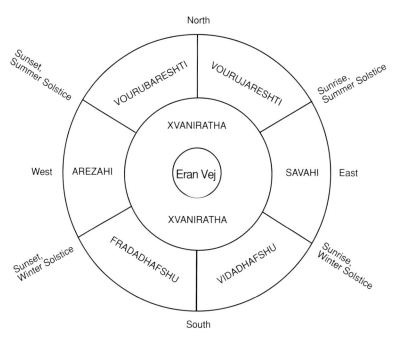

The mythic regions or keshvars. (After Corbin)

While we see the physical landscape in horizontal terms (we speak of 'landscape format' for a picture that is wider than it is high, for example), it is best to think of this visionary geography as intersecting that in a *vertical*, or ascending polar, direction. Allusions in the Iranian spiritual literature to northern regions are actually symbolic references to this esoteric orientation. (Even as I write this, I recall a curious LSD-vision I had a quarter of a century ago, in which I found myself suspended over what I 'knew' to be the North Pole. But I was in a kind of upside-down and 'inside-out' or laterally-inverted space that I cannot now describe. This was, I think, a direct, neurological expression of this intersection of the worlds. As an aside, I might mention that during the vision two angelic arms appeared out of a cloud, holding an opened, blank book and a quill pen in a gesture of invitation. While this had a kind of cosmic corniness about it, it occurs to me now that perhaps this is that book!)

The paradisal world of Eran-Vej, mythologised as the *Var* of Yima, secretes light, and the beings who inhabit it are the mythical heroes who will eventually repopulate the Earth when it is macrocosmically Transfigured, which, by correspondence, also means in personal post-mortem terms. Personal and general eschatology are often compressed within the symbolism.

One of the mountains in Eran-Vej is Hukairya, which reaches to the stars and is the source of the Waters of Life. Around the spring on the mountain grow marvellous plants and trees, and especially the all-white Haoma which can provide immortality and from which the Elixir of Life will be made at the time of Transfiguration. Close to it is another mountain, made of ruby, the Mountain of the Dawns - the first to be lit by the rays of the rising sun. A third mountain in Eran-vej is the Peak of Judgement from which springs the Bridge of Chinvat, leading to the Beyond.

This is, obviously, a symbolic geography, and relates to the individual conscious-ness. The 'dawn' is the dawn of immortality, either at death or in mystic trance - 'dawn' and 'intelligence' are the same in Mazdean lore and language. The Bridge of Chinvat is the ordeal the soul has to endure: to the ungodly the bridge can become as narrow as a razor's edge; to the spiritually healthy, it allows easy passage. One's Overself, the primordial 'I', meets the soul at the entrance to the Bridge. This idea of a narrow way or passage from mundane to supramundane states is another of the key themes of shamanism.

This inner symbolic or visionary geography, the scene for psycho-spiritual events, was translated to the physical landscape by the ancient Iranians - creating a *psycho-geography*, to use Corbin's phrase. The liturgical hymns refer to the 'the mountains of dawns, to all the mountains...' making the connection between the symbolic and the sensory, physical. In Iran, the archetypal mountains were projected on the Elburz, the chain of peaks that run east to west across northern Iran. In mythological terms, the Earth threw up its mountains when the great demonic Powers of Ahriman stirred out of the abyss, causing a war between light and dark on the physical plane. The mountains, on the skyline, around the edge of the world, were at once buttresses against the Ahrimanic forces and Earth's attempt to maintain contact with heaven.

The Interworld at the Sacred Centre

Mazdean philosophy was carried over into Islam by the twelfth-century mystic, Suhrawardi, and was modified and embellished in succeeding centuries, particularly in the Shi'ite faith. The Interworld, the Centre, the Celestial Earth, became 'the World of Hurqalya'. This was the 'Earth of the Emerald Cities', of which there were three, the third being Hurqalya which gave its name to the mystic region as a whole. Hurqalya has a cosmic mountain, Qaf, which supports an emerald stone on its summit - the *smaragdina*. Qaf is the mother of all mountains, and 'marks the boundary between two worlds, the one visible and the other invisible to the senses'.[9] It, or rather the archetype it represents, 'has been projected... on spaces of empirical geography (the Caucasus and its foothills on Iranian soil), which then became the theater of mythical events.'[10]

The Centre, the paradise of Yima, Eran-Vej, the 'eighth climate', the Earth of Hurqalya - all esoteric versions of the omphalos - mythically represent the Interworld, at one level of correspondence the soul or mind, existing between the material and non-material. It is the centre of the *worlds*, a zone 'mediating between the sensory and the intelligible' as Corbin put it, and he admitted that 'it is difficult in our language to find a satisfactory term' for this interworld state. In Sufi tradition it is called *barzakh*. 'The sensory world has its analogue there,' wrote Corbin. It preceded the sensory world, he said, and 'is the phenomenon of the Earth in its pure state, since it directly reflects the image premeditated by the soul.' The seventeeth-century Islamic mystic, Muhsin Fayz Kashani, taught: 'This intermediate world... is the world through which spirits are embodied, and bodies spiritualized.'[11]

The Interworld is not the world of sensory perception, yet not the realm of pure spirit either. It has characteristics of both, and the mythologised landscape results from it. It is a realm we need to bring back into focus in our culture. It is apprehended by *Imagination*. I write this with a capital 'I' to distinguish it from the insipid thing we normally mean by that word, and it does *not* mean 'unreal'. In Mazdean tradition, the light that is secreted from paradise is *Xvarnha*, the Light of Glory; the primordial, universal force permeating all things. Even material forms are in their essence this light, so our souls are composed of it. *Xvarnha* is the medium through which the Imagination works, but as the soul, the spirit or the mind, is also composed of this sacral light, it is itself, therefore, the medium.

The act of transfiguring the Earth into its celestial form is thus done simultaneously *by* and *through* the soul, the spirit, the mind. The vision of *barzakh*, the Interworld, the Spirit Earth, the *aluna* of the Kogi Indians, or whatever else we want to call it, is accomplished by the lens of consciousness, not by the physical eyes; yet the sensory material that is received by the mind through the physical senses is used, or, rather, *re-created*. (This may be difficult to grasp, yet it is the crux of the alchemy involved, and is a directly-accessible experience to everyone, to every reader of this book, for example, as will be explained below.) It is the 'transmutation of sensory data'.[12] The metamorphosis of the Earth reveals a landscape of *Xvarnah* - 'earthly landscapes then appear haloed in the Light of Glory, restored to their paradisal purity'.

Supernature

Before looking more closely at this mechanism of perception through Imagination, it is important for us to realise that the experience of the Interworld is a *real* one, not some weakly-imagined concept, an abstract cerebral philosophy or loose poetic image. It can be experienced with as much (indeed greater) reality than walking down the street. Corbin wrote that the Imagination...

> ...does not *construct* something unreal, but *unveils* the hidden reality; its action is, in short, that of the *ta'wil*, the spiritual exegisis practised by all the Spirituals of Islam, whose special quality is that of alchemical meditation: to occultate the

apparent, to manifest the hidden. It is in this intermediary world that those known as the *urafa*, the mystical gnostics, have meditated tirelessly, *gnosis* here being taken to mean that perception which grasps the object not in its objectivity, but as a sign, an intimation, an announcement that is finally the soul's annunciation to itself.[13]

To some, the nature of this interworld is that of an actual Spirit Earth, an environmentally-true spiritual dimension of the physical Earth; to others, it is hallucinatory perceptions, resulting from specified altered states of consciousness. In a way, *both* views are true (an almost unbearable ambiguity for Western thinkers!), for the Interworld is the conjunction of inner and outer.

The nature poet, William Wordsworth seemed to understand the ambiguity when he wrote:

> ... And I have felt
> A presence that disturbs me with the joy
> Of elevated thoughts; a sense sublime
> Of something far more deeply interfused,
> Whose dwelling is the light of setting suns,
> And the round ocean and the living air,
> And the blue sky, and in the mind of man...[14]

He had once known what the Persians would have called *Xvarnah*:

> There was a time when meadow, grove and stream,
> The earth, and every common sight,
> To me did seem
> Apparelled in celestial light,
> The glory and the freshness of a dream.[15]

The poet lamented that 'it is not now as it hath been of yore', and as he had grown older the visionary dimension of his youthful perception had dimmed. He did not lose, however, the memory of the transfigured Earth:

> But yet I know, where'er I go
> That there hath past away a glory from the earth.

The reverse was the case with the Irish poet, painter, journalist, agiculturist and great nature mystic, George William Russell, or 'AE'. He claimed that he did not always have an 'intimacy with nature'. 'I never felt a light in childhood which faded in manhood into the common light of day... I was not conscious in my boyhood of any heaven lying about me,' he wrote.[16] He lived in the city, but as his adolescence progressed, he found himself increasingly drawn to the hills - 'a far flush of blue on the horizon'. As he walked the country lanes during his visits there, he became 'astonished' at the intimations 'of another world, of an interior nature' that 'began to overpower' him. His senses 'were expectant of some unveiling to take place':

> The tinted air glowed before me with intelligible significance like a face, a voice. The visible world became like a tapestry blown and stirred by winds behind it. If it would but raise for an instant I knew I would be in Paradise. Every form on that tapestry appeared to be the work of gods. Every flower was a word, a thought. The grass was speech; the trees were speech; the waters were speech; the winds were speech. They were the Army of the Voice... I listened with my whole being, and then these apparitions would fade away and I would be the mean and miserable boy once more.[17]

We have hints here, perhaps, of Julian Jaynes' proposed bicameral condition, discussed earlier.

Happily (for him and us), Russell eventually 'broke through' into the direct vision of the Spirit Earth. Here is a typical example of his visionary perception, and the context in which he placed it:

> I believe that most of what was said of God was in reality said of the Spirit whose body is Earth. I must in some fashion indicate the nature of the visions which led me to believe with Plato that the Earth is not at all what the geographers suppose it to be, and that we live like frogs at the bottom of a marsh knowing nothing of that Many-Coloured Earth which is superior to this we know, *yet related to it as soul to body...* I wish to convey, so far as words may, how some apparitions of that ancient beauty came to me in wood or hillside or by the shores of the western sea. Sometimes lying on the hillside with the eyes of the body shut as in sleep I could see valleys and hills, lustrous as a jewel, where all was self-shining, the colours brighter and purer, yet making a softer harmony together than the colours of the world I know. The winds sparkled as they blew hither and thither, yet far distances were clear through that glowing air... There, too, in that land I saw fountains as of luminous mist... and shining folk.. .They were, I believe, those who in the ancient world gave birth to legends of nymph and dryad.[18] (Emphasis mine.)

It is easy to see the remarkably close similarities between Russell's spontaneous visions, together with his feelings about them, and the Iranian ideas of the Paradise of Yima, of Eran-Vej, of the world of Hurqalya. The transfigured Earth, the luminosity, and the sense of the world soul (and ensouled Earth) are all there. In fact, Russell even spoke of a 'Planetary Spirit... manifesting through the substance of Earth'. But Russell was a modern Irishman, not an ancient Iranian: clearly, the source of such visions has to be the deep, collective pool of human consciousness.

Russell developed his natural gifts with intensive meditation. Light was as important an aspect of his altered states as with any Zoroastrian mystic. The more his meditative exercises proceeded, the more he became aware of a growing inner luminosity, 'as if I had unsealed in the body a fountain of interior light'. At times, he recalled, 'there broke in on me an almost intolerable lustre of light, pure and shining faces, dazzling processions of figures, most ancient, ancient places and peoples, and landscapes lovely as the lost Eden'.[19]

The Irish nature mystic identified several species of consciousness within himself: 'I know that my brain is a court... and I am never alone in it.' There were the thoughts of others; he had one experience at work, for instance, when he was suddenly flooded by the detailed images of a shop and two individuals he had never seen before. They turned out to be - in every detail - related to a man working alongside him whose thoughts had turned to home. Russell wondered how many thoughts we assumed were our own were in fact those of someone else. There was also the type of vision in which Russell felt his mind 'intersected' that of someone else and he saw fleetingly through their eyes. He figured that this was caused by the accidental but precise correspondence of moods between the individual concerned (who would most often be completely unknown to him) and himself. Russell's detailed analysis of his mental life revealed that other images were symbolic material refashioned from his own storehouse of individual memories by an interior architect he identified as a kind of immortal oversoul, a transcendent 'I', a spiritual umbilical cord that linked each person to the godhead beyond time and space. Yet other forms of consciousness seemed to be the 'memories' of this immortal overself, transpersonal images from past lives it had inhabited, and transcendental visions of the spirit, of the soul.

Finally, there were visions of the past superimposed on, or emerging out of, the physical scenery around him that he concluded could only be explained by his tuning into 'the memory of nature' or 'the memory of Earth' itself. For instance, while waiting for someone in a ruined chapel, he suddenly saw the place as it had been, and saw every detail of people in the congregation. Sometimes, though, he did not know whether he was seeing the past or the future. While in the hills alone, he saw on two separate occasions years apart, 'an airship glittering with light' that seemed to be part of some aerial battle or manoever. More came, floating majestically over the hill slopes. They were unlike anything he had seen. Either they were from time to come, or were from some previous cycle of civilisation of incalculable antiquity. Russell believed that 'memory is an attribute of all living creatures, and Earth also, the greatest living creature we know... we can evoke out of the memory of the Earth images of whatsoever we desire...The fact that Earth holds such memories is itself important, for once we discover this imperishable tablet, we are led to speculate whether in the future a training in seership might not lead to a revolution in human knowledge.'[20]

All in all, Russell decided that the 'self which sits in the gate of the body does not know what powers or dignitaries meet in the inner palace chambers of the soul'. 'If you will but awaken the inner sight,' he urged his readers, 'Hy Brazil, Ildathach, all the lands of Immortal Youth will build themselves up anew for you no longer as fantasy but in vivid actuality.'[21] The Golden Age had never left the Earth, he averred; it surrounded us still, but we had become blind to it.

Russell referred to his visions of the Spirit Earth as 'supernature', the identical phrase that Lévy-Bruhl coined for the same thing, and also made the intriguing statement that there were special places in the physical world where he could 'see' more easily than others: 'The whole west coast of Ireland from Donegal to Kerry seems charged with a magical power, and I find it easiest to see while I am there. I have always found it comparatively easy to see visions while at ancient monuments like New Grange and Dowth...'[22] Yet another aspect of the 'Sophianic' Mystery of the Earth - the environmental effects of certain places that we have touched on in different ways in earlier pages.

The Doors of Perception

Russell saw his visions solely as manifestations of spirituality and translated them in terms of Irish traditions - the fairy folk, Tir-na-nog and so on, which were to him real places perceived by the mind's eye. Aldous Huxley, on the other hand, whose interest in visionary states was catalysed in the 1950s by his experimentation with the hallucinogen, mescalin, was well aware that in visionary or hallucinatory states one had to take into account one's neurological inheritance, and that it was a person's biochemistry that provided the wherewithal for the experiences of the Otherworld to occur, whatever their actual nature, and towards which he maintained an equivocal attitude.

For Huxley, mescalin tended to transfigure the visible world around him rather than admitting him to interior, visionary landscapes. For instance, while under the influence of the drug he confronted a garden chair onto which the sun, streaming through lattice-work, cast dark strips of shadow:

> That chair - shall I ever forget it? Where the shadows fell on the canvas upholstery, stripes of a deep but glowing indigo alternated with stripes of incandescence so intensely bright that it was hard to believe that they could be made of anything but blue fire. For what seemed an immensely long time I gazed without knowing, even without wishing to know, what it was that confronted me... Garden furniture, laths, sunlight, shadow - these were no more than names and notions, mere verbalizations, for utilitarian or scientific purposes, after the event. The event was this succession of azure furnace doors separated by gulfs of unfathomable gentian...
>
> Confronted by a chair which looked like the Last Judgement - or, to be more accurate, by a Last Judgement which, after a long time and with considerable difficulty, I recognized as a chair - I found myself all at once on the brink of panic.[23]

Although he was experiencing ever increasing beauty and significance in the world around him, Huxley felt things were going too far; he sensed that he might be overwhelmed by the *Mysterium tremendum*. The mescalin had affected the normal filtering process of the mind, allowing in infinitely more material from 'Mind at Large' (Huxley's borrowed phrase) to conscious awareness than normal. Flowers in his garden strained to the heavens, their colours blazing on the 'brink of being supernatural'; trees seemed to 'belong to some sacred grove', and 'Eden alternated with Dodona, Yggdrasil with the mystic Rose.'[24] Foliage and sunlight wove an intricate pattern 'of the most delicate green lights and shadows, pulsing with undecipherable mystery'. Colour had its own power, independent of the object it described; light was intense.

Despite the fact that his own experiences concerned mainly the outer world, Huxley was most intrigued by the inner vistas of the psychedelic (Huxley invented that term) experience, which most of the great early experimenters had described. He proposed an unforgettable model of the visionary world:

> A man consists of what I may call an Old World of personal consciousness and, beyond a dividing sea, a series of New Worlds - the not too distant Virginias and Carolinas of the personal subconscious and the vegetative soul; the far West of the collective unconscious, with its flora of symbols, its tribes of aboriginal archetypes; and, across another, vaster ocean, at the antipodes of everyday consciousness, the world of Visionary Experience.
>
> ... if you go to the antipodes of the self-conscious mind, you will encounter all sorts of creatures at least as odd as kangaroos. You do not invent these creatures any more than you invent marsupials. They live their own lives in complete independence. A man cannot control them. All he can do is go to the mental equivalent of Australia and look around him...[25]

Huxley was quick to note that the great common denominator in peoples' experiences of this visionary antipodes was the *light* that was seen there: 'Everything seen by those who visit the mind's antipodes is brilliantly illuminated and seems to shine from within. All colours are intensified to a pitch far beyond anything seen in the normal state... the visions met with... are always intensely and, one might say, praeternaturally brilliant in colour.' Every vision was unique

> ...but all recognisably belong to the same species. The landscapes, the architectures, the clustering gems, the brilliant and intricate patterns - these in their atmosphere of praeturnatural light, praeturnatural colour, and praeturnatural significance, are the stuff of which the mind's antipodes are made. Why this should be so we have no idea. It is a brute fact of experience which, whether we like it or not, we have to accept - just as we have to accept the fact of kangaroos.[26]

This light could have its demonic aspects, however, as Huxley recognised. He referred to the account of a schizophrenic girl, who saw the world transfigured into the harsh glare of 'the country of lit-upness'.

In the outer experience of vision, such as Russell's experiences or his own with mescalin, Huxley suggested that 'some of the brightness of visionary experience spills over... Though still recognisably itself, the Old World takes on the qualities of the mind's antipodes.' This is, of course, the very essence of the Interworld; this is the haloing of the material landscape with *Xvarnah*.

Huxley compared the peyote vision of Weir Mitchell with a traditional description of paradise to show that they both originate from the same 'antipodean' source of vision. Mitchell's experience began with what we would now classify as entoptic images - 'star points'... 'fragments of stained glass'... 'zigzag lines of very bright colours'. These gradually transformed into representational (iconic) imagery: an elaborate gothic tower, with eroded statues and festooned with huge gemstones 'like masses of transparent fruit', which in turn changed into 'a mountain, a cliff of inconceivable height, a colossal birdclaw carved in stone and projecting over the abyss, an endless unfurling of coloured draperies...' Finally, there was vision of purple and green waves crashing on a beach 'with myriads of lights of the same tint'. Huxley invited comparison of this with the *Ramayana*'s description of Uttarakuru, the Otherworld of the Hindus:

> The land is watered by lakes with golden lotuses. There are rivers by thousands, full of leaves of the colour of sapphire and lapis lazuli; and the lakes, resplendent like the morning sun, are adorned by golden beds of red lotus. The country all around is covered by jewels and precious stones, with gay beds of blue lotus, golden-petalled. Instead of sand, pearls, gems and gold form the banks of rivers...

Clearly, then, in order to see and experience the paradisal Interworld, altered states of consciousness are required. The content is sensory, and the only source of sensory material is through the senses. 'The raw material for this creation is provided by the visual experiences of ordinary life,' Huxley acknowledged, but added that 'the moulding of this material into forms is the work of someone who is most certainly not the self.'[27]

As we have noted in previous pages, the methods of obtaining these altered states in which visionary landscapes and transfigured outer perception can occur are legion, ranging from incarceration in caves, through trance dancing, drumming and meditation to the ingestion of hallucinogens - each doubtlessly lending its own character to the experience. The Islamic mystics used a specialised alchemical meditation to transmute sensory data in order to experience, or 'unveil', the Interworld. Corbin wrote that the perception of the Spirit Earth, in Mazdean terms the Angel of the Earth, 'takes shape exactly at the point where the data of sensory perception are raised, as it were, to the diaphanous state by the active Imagination'. The aim was to become an inhabitant of the Earth of Hurqalya here on the sensory, physical plane of Earth (such a spiritual master was known as a *Hurqalyavi*).

The frontier of the Interworld

There is a certain state of altered consciousness that is particularly suited to the perception of the Interworld, one that is quieter and more reliable than the roller-coaster package tours provided by drugs, that does not require the particular application that meditational techniques demand, nor the specific social contexts needed for trance-dancing and drumming. It is a curious condition accessed in sleep

- an alert form of consciousness that can be fostered while still within the physiological state of sleep. Corbin notes that Suhrawardi, during a period of overwork and spiritual ordeal, had a major vision 'while still in an intermediate state between waking and sleeping'.[28] This spectrum of altered consciousness, available to us all, has special associations, as we shall see, with out-of-body experience, that crucial element of shamanic trance that we saw earlier was such an important factor in the creation of shamanic landscape lines.

Those remarkable manuals of altered states of consciousness, the first-millenium BC *Upanishads*, spoke clearly on these intermediary states between waking and sleep. The eighth-century AD Vedantic theologian, Sankara, in a commentary on Verse 4 of the *Mandukya Upanishad*, wrote:

> Waking consciousness, being associated with many manners of relationship and seemingly conscious of objects as external (although in reality they are nothing but states of mind), leaves in the mind corresponding impressions. That mind in the dream, maintaining none of the external connections, yet possessed of these impressions left upon it by the waking consciousness, like a piece of canvas with pictures painted upon it, should experience the dream state as though it were a waking state, is due to it being under the influence of ignorance, desire, and impulse to action. Thus is it said in the Brihadaranyaka Upanishad:

> 'When, on falling asleep, one takes along the material of this all-containing world, tears it apart and builds it up, oneself, and by one's own light dreams; that person becomes self-illuminated.

> 'There are no chariots there, no spans, no roads. Yet he projects from himself chariots, spans and roads. There are no blisses there, no pleasures, no delights. Yet he projects from himself, blisses, pleasures and delights. There are no tanks there, no lotus-pools, no streams. Yet he projects from himself tanks, lotus-pools, and streams. For he is creator.'[29]

Sankara then refers to the *Brihadaranyaka Upanishad*, which includes these lines:

> Striking down in sleep what is bodily,
> Sleepless, he looks down upon the sleeping senses.
> Having taken to himself light, he has returned to his own place:
> That Golden Person, the Lone Wild Gander.
> Guarding with his breath his low nest,
> Out of that nest the Immortal goes forth
> He goes wherever he pleases, that Immortal
> The Golden Person, the Unique Wild Gander.
> In the State of Sleep, soaring high and low,
> A god, he puts forth for himself innumerable forms...

The 'Lone Wild Gander' recalls the goose-symbol of magical flight common to shamanism - 'soaring high and low'. Joseph Campbell related this material to 'out-of-body experiences in the trance state' and of scenes 'of an intelligible sphere, known to the eye of the mind, unseen by the light of day'.[30] Campbell applied this to San rock art, but it can be applied to any mystical tradition, of which shamanism was the first flowering. Zarathustra, in his mythic journey to Eran-Vej, for example, is required to 'take off his dress' in order to reach the Interworld. There, he *casts no shadow*. All this is, of course, symbolic language. As Corbin pointed out: 'to take off the "material dress" is to foretaste the state of the Body of Light, or resurrection body... Not to cast a shadow is the property of the *glorious body*, is to be at the center.'[31] It is always the high noon of mythic time in the Interworld, when shadows are not cast, for one can only be there in an out-of-body state, whatever that implies; one can be there only in mind, the astral body or whatever concept one chooses for the out-of-body locus of consciousness. (The Mazdean traditions also refer to a 'Cable of Irradiation' by which to climb to the luminous Centre, a specialised form of the spirit-flight-line complex discussed earlier.)

The curious state of consciousness between waking awareness and sleep is known in modern research terminology as 'lucid dreaming', and its consideration opens a veritable 'can of worms', not least because it has a close association with, or similarity to, out-of-body experience, as we shall see. In a lucid dream, one is fully conscious *within* a dream; physiological sleep is not disturbed. Some people have caught fleeting moments of such a condition, and others will know the state quite well, but the majority to whom the condition is unfamiliar may mistakenly think that what is being discussed are merely vivid dreams. This is not so; I am referring to a distinctive and very important state of consciousness - virtually a separate reality.

The term 'lucid dreaming', first coined by Frederick Van Eeden in 1913,[32] is unfortunate in this respect. Methodical, scientific research on the state only got under way in the 1970s, and was first clinically demonstrated in 1975 by British dream researcher Keith Hearne.[33] He had a volunteer subject who said he regularly experienced lucid dreams, but how could Hearne as experimenter study the state unless he knew his subject was having a lucid dream? He hit on the idea of using eye-muscle signals: when dreaming, most of one's muscles are paralysed, except for the respiratory muscles and those of the eyes (for some unknown reason one produces 'rapid eye movements' - REMs - beneath the closed lids during dream periods of sleep). In a set of sessions, Hearne's subject was duly wired-up in the dream laboratory, and his various physiological parameters were monitored. Within a couple of nights the volunteer 'awoke' in a dream without waking up from sleep or disturbing the progress of the dream, and he made a pre-arranged sequence of movements with his eyeballs. These showed up as signals on the monitoring equipment, which also confirmed that the subject was soundly asleep! For the first time it had been possible for a person to communicate to the 'outside world' from within a dream.

(In order to avoid discussion on the nature of this state of consciousness becoming too academic, I will make occasional brief references to my own experiences of it in following paragraphs. Although I am doubtlessly simply a beginner, and although I rarely discuss my inner life in public, I thought it might be helpful to indicate to those readers unfamiliar with this 'interworld state' what it *feels* like to a contemporary person who is not enmeshed in any particular religious belief system.)

It is perhaps important to clarify that the lucid dream condition is not exactly that of hypnogogic or hypnopompic visions - those transitional states between falling asleep and awakening, respectively, when pictures can flash in front of the mind's eye. Although it may be possible with training to 'slow down' these transitional states and 'enter' more stable and prolonged lucid dream conditions, most people seem to experience lucid dreams by becoming self-consciously aware during and within full, dreaming sleep, particularly towards the latter part of a sleep cycle when periods of dreaming (of REMs) are at their longest - usually from about 5 am, when the sleep cycle is a normal nightly one. That has certainly been my experience.

When one 'awakes' within a dream, 'real' three-dimensional space is experienced. Scenery takes on a crisp detail, and the perspective of objects as one moves around changes in a totally authentic manner. Colours become brighter and purer. Lighting ('one's own light') is convincing. Nor is the lucid dream simply visual: sounds are heard - characters in the dream can be spoken to and questioned, and objects can be touched, held, felt. In one of my own lucid dream states, for instance, I have felt the waxy texture of a leaf on a tree, and felt the resistance of the branch it was growing from as I tugged at it. Total sensory realism. When awake in a dream one can, by applying some skill and will, direct the course of action, or change it into another sequence of events, another adventure. This 'pure' sensory world can be manipulated in a way that is exhilarating.

It is only by accident or because one has a meditator's control of mind, however, that one can extend beyond the illusionary veil of these sensory re-creations and enter truly spiritual and mystical mind states that the 'fluid' nature of lucid dreaming or interworld consciousness makes more readily accessible. It is in this use of the state that mental and spiritual training becomes necessary.

One of the practical difficulties of functioning in the intermediary, lucid dream state is to preserve the necessary precise balance between waking consciousness and sleep. It is all too easy, on the one hand, to lose the lucidity of the experience and sink back into a normal, non-self-aware sleep condition, or, on the other, to extinguish the finely-tuned state of consciousness involved by 'waking up' to the outer, material world of one's sleep environment. There are varying layers of the lucid dream state, and with experience and training one can get deeper without falling back into an unaware sleep state. I discovered that by looking at the backs of my dream-body's hands, I could often stabilise the condition when it threatened to break up. Subsequently, I learned that this is a well-known technique.

In the deeper types of lucid dream, the illusion of the sensory world fully re-creates the physical world (or perhaps the physical world is a dense illusory form of the lucid dream state!), but it is a magic sensory world in which virtually anything is possible.

The sense of movement, particularly, while utterly realistic, is often in the exhilarating form of 'bouncing' light as thistledown, floating or flying. It is here that the distinction between out-of-body states and lucid dreaming becomes hard to make - especially when the re-created sensory environment happens to be of one's own bedroom or another known physical location, as sometimes happens.

The out-of-body experience is known of in modern societies today only in the forms of spontaneous cases, in near death experiences, and, I suggest, in some of the reported 'UFO abductions', which seem to be spontaneous out-of-body (or lucid dream) experiences interpreted in terms of extra-terrestrial craft and beings - the archetype of the depersonalised (alien) machine (spacecraft) has truly invaded the modern soul. (It seems that it may be possible for people to enter lucid dream states directly from the waking condition, and research is currently under way to study this.) The causes of these various circumstances of out-of-body experience can be extreme physiological or psychological stress, illness, traumatic accidents, fatigue, reverie, drugs, or the effects of external energy fields - especially from certain geophysical phenomena.

The Metachoric Earth

It is difficult for people who have felt themselves 'exteriorise' from their bodies with utmost realism to accept that they may have undergone a lucid dream experience - even though many out-of-body experiences in normal healthy people occur when they are in a semi-sleeping or quiescent state. Nevertheless, modern scientists are not at all convinced that 'anything leaves' the body during the so-called out-of-body experience. In the 1960s, Celia Green proposed a 'metachoric' state, in which an hallucination of the external world is instantly and seamlessly melded with the actual perception of the external world.[34] There may be only a slight difference between the actual and hallucinated versions: Green suggested, for example, that the apparition of a 'ghost' may in fact be a hallucination re-creating the actual scene in front of the witness but containing the extra element of the ghostly figure.

As unlikely as this idea sounds, it has to some extent been vindicated since the advent of lucid dream research, particularly in the phenomenon known as the 'false awakening'. In this, a person may awaken and arise, shower, dress, and perhaps even have breakfast before discovering that they are, in fact, still sound asleep in bed! People experiencing this in dream laboratories have thought they have got up and walked around the laboratory, observing the surroundings in extreme detail, when the observers and monitoring apparatus showed conclusively they were still fast alseep. Stephen LaBerge, a lucid dream researcher at Stanford University who has personal experience of the states he studies experimentally and academically, once 'rolled' out of his sleeping body and walked around his bedroom, even looking back at his sleeping form. It seemed he was having an authentic out-of-body experience, but he noted a detail in the otherwise convincing home environment that he knew could not be true, and which revealed the whole experience to be metachoric. He physically awoke to the bedroom without the added detail.[36]

The mind can indeed 'project from itself chariots, spans, and roads' and re-create in a twinkling its external environment.

Crossing the frontier

Typical of the out-of-body condition is that its onset often contains a powerful version of one of the 'tunnel' entoptic form constants which were described earlier. Those who find themselves out of their bodies during near-death states, for example, frequently report a journey along a tunnel towards a distant light, where they usually see an 'Elysian Fields'-type of paradisal scene and may converse with a glowing being of great sacral power. Again, UFO 'abductees' often mention being 'drawn' up a 'traction beam' of light towards a spacecraft (which is, incidentally, almost always only inferred; a curiously-illuminated interior being what is actually seen).

In my own interworld experiences I have similarly encountered the tunnel entoptic form. In one case I found myself running along a darkened tunnel in a dream. I recognised the entoptic nature of the image while in the dream, and immediately began to become increasingly self-consciously aware. Instead of waking up, however, the scene changed suddenly, and I was running in open country illuminated by the 'sun' off somewhere to my left. Ahead were great marble archways, or, more precisely, trilithons, arranged one behind the other forming a kind of corridor. I took off and flew headfirst and with increasing speed through them, all the time becoming more vividly conscious. I emerged at the far end and soared upwards into a blue sky, flying and arching through space in what felt to be a totally authentic fashion and fully and vibrantly conscious. I went on to fly over scenery that had a stable geography (I was able to return and fly over certain parts again), to study features in the vast sunlit landscape in intricate detail, and to spy down on apparent human beings moving about their business. Some of their technology and dress were unfamiliar, but otherwise everything looked completely 'real' and 'normal'.

On another occasion, I 'awoke' to find myself hurtling along a narrow river, only a few feet above the water surface. I thought I was attached to the front of a speed boat (the dream I had 'awoken' out of involved my being on a jet plane), but I discovered that I was flying free, by myself. The 'sun' was - again - low and shining outside my field of vision to my left somewhere, lighting up the water a golden brownish colour and the willows overhanging the river a marvellous golden yellow. The arching trees and water course formed the 'tunnel' entoptic image that I was rocketing along. Psychologist, Susan Blackmore underwent an extraordinary three-hour-long out-of-body episode, which started by her finding herself 'thundering along' a tree-lined road as if in a carriage drawn by a number of horses, 'only I was very close to the ground'. Blackmore recognised that the road was effectively 'a tree-lined tunnel'.[37] Later, Blackmore became convinced that her experience had been a form of lucid dream.

While some of my own conscious 'Otherworld' journeys contain matter that I could interpret as emerging from my own neurological processes, and to be therefore lucid dream-style consciousness, I have had other experiences which I find more difficult to think of in that way. The earliest one I can recall, for example, was when as a very young child I suddenly found myself watching 'me' playing with my toys. I rushed into the kitchen to tell my mother, who did not have the time or temper to cope with a child babbling that it had seen itself playing! So it is, in our culture, that states of consciousness other than the narrow spectrum of states that are agreed on as being 'normal' are edited out.

Of course, I now deliberately encourage my 'interworld' states, especially during sleep (and, when achieved once, it is easier to repeat the experience) and observe them closely. I have flown over wondrous landscapes lit by an inner sun, observed other beings, floated over and through cities that never were built in the physical world, gazed at clouds scudding across the face of a moon that never shone in mundane skies, and soared off sea cliffs at twilight along lonely shorelines of unknown lands, hearing murmuring waves shifting beach boulders beneath me as I passed. The sense of reality in such experiences is total - far more so than even vivid dreaming or strong visualisation. Sometimes they are long and complex, at other times they are brief, as in one curious but beautiful instance where I 'awoke' to full, intensely clear consciousness in a glade within a pine forest. I was suspended upright in the air with my feet just a few inches above the topmost blades of frost-bloomed grass, floating almost imperceptibly backwards...

In analysis, both during the experiences and afterwards, I do detect elements that come from my personal memories and daily, waking life, even though integrated into scenes and events that are totally novel to me. There are also, I suspect, elements that are *transpersonal* - originating from sources that are not to do with my personal, individual life and consciousness. This is, of course, deep water as far as modern scientific thought goes, and I will not elaborate on it here. For myself, I simply do not know if a person's spirit or consciouness leaves the physical body in these types of experience; I do not know if one really moves around the external environment, as sometimes seems to be the case, or, on other occasions, enters other dimensions of the world. By the same token, we do not know if the ancient shamans flew their spirit ways across their actual tribal landscapes, or across metachoric versions of them. (The shamanic markings would have been made in either case, of course.)

To most modern scientific researchers (there are exceptions), such experiences are exclusively hallucinatory, resulting from neurological mechanisms. While there can be *no* doubt that that is at least partially true, is it the whole story? Does the brain act like a trans-dimensional crystal set, picking up the traffic not only from our own mentality, but from transpersonal and even spiritual sources, as Russell maintained? Can we walk, or soar over, the Spirit Earth? The modern mind likes to feel sure whether or not it is dealing with a neurological construct or a neurological window into another reality. It will, alas, have to live with the ambiguity, because there is as yet no way of truly deciding between the two possibilities.

My own guess, for what it is worth, is that the idea of 'inner' and 'outer' is itself a fallacy, and so the need to know whether we are dealing with an experience produced solely by the brain or an actual perception of some level of 'environment' is a wrongly-conceived question. Just look at our 'normal' experience of consensus reality. What is it that we are experiencing? Various forms of raw energy impinge upon our sensory receptors and are translated into what are effectively hallucinations - they are certainly neurological constructs - which we say represent the 'real' world. Take sight, just as one of the five sensory examples. Light energy hurtles at 186,000 miles a second into the eye tissue and onto millions of swaying, shimmering rods and cones in the retina; raw elemental energy explodes across a soft, organic marsh of receptor cells that translate it into nerve signals that are transmitted to the visual cortex as electro-chemical processes.

These processes, which are not the energy that impinged on the sensory apparatus of the eye in the first place, create a stable, highly-edited mental view of the 'outer' world. Light is created within the darkness of the skull. This type of translation is true for all the senses. Our knowledge and experience of the 'real world' is a mental construct that shares the same mechanisms as do hallucinations. This 'real world' construct is largely a learned structure, culturally determined to a surprising extent. As Weston La Barre has remarked, 'a surprisingly good case could be made that much of culture is hallucination'.[38]

We have noted with Aldous Huxley what a greater reality floods in when the culturally-determined editing systems are disrupted by hallucinogens or other mind-altering techniques. Similarly, commonly-agreed versions of reality differ from culture to culture; so in ancient and non-Western societies the actual perception of the world could be substantially different to our own, and only 'unreal' to us because of the particular editing system our culture employs.

Hence all we know, in fact, is what is produced in our minds - we *do not have direct contact with 'outer' things. We never experience them in their unmediated 'thingness'*. Our knowledge of them is constructed within our mind-brains.

A hallucination originates somewhere within the cortex responsible for the sensory mode involved. Its source might be as valid as normal sensory input, and the brain uses the same equipment that it uses to process sensory data to present us (whatever 'we' are) with the hallucination. A 'signal' is clothed in cognisable form for us to perceive, whether it be a sensory nerve impulse or the mysterious source of the hallucination. The organ of the brain, like a church organ, is simply an instrument that responds to fingers on the keyboard. The point is that different fingers play different tunes - and the question sometimes arises as to whom do the fingers belong?

The sense of 'I' and 'not-I', subject and object, inner and outer, is largely a function of a spectral mental vehicle we call the ego. In altered states of consciousness, and, equally, in differently-rigged consensus-realities of different cultures, that structure can have a different form, can be a weaker mental artefact or even dissolve entirely. Then there is no inner or outer. There is, indeed, as Sankara put it, 'only Mind'.

There is no little person inside our heads: that too is a hallucination. If we have the sense of going 'out-of-body', Keith Harary, the American lucid dream researcher and experient, has reminded us, we are making an assumption that we were *in* our body in the first place. In fact, body-centred consciousness is a sustained hallucination closely linked to that of the personal ego. Our locus of cognition is simply a mental model, and that model can become mobile, and change. When experiencing mind-change, one's 'body image' can alter dramatically, even to the point of disappearance, and the hallucinated inner person can move around within the body as well as leave it altogether, adrift on the sea of Mind at Large. Susan Blackmore suggests that the out-of-body experience is, effectively, simply another model of self, in a sense hindering the process of entry into deeper and more profound levels of consciousness. The importance of the out-of-body or lucid dream experience is that it signals that 'something is happening' in one's consciousness, of it becoming more fluid.[39]

Metaphysically, the surroundings experienced in lucid dream or out-of-body states are no more or less illusionary than those experienced in waking consciousness - everything is *maya*, illusion, except the direct, unpolluted experience of Mind. The advantage of the out-of-body experience, lucid dreaming, the experience of the Interworld, or whatever label we give it, is that the surroundings are less dense, more diaphanous and malleable; they provide a flimsier veil of illusion to draw aside.

All these kind of states are potential mental gateways to ever-increasing depths of consciousness - that is their real importance. The entry to Eran-Vej, the Interworld, is 'the necessary prelude to the direct vision of the archetypal Powers of light'.[40] Similarly, while on the trance journey, the shaman can sometimes pass through the 'sun door' into the 'realm of eternally awakened consciousness', in Joan Halifax's evocative phrase.[41]

The sun is one symbol of this eternal light at the beginning and end of all things, beyond time, life, death, inner, outer and all dualities - the Light of Lights to the ancient Persians, the Clear Light of the Void to Zen Buddhists. In Indo-European traditions this light became anthropomorphised into a resplendent deity, *Diw*, which gave its root to many later gods such as Zeus, Tiw, and god-words such as *Deus*. I have little doubt that the sunbeams that entered the Neolithic chambered mounds (and still enter some, like Ireland's Newgrange), the Egyptian temples, the shamanic caves, and the like, were symbolic expressions of this ineffable spiritual experience, and that it is in such cosmological contexts that ancient astronomy needs to be appreciated.

The straightness of the sunbeams lancing through the inner sacred darkness of the ancient temples and holy caves would be yet another symbol of the *sanctity of the straight*, the line-straightness-spirit complex that had as one of its manifestations the linear landscape markings we considered earlier.

The Interworld is the threshold of the pure spiritual realms, whatever that phrase actually means, and is a refined form of sensory experience. It has cast its reflection on the physical world in the form of mythologised and shamanised ancient land-scapes around the world. These mind-modified landscapes are of course filtered through different cultural belief systems, as has been obvious in the handful of examples we have looked at in these pages.

Reclaiming Paradise

This symbiotic state of Earth and mind is culturally absent for us, as I have said. It does not matter whether or not it is a neurological blueprint or another level of being - it remains an important state. Can we recover it? And if so, to what purpose?

The first answer is that, yes, we can recover it. The experience of the Earth of Visions is but a hair's breadth away for any one of us. There are a wide variety of techniques that can be used to attain it, some of which I have mentioned in passing - it is beyond my brief here to go into any more detail regarding these. The state of consciousness involved is studied in university lucid dream research programmes, as we have seen, and is used in 'occult' circles. I feel it is most important for this state of mind to become much more commonly accessible, to have a higher cultural profile, and to be eased a little out of the tight confines of scientific and academic thought on the one hand, and occult belief-systems on the other.

As to the purposes of reclaiming and reinstating this intriguing level of human experience - they range from the pragmatic to the sublime.

Pragmatically first, we need to re-acquaint ourselves at a cultural level with actual visions of paradise; with the knowledge of the archetypal Spirit World. If we did this on a sufficiently broad and deep level, it would *inevitably* filter through to our collective cultural perception of our material, physical environment and our awareness of the appropriate protocols for living with it.

Without this direct 'knowledge of paradise', the ecological sensitivity we now see developing at the eleventh hour in modern society will forever lack the essential drive and inner significance that it will need to change our worldview and habits on a sufficiently significant scale. Whether the vision of the Interworld is a neurological imprint, or an actual glimpse into another level of reality hardly matters: the *experience* is what counts; it is that which has the power.

Even more pragmatically, direct modern knowledge of the Interworld could lead to conscious acts in the material world. In my own interworld journeys, just for example, I have studied the strange cities 'there'; these usually have modest buildings in them, but sometimes contain the most amazing large-scale (what we would call 'public') buildings. They are totally 'real' but rather different to modern buildings. If I was an architect, I would have been able to produce genuine architectural plans of such structures after seeing them. If this was put into large-scale practice, we could foster a *fully-conscious* process of producing in our physical environment an architecture already prefigured in the Interworld, an architecture *imprinted by mind* in the most direct sense.

Again, on another lucid dream/interworld journey, I have closely examined an unfamiliar type of tricycle machine. As trivial as this particular example is, the point remains that it was so solid and detailed that if I had been an engineer I would have been able to have produced an engineering drawing of that 'machine'. It could be built in the physical world. There are undoubtedly other, more significant examples of this archetypal 'machinery' in the Interworld. George William Russell's visionary airships (above) are another case in point. He asked himself when or where such vehicles had been launched. 'Was it ages ago in some actual workshop in an extinct civilisation, and were these but images in the eternal memory?' he wondered. 'Or were they launched by my own spirit from some magical arsenal of my being...? Or were they images of things yet to be in the world, begotten in the eternal mind... and from which they stray into the imagination of scientist, engineer or poet to be out-realized in discovery, mechanism or song?'[42]

In the realm of art, William Blake, for instance, referred to the 'wonderful originals' in the mind realms, and discoveries by scientists and mathematicians have likewise been claimed to have been seen by the mind's eye before they became intellectual actualities. Politicians could absorb how interworld cities (I assure the reader they do exist, whether as spiritual places or neurological models) are governed; economists and ecologists could together study the lessons the Interworld had to give.

We can all look into the storehouse of Russell's 'eternal mind'. In the way the Tukano Indians of South America can manipulate their entoptic imagery, we could doubtlessly learn to focus in on specific aspects of the Interworld that had relevance to our work and times. Instead of allowing insight, invention and inspiration to remain a hazy, hit-or-miss affair, our engineers, architects, town planners, and so on could directly access the prefigurative, archetypal state possessed by the Interworld. In such a collective, culturally -significant process, the ages-old wisdom of the mind would begin to guide our collective hands and thinking. It would also be a profoundly valuable extension of hospice care: death could be recognised as the ultimate version of mind change, and trained for accordingly.

All this is the *least* benefit that direct access to the Interworld could bestow. At the sublime end of the spectrum, many of those who entered regularly through the gateway into the Interworld would inevitably and eventually come into contact with the higher realities that are more readily accessible from that state. It would become the starting place for countless personal journeys into the Beyond. It would be a background beat to the more pragmatic usages of the state, and if conducted on a sufficiently broad basis within our culture it would, over a generation, bring a more mystical colouring to our ways of thinking and behaviour. To be sure, I think it would generate a new development of the human mind.

I am not envisaging the British Prime Minister conducting shamanic drumming sessions in 10 Downing Street (though it would be a delight if that happened), nor the President of the USA engaging in trance dancing on the White House lawn (though that would be fun, too, and would doubtlessly improve all sorts of policies). I am not suggesting some crazed, pill-popping, chaotic misuse of the interworld consciousness, which in any case is rarely experienced in such situations. No, obviously, we can quite readily now develop mind-change techniques appropriate to our times and culture, which are healthy, safe, natural and long-lived; techniques that are socially integrated.

The point is, access to the Interworld is a readily-achievable goal. With the improvements in accessing techniques serious cultural interest would encourage, large-scale (though never, I suspect, mass) experience of the Interworld would become routine. There are already enormously skilled technicians in interworld access techniques available today in both academic, 'fringe' and occult areas. Although I suspect there would be resistance from those who had a vested interest in maintaining certain belief structures, in both academic and occult circles, the level of consciousness in question can be wrested from their dominion. If Kalahari Bushmen are *all* free to enter such a state three or four times a month, why not ourselves? (Indeed, if we could bring about such a thing in our modern societies, the better the chance that the remaining Bushmen will long be with us!) We need a new, culturally effective experience of consciousness in our times, and a democractic access to that experience.

If all this sounds an utterly unlikely scenario, I agree that is the case only in so far as we think it to be. What I describe is in fact a process that can be initiated on a perfectly practical, even technical, basis. It would, however, *lead* to a spiritual worldview - that is the marvellous inevitability of such a process once started. But, alas, on the one side we have those who think such states of consciousness do not exist and would scorn such a proposal, and on the other there are those who do accept the reality of such mental realms but consider them to be so far removed from mundane consciousness that only a few mystics and spiritual masters can ever attain them. (This is true only for fully spiritualised, mystical consciousness, not the visionary states being discussed here.) Ironically, such reactions are the *only* thing stopping it happening!

The scepticism can be side-stepped by action. If enough people had the will, the interworld state could readily be made a cultural fact of life in our present Western-style societies, and in our lifetimes. We are talking about bringing a marginalised state of consciousness to the fore once more: what I think the Egyptian initiates called 'coming forth by day'. We *must* re-acquaint ourselves with paradise; it needs to start dynamically informing our worldview once more. I do not believe that if our policy-makers in industry, commerce, economics and politics, our scientists, technologists, architects, engineers, artists and poets regularly accessed the interworld realms of consciousness as a broadly-based, culturally-acceptable phenomenon, it could fail to have profound and beneficial effects on our worldview. We would *not* be returning to the gods and religions (necessarily) of the ancient world, but the archetypal realities they represented would assume forms in ways meaningful to us today. But though we would celebrate the Sacrament of the Earth in a new way, it would unavoidably be conducted in accordance with primordial principles.

It hardly matters whether we view the interworld state as a hallucinatory re-creation of sensory material or as some spiritual prefiguration of the material world. What is important is that we carry within us - the human mind carries within itself - the transpersonal, timeless blueprint of paradise. It is a blueprint that needs taking down from the shelf and dusting off - there is an important state of consciousness we need to rehabilitate within our culture.

PART TWO

A Guide to the Open Secrets of Avebury

I remember a Kamba man in Kenya, Kamoya Kimeu, a companion in the stone desert west of Lake Turkana - and a dozen other men - telling me, you know how to see, learn how to mark the country. And he and others teaching me to sit down in one place for two or three hours and look.

When we enter the landscape to learn something, we are obligated, I think, to pay attention rather than constantly to pose questions. To approach the land as we would a person, by opening an intelligent conversation. And to stay in one place, to make of that one, long observation a fully-dilated experience. We will always be rewarded if we give the land credit for more than we imagine, and if we imagine it as being more complex even than language. In these ways we begin, I think, to find a home, to sense how to fit a place.

Taken from an essay by Barry Lopez entitled 'The Rediscovery of North America', originally published by the University Press of Kentucky.

5

INTRODUCTION

In Part One we have explored evidence regarding the ancient worldview, starting out with actual mythologised landscapes and ending with a study of an important state of consciousness. Here in Part Two, we turn back to the physical landscape once more, a particular physical landscape, in fact; hopefully now able to look at it with a slightly enhanced perception.

The specific landscape I have selected is that of the Avebury complex in Wiltshire, southern England. It is a relatively large and well-preserved Neolithic landscape, dating approximately to the fourth and third millennia BC, and is one of the most important survivals of its kind in the world (it is included on the World Heritage List). I have chosen this particular landscape to study not only because of all these factors, but also because it is a *ceremonial* landscape: in Part One we learned that if a landscape was seen by its ancient inhabitants as a sacred topography, it was also a landscape of the mind. That is the meaning of sacred geography. Is it therefore possible, by looking in certain ways at the ceremonial arrangement and juxtapositions of monuments and natural contours to at least *start* to share the worldview of the ancients? I hope to convince the reader that this can be demonstrated at Avebury. Furthermore, as we know virtually nothing about the builders of the Avebury complex, nor what they used it for, I suggest that a 'Dreamtime' perspective on what they have left is the *only* way we are likely to get a hint of what they thought.

While the reader can use this part of the book as a practical guide to the Avebury landscape, one which show aspects of the complex unavailable in any other guide to the place, it is also a *conceptual* guide, so even if the reader never visits Avebury, the findings and processes described in the following pages will, I trust, still be of value and interest, and have application on a general level.

It is so important that in exercising our investigations, theories and speculations, we never let our feet lose contact with the good, ancient Earth that sustains us. The paradox is that by greater intimacy with the physical Earth, we can more readily 'see the Earth as an Angel' - an alchemical shift of perception that transforms Earth into Mind. It is the great lesson the ancient peoples left us in their sacred sites and landscapes.

14. The south-west arc of Avebury henge. (Author)

15. The Cove. (Author)

16. The Barber Stone looms menacingly out of the evening shadows towards the camera. (Author)

17. Silbury Hill from the south-east. Note the 'ledge' near the top of the mound - this has considerable significance as will be described later. (Author)

18. The eastern entrance facade of West Kennet Long Barrow. (Author)

19. The tree-topped mound of East Kennet Long Barrow, silhouetted against a sunset sky. (Author)

20. The Devil's Den. (Author)

21. Silbury Hill (left) viewed in early morning light from the south.
To the right is the ridge of Waden Hill. (Author)

6

THE AVEBURY COMPLEX

The village of Avebury in Wiltshire is situated a little under 80 miles west of London, and approximately 10 miles south of Swindon and the M4 motorway. It can be accessed directly from Swindon (A4361) or from junctions 15 (via Marlborough) or 16 (via Chippenham) on the M4.

The village, of medieval origins, has spread into the great enclosure of Avebury henge and stone circle, which is also bisected by the busy A4361 road. Here are the pubs, restaurants, book and souvenir shops, car parks and museums, and this is the obvious starting point for any visitor to the complex.

Although Avebury henge has managed to retain a powerful aura of dignity despite the encroachments of the village, it must always be borne in mind that it is but one element in a whole surrounding prehistoric landscape which is formed by a remarkable blending of built monuments and natural topography. This prehistoric landscape derives from the Neolithic period and the following Bronze Age. Although the Bronze Age culture has left different kinds of monuments to those of the Neolithic peoples, and presumably had different religious concepts, there are some hints, which will be mentioned later, that the Bronze Age *tumuli* (round barrows) which dot the Avebury district were placed with some consciousness of the existing Neolithic arrangement. Nevertheless, the landscape is fundamentally and primarily of Neolithic origin, and it is that which is of main concern to us here.

The following overview provides an archaeological account of the key Neolithic sites within the ceremonial landscape, as that basis is required for the proper understanding of the 'open secrets' to be described later. Although it is possible here only to give a brief description of these places - the bibliography lists books that can give greater archaeological detail for those who want it - the essentials are covered and the most important recent archaeological findings are included.

A prehistoric focal point

The Avebury region seems to have provided a focus for ceremonial monuments across a substantial region of Wiltshire countryside, but there is what could be described as a 'core' or 'inner' landscape that encompasses Windmill Hill to the north, Overton Hill and the Sanctuary in the east, East and West Kennet long barrows on the south and long barrows around Beckhampton to the west. This almost coincides with the visual circuit of the landscape as viewed from around Avebury, which, however, effectively extends to glimpses of downs a few miles further away to the east and south, and to the bulk of Oldbury Hill and Camp on the western skyline.

We look first of all at the core ceremonial landscape, traversing from north to south across it, selecting the Neolithic sites of major importance plus some of those of special significance to the 'open secrets' to be discussed later. Ordnance Survey grid references are given for each site. (O.S. Landranger sheet 173, 'Swindon and Devizes', 1:50,000 scale; Pathfinder sheets SU 07/17 and SU 06/16, 1:25,000 scale. How to use grid references is given on Landranger maps.)

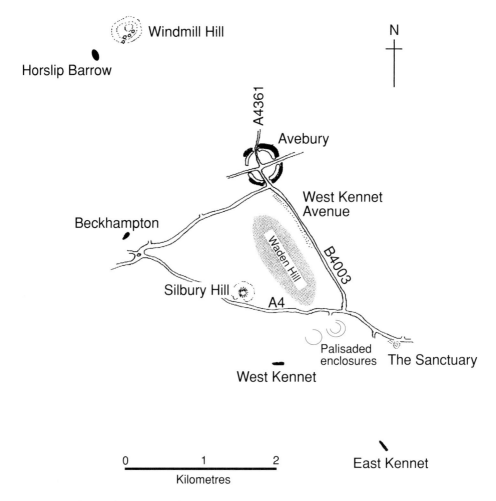

The core landscape of the Avebury complex, with selected features indicated.

Windmill Hill (SU 087714)

This softly-contoured hill a little over a mile north-northwest of Avebury henge can be considered the 'grandmother' of Avebury's sacred landscape, for Neolithic use of it had commenced by or before 3700 BC, long before the henge and some other features of the Avebury complex had been built.

Excavation has revealed that around 3400 BC, after a period of cereal-growing and probable settlement on the hill, three roughly concentric rings of ditches encircling its summit were dug. These had causeways crossing them which varied in width and do not seem to have been formal entrances. Windmill Hill gave its name to this type of Neolithic causewayed 'Camp', and the style of pottery found at the site, and is the largest such example in Britain, covering some 21 acres (9 ha). It is thought that Neolithic causewayed camps were the focus of self-contained geographical areas.

Apart from many hundreds of pottery vessels and fragments found by the excavators at Windmill Hill, large numbers of bones, human and animal, were found scattered amongst domestic debris in the ditches. There were also two complete child burials found in the ditches, their heads laid to the east. One child had been buried close to the bodies of a goat and young pig. A complete dog skeleton was also uncovered elsewhere in the ditches. These interments probably had ritual significance, as had curious objects found in the ditches - small chalk 'cups', with holes or indentations engraved into them; chalk plaques with incised lines; chalk phalli; headless and armless figurines, and stone disks with shaped edges. At least some of the pottery vessels seem to have been votive offerings, and some of the pottery was not local.

The scatter of human bones seem too fragmented to have been deliberate burials, and it is thought that they may have resulted from bodies that had been left out on wooden platforms for natural decay and defleshing by the elements and carrion birds and animals. The foundations of a square enclosure outside the outer ditch may have been a mortuary house. Aubrey Burl has suggested, however, that some of these bones may have been deliberately brought to Windmill Hill for ritual purposes, and we shall return to this idea later.

So many animal bones were found, that it is assumed that there were great feasts on the site, presumably of a ritual, ceremonial nature.

The presence of pottery from outside the region, and stone axes from various parts of Britain, all suggest that Windmill Hill had major importance, and it seems it was a multi-function site, combining a kind of trade-exchange centre with seasonal festivals of a religious nature, linked with ceremonies associated with the dead (and perhaps rebirth).

It is difficult for today's visitor to the site to appreciate all this, or to picture the gleaming chalk-white banks of the ditches which would have made the hill a great landmark, for the Neolithic phase of the hill is now barely apparent. The most dominant visual features are the great Bronze Age round barrows that crown the hill - evidence that Bronze Age peoples still acknowledged sites in the Avebury landscape that had been identified as sacred by the Neolithic societies they supplanted.

Horslip Long Barrow (SU 086705)

A rise in a field two hundred yards to the west of the path that leads up to Windmill Hill (at the point where the metalled surface gives way to dirt track) is all that can now be seen of this site. It is situated on the lower southwesterly slope of Windmill Hill, and is oriented northwest-southeast and was originally about 50 m in length.

It was excavated in 1959. In the ditches along each side of the feature, the contents of which provided the earth for the mound itself, the archaeologists found large blocks of chalk which may once have formed a revetment around the mound. Slabs of sandstone found in the plough soil above the mound, which appears to have been deliberately levelled, were identified as coming from the Mendip hills, far to the west. There were no traces of burials or internal structures such as a stone chamber. Pieces of ox bones and antlers were encountered plus fragmented artefacts from the early Neolithic to the present day. Radiocarbon dating of the antlers indicated a date very early in the fourth millennium BC, so the barrow was probably in existence during the earliest phase of use of Windmill Hill.

Air photographs revealed a possible second long barrow alongside this feature, but explorations in 1959 revealed no ground evidence of it.

Avebury Henge (SU 103700)

A henge is a Neolithic enclosure, circular or tending that way, formed by a surrounding ditch and bank. (See plate 14.) Not all henges contain stone circles by any means, but it happens that the Avebury henge encloses the largest stone circle anywhere. The enclosing ditch was originally up to 33 feet (10m) deep, but is now silted up to over half that depth. This ditch was dug out of the solid chalk with antler picks: it is estimated that 100,000 tons of chalk were removed in this way. The bank is on the outside of the ditch, which tells us that it was never intended for defensive purposes. There were four original entrances to the henge, still used today - the motor road uses the north and south entrance, the village high street the western one, and a lane runs out from the eastern gap.

The henge is 28.5 acres (11.5 ha) in area and has a mean inner diameter of 1140 feet (347 m). The stones of the great circle stand on the inner lip of the ditch, forming an overall plan that is in fact far from circular. Many of these stones are lost or still buried.

Within this great circle are the remnants of other stone settings, the exact nature of which are not all that clear. The usually accepted concept is that there were two inner circles - one in the north half of the great stone ring, the other in the southern sector - which in turn had stone settings in their centres. The north circle had a 'cove', of which two stones still stand today, and the south circle had a massive stone, the Obelisk, now lost, surrounded by a rectilinear arrangement of small stones. Little survives of the north circle's ring of stones; the south circle has fared a little better. (See plate 15.)

Altogether, it is thought that around 4000 tons of stone were moved to make the megalithic parts of the henge, mostly in the form of sarsens dragged on wooden sleds from the surrounding downs. It was a colossal undertaking.

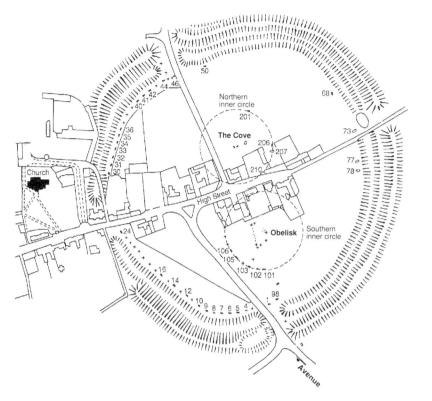

Plan of the henge at Avebury. (Slightly modified after I.F. Smith.)

This idea of the pattern of the megalithic arrangements inside the main Avebury circle are contentious, however, and there are differing versions that can be inferred from the various antiquarian drawings and observations. Avebury was lost to scholarship until 1648, when the antiquarian John Aubrey 'discovered' it. He saw that the great grey stones interspersed amongst the buildings, fences and smallholdings of Avebury village formed one site complex or temple. Staggered by what he had found, Aubrey wrote that Avebury 'does as much exceed in greatness the so renowned Stonehenge, as a Cathedral does a parish Church'. He and William Stukeley, half a century later, were the main antiquarian students of Avebury, though others, such as Walter Charleton, also produced groundplans of the henge. The thing is, these plans vary considerably in certain particulars, not only from one antiquarian to another, but even from one drawing to another by the same man! It seems that not only did they put in what they saw, but they sometimes marked a stone as an observable fact when they had actually only been told by locals that a stone was once known to have stood there, or they idealised certain features to better fit in with their personal theories. Much of their work was really quite accurate, but there were these areas of contention.

Various antiquarian plans show four stones forming the Cove, and previously unknown early plans by Aubrey and Charleton, discovered as recently as 1988 by Professor Peter Ucko, showed portal stones - standing stones like gateposts - at three (Aubrey) or four (Charleton) of the henge entrances. No signs of these stones exist today, nor did they appear in later plans by Aubrey or Stukeley.

Between 1934 and 1939, Alexander Keiller conducted a great deal of work at Avebury, clearing away old buildings, fences and tree stumps, and re-erecting some fallen or buried stones, and marking the stone holes of missing ones with concrete plinths. Many stones are lost or no longer visible because there was a practice in medieval times of toppling and burying them - perhaps because they were thought by the Church to be a bad pagan influence on the villagers - and in the eighteenth century local farmers developed techniques for breaking up the stones to use in walls and buildings. An ironic relic of the medieval desecration was uncovered when Keiller raised a fallen stone in the southwestern quadrant of the great circle - the crushed skeleton of an itinerant barber-surgeon of the fourteenth-century was revealed. It had obviously been one stone burial that had gone wrong. The man's tools and coinage were preserved. His bones were shipped to London, but fate really had it in for the fellow, because they were completely destroyed by bombing in World War Two! The re-erected stone is now nicknamed the Barber Stone. (See plate 16.)

The Avebury henge we see today is thus largely a result of Keiller's reconstruction, though much earlier work had revealed the true depth of the ditch and the ritual burial of a woman of short stature in it.

Ucko and colleagues have conducted resistivity tests of the area within the henge and selected areas outside. This non-intrusive geophysical method produces electronically-generated images of any disturbances beneath the modern ground level, so stone holes can, theoretically, be detected without physical excavation. (In practice, there may have been so much former ground disturbance that it is difficult to interpret any pattern). These tests failed to confirm the presence of portal stones and certain other details claimed by the antiquarians, but concentric rings of post holes within the henge, perhaps left by a timber temple, were indicated by the electronic survey. Forty previously undetected stones and stone holes within the henge were also located.

No significant excavation has yet been conducted in the northeast quadrant of the henge, and clearly, at many levels, a great deal of archaeological work remains to be done at the site. From what is known, archaeologists reckon that the henge is a relatively late addition to the Neolithic landscape around Avebury, and dates to perhaps the middle of the third millennium BC, say between 2600 - 2300 BC. It clearly had been a major ceremonial complex.

Beckhampton Avenue and the Longstones

William Stukeley claimed that in his day the remnants of an avenue of stones led out from the west entrance of the henge. He recorded stones in Avebury's high street and conjectured a link with the two extant megaliths known as the **Longstones**, or 'Adam and Eve', to the west of the henge (at SU 089693). No clear evidence of this avenue is now visible, nor any of the high street stones marked by Stukeley on his plans. Aubrey had not commented on such an avenue. It is thought possible that Stukeley had marked recumbent field sarsens that simply had never been removed, rather than deliberately-placed megaliths. Certainly, only three of his recorded stones were standing. (It is also worth remarking that Stukeley was trying to fit the whole of the Avebury landscape into the scheme of a great terrestrial snake or serpent, and he needed an avenue to the west of the henge to make a convincing serpentine feature stretching through the henge, down West Kennet Avenue [below] and to the Sanctuary [below] on Overton hill which was its 'head'.) Ucko and colleagues carried out extensive resistivity surveys along the supposed course of Beckhampton Avenue, but no regular pattern could be detected beneath the ground. Because of much ground disturbance, however, this survey cannot be definitive and so the question of whether there ever was a Beckhampton Avenue remains open. On balance, Ucko thinks that it is unlikely.

Stukeley considered the Longstones to be a cove on the course of the avenue. Another interpretation has been that the larger stone, 'Adam', was part of a megalithic structure and 'Eve' was a stone in the supposed Beckhampton Avenue leading to it. Adam, which weighs over 30 tons, was re-erected in 1911, though great difficulty was found in doing this, even using powerful railway jacks. Steel ropes tested to 50 tons snapped without the stone budging. The job was eventually accomplished by using timbers and wedges over a period of time - virtually as the original megalith builders had done! Stukeley had recorded the finding of bones near Eve, and the archaeologists in 1911 found a crouched skeleton by the inner face of Adam. It had been buried with a bright red pot, which was dated to around 2300 BC. This might, of course, be later than the erection date of the stones.

Long barrows near Beckhampton

A few hundred yards to the east of the Longstones is the site of a long barrow archaeologically identified as **South Street** (SU 090692). Prehistoric plough marks were found beneath the base of this feature, which is now virtually indiscernible. No burials were recorded at the site, and though some large stones were found near it, there seems to have been no inner chamber - though it had had inner wickerwork divisions. It has been dated to the late fourth millennium BC.

About three hundred yards southwest of the Longstones is the **Longstones Long Barrow** (SU 087691). This is still a substantial mound and can be seen in the field immediately to the north of the traffic island on the A4 next to the Waggon and Horses Inn at Beckhampton. Stukeley observed that its axis points to the Longstones.

The barrow has been badly mutilated over the centuries, but still stands 6 m high, 84 m long and 35 m wide. The only reported artefact to be recovered from it was a Bronze Age urn. This again shows that the Bronze Age peoples of Avebury maintained a respect for the old Neolithic sites.

West Kennet Avenue

Running from (or to) the south entrance of Avebury henge are two lines of stones. This stone avenue averages 50 feet (15m) in width and has been assumed to have originally linked the henge with the Sanctuary (below) on Overton Hill. The avenue was first recorded by John Aubrey, but Stukeley paid much attention to it, making a record of the stones extant at his time which proved valuable to later archaeologists. Keiller reconstructed what he could of the feature.

The course of the avenue southwards has a distinct kink near the henge entrance, then proceeds to the top of a ridge where two of the tallest surviving stones still stand. From there it drops downhill in a curving course, with the east slope of Waden Hill to the west, and the lane (B4003) linking the village of Avebury with the A4 on the east. Between the eleventh and sixth pairs of stones from the end of the presently-visible length of the avenue, a 'Neolithic occupation site' is located. Nothing is to be seen of this now, but archaeologists discovered dense scatters of pottery and flint, as well as two pits containing flint tools, polished axes, animal bones, domestic waste and charcoal. There were also post holes, suggesting that this had been some building that had been carefully incorporated in the avenue's course.

Burials were found at the foot of some of the stones in the avenue, but these were added some time after the stones had been erected.

When Keiller set about reconstructing the northern section of the Avenue, the only length of it currently visible to the visitor, there were only 13 stones visible, and of those only four were standing. Keiller and his team uncovered several buried stones and re-erected them, marking missing stone positions with concrete plinths as they did in the henge. Although the general course of the restored avenue appears sinuous, the archaeologists noted that in fact it was laid out in straight sections articulated together.

The course of the remaining two-thirds of the Avenue, still invisible, is supposed to run generally southeast to the Sanctuary (below), and it is known that some stones of the Avenue are still buried. However, it is possible that it ran more or less south to the recently discovered West Kennet palisaded enclosures (below) and then struck eastwards to the Sanctuary from there.

Falkner's Ring (SU 110693)

From within the Avenue a standing stone in a hedge is visible a few hundred yards to the east. This is the sole survivor of a circle of 12 sarsen stones.

Silbury Hill (SU 100685)

This site, a mile south-west of Avebury henge, was the tallest mound in Neolithic Europe. It stands 130 feet (40 m) high, contains over 12 million cubic feet (339,600 cu m) of chalk and earth and covers over 5 acres (2 ha) at its base. It has a platform-like flat summit, about 100 feet (30 m) across. (See plate 17.)

It was built in three phases. Sometime around 2700 BC, a ring 120 feet (36.5 m) in diameter was closely staked out on a small hillock alongside the Winterbourne stream that runs at the base of the western flank of Waden Hill. Threads of woven grass were placed radiating from the centre of the ring. Gravel from the stream was spread out within the ring and then topped with turfs. Following this, two-foot-thick layers of soil, clay, chalk and gravel were placed over the previous deposits. These layers, each distinct from one another in colour and texture, brought the whole drum-like mound to a height of about 15 feet (4.5 m).

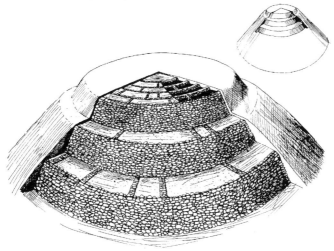

The inner structure of Silbury Hill, showing the stepped-cone arrangement beneath the earthen outer cover and the apparently deliberately-left top ledge.

In the second phase, this was enclosed within an area 350 feet (107 m) across, surrounded by a large ditch (never fully completed). A second mound was constructed over the first using chalk blocks. It was built in sloping steps and held together by an intricate arrangement of interconnecting walls. Work seems to have halted when this chalk mound reached a height of about 55 feet (16.7 m). The third phase involved the filling in of the first ditch and the digging of a much larger one. The previous mounds were engulfed by the giant mound we see today, constructed once more of chalk blocks built in a honeycomb fashion with the spaces filled with chalk rubble. It was a stepped-cone construction, each step being about 15 - 17 feet deep. (The structural engineering was such that a dynamic tension in the chalk walling ensured that the artificial hill's form did not slump, and the still distinct shape of Silbury Hill testifies to the Neolithic engineers' skill.) This chalk structure was then covered by earth and smoothed.

The work-effort on this structure was obviously enormous, and this is only emphasised when one considers that at least part of its construction was very probably being undertaken at the same time that the henge was being built.

To archaeologists up to the late 1960s, Silbury Hill was simply the world's largest Bronze Age burial mound, a giant tumulus, but in excavational investigations undertaken by archaeologist R.J.C. Atkinson between 1968 - 1970, this view was dramatically altered.

Legend spoke of a king in golden armour being buried in Silbury, so for a long time there was speculation that the mound contained a particularly rich burial. Previous excavations had failed to find anything significant within the hill, however, and much was expected from Atkinson's team. The BBC had their new colour TV cameras on hand to catch the moment when the break through into the expected burial chamber occurred. Atkinson tunnelled in from the south side of the mound into its very heart. He caused surprise by confirming Silbury as a Neolithic structure rather than a Bronze Age one. He caused popular disappointment by finding no chamber and no burial within the artificial hill. But the archaeologists found something just as remarkable: the original turfs, cut off from sunlight for nearly 5000 years, still displayed green grass! So well preserved were these turfs that they still contained the flying ants that had been busying themselves amongst the blades of grass when they were dug, and it was possible for experts to determine that they had been turned either late in July or early in August. This information, we shall see, has considerable significance.

Silbury Hill is thus an apparently empty mound, yet built with immense care and skill. It sits in the Avebury landscape like a Christmas pudding, silent and enigmatic. We shall shortly learn that it is the key to the newly-discovered 'open secrets' of the Avebury complex.

West Kennet Palisaded Enclosures (SU 110682)

Although there were slight hints in earlier air photographs and archaeological explorations, it is only in very recent years that the foundations of two great structures have been found on either side of the River Kennet close to West Kennet Farm on the A4, and less than a kilometre northeast of West Kennet Long Barrow (below). This recent work, which is still ongoing at the time of this writing, is revealing two circular ditch enclosures. Palisade Enclosure 1 has been confirmed as having two concentric ditches enclosing an approximately circular area over 200 m across. Test trenches have revealed that these ditches held oak posts forming a dense timber palisade. They rotted *in situ*, and may have been burned. Animal deposits had been placed at the bases of some of the posts. An intriguing feature of this enclosure is that the River Kennet cuts right through its centre - it was built *over* the river.

Only part of one ditch of Palisade Enclosure 2 has so far been located, but this, too, contained timber posts. Within the circuit of the ditch, however, there has been discovered two smaller concentric circular ditches belonging to a former timber building 40 m in diameter.

Air photos and magnetometer surveys show some curious straight lines associated with the second palisaded enclosure: there are the remnants of two radial lines

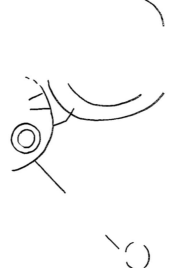

The ditches so far uncovered of the palisaded enclosures. (Redrawn after an interim plan by Alasdair Whittle.)

within the enclosed area, while a longer line runs out from the southeast sector of the ditch to another circular marking over 200 m away. Test excavation of one of these lines suggests that they were some kind of fencing. A linear feature also links Palisade Enclosure 2 with the other enclosure.

A great deal of timber was used in the palisades of these sites. Conservative estimates suggest that the posts may have been almost 30 feet (8 m) high, and densely packed together. Alasdair Whittle, the archaeologist leading the investigations, estimates that perhaps 20,000 linear metres of wood was used.

The features are tentatively dated to the later Neolithic period. It may yet transpire that West Kennet Avenue came south to them, and another section went up to the Sanctuary from there, rather than it being a continuous ritual way between the henge and Sanctuary.

While these enclosures are new discoveries of major importance within the Avebury landscape, there is nothing for the visitor to see.

The Sanctuary (SU 118679)

Archaeologists have found evidence of six concentric rings of post and stone holes on this site atop Overton Hill, hard by the prehistoric Ridgeway track (and the A4 road). These various holes are now indicated by concrete markers as nothing has survived from the site, which was finally destroyed in the eighteenth century. Nearby Bronze Age round barrows are now visually more dominant, and the visitor has to make a conscious effort not to be distracted by them from the importance of the Sanctuary site.

Interpretation of the various holes is difficult. The post holes may have resulted from a sequence of circular timber buildings, with the stone circles enclosing the last of these, or the post holes may record arrangements of ritual poles, like totem poles. The consensus amongst archaeologists today, however, is that the post holes relate to a series of wooden buildings, the first, small, hut being erected around 3000 BC. This may have been the dwelling of a holy person, a shaman perhaps. This was followed over succeeding centuries by three further phases of construction, in which stone settings began to be incorporated. The final phase was probably contemporary with the erection of the West Kennet Avenue, and consisted of a ring of 42 stones 138 feet (40 m) in diameter acting as an outer limit or temenos of the site.

Two rows of stones, presumed to be the West Kennet Avenue, formerly connected with the Sanctuary stone circle on its west side. A short alignment of stones outside the northwest quadrant intriguingly points to Avebury henge, out of sight from this position.

The function of the site is unclear, but many human bones and evidence for feasts have been uncovered there, suggesting that the buildings may have been mortuary houses of some kind, where ritual celebrations took place.

John Aubrey was the first to record the site, and he claimed the local people even then referred to it as 'The Sanctuary'. Stukeley considered it the head of his landscape snake, and recorded, with some outrage, its destruction by locals. It was Stukeley's work which helped in the rediscovery of the site by archaeologists this century.

West Kennet Long Barrow (SU 104677)

It was also Stukeley's work which helped archaeologists in their assessment of this site, which has undergone two excavations, by Thurnham in 1859 and Piggott and Atkinson in 1955-6, and is now in something of a restored condition. Stukeley had mentioned drystone walling at the eastern facade and around the flanks of the mound which has now disappeared.

West Kennet Long Barrow is a huge feature, some 330 feet long and ten feet high. It is oriented east-west. Within the east end of the barrow there is a stone-built passageway with two chambers on either side and a terminal chamber at its western end. This megalithic chambering occupies only a tiny part of the barrow's total volume.

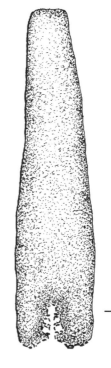

Plan of West Kennet Long Barrow, showing how small a portion of the total volume of the mound is occupied by the megalithic chambers at the east end.

The first stage of the barrow was probably commenced sometime between 3700 and 3500 BC. It was thus contemporary with the activities on Windmill Hill (above) - an association I consider to be important, as will be discussed later. This early construction consisted of a core of sarsen boulders laid directly on the old ground surface, capped with chalk rubble from flanking side-ditches. When fresh, this feature would have created a stark white marker in the landscape, eminently visible from the summit of Windmill Hill.

The eastern chambers may have been part of this original feature, or may have been added later. The passage leads into the barrow from the east-facing, slightly crescent-shaped forecourt. The human bones - from at least 46 individuals - found within the chambers had a semblance of patterning in their placing: the large chamber at the west end had skeletal remnants mainly of males; the northwest and southwest chamber pair had a mix of male and female remains; the southeast chamber had primarily the bones of youngsters while the northeast chamber had mainly old people's bones. There were also what seem to have been carefully-selected animal bones with the human deposits.

The west chamber burials of the men included skulls, but there is a general paucity of skulls and long bones in the other chambers, and these may have been taken away for ritual purposes, or, possibly, because it was important to leave the skulls only of the dead men in the western chamber - a hint here, perhaps, of some bicameral

Nineteenth-century engravings of the passage (left) and western end chamber (right) in West Kennet Long Barrow, by excavator John Thurnham. (The covering of the passage, now reconstructed, is missing in these depictions.)

hallucinatory function, as suggested by Julian Jaynes' theory (Part One). However, the fact that some skeletons are even more incomplete than ritual selection would account for, plus the presence of apparently stray bones, indicates that the early usage of this site may have incorporated a range of mortuary practices. Also, as new bones were added, earlier deposits may have been moved and tidied up within the chambers.

West Kennet Long Barrow was certainly no mere grave - it was a used ritual centre, and whatever the precise usage was, it seems to have fallen into two stages: an early period, and then a secondary phase conducted over a long period to later Neolithic times. (See plate 18.) Eventually, at a period when Silbury and the henge would have been in use, the monument was closed down: the five chambers and the passage were filled completely with coarse rubble and the eastern forecourt and frontage was blocked off by the erection of massive stones. This all seems to have been done either in one operation or over a relatively short period of time.

There have been no radiocarbon dates from West Kennet Long Barrow - its dating has relied on what appear to be primary pottery deposits which match those found on Windmill Hill. I think that has significance over and above its use as a dating aid, as I shall indicate later.

One of the enigmas of this barrow, like certain others elsewhere in Britain, is its considerable length. It is hard to see why such a long earthen mound was required for the relatively small chambered area. There is some evidence, noted by at least two archaeologists, that the original West Kennet barrow may have been shorter than what we see now. It may have had an earthen 'tail' added much later, extending its length westwards. The reasons this might have been done are revealed in the next section of this guide.

East Kennet Long Barrow (SU 116668)

This is an even mightier barrow than West Kennet, being 345 feet in length and 14 feet high, and makes a noticeable tree-capped landmark. (See plate 19.) It is oriented south-east to north-west and has not been excavated, though in all probability it, too, contains stone chambering. It can only be assumed that its date is similar to that of West Kennet.

Archaeologist Caroline Malone has noted than a faint air photograph of 40 years ago shows a crop mark that may show a cursus running past the north-west end of the barrow, but no other evidence for this has so far been found.

The outer landscape

The above descriptions cover the 'core' Neolithic landscape of the Avebury complex, and it is that which primarily concerns us here. We will see that the more distant skylines do, however, become incorporated into sightlines between monuments within the core landscape, so it is worth mentioning in passing a few of the many other Neolithic monuments scattered more distantly around the Avebury region.

Visible to the west is **Oldbury Hill** (SU 050693) a prominent landmark which became an Iron Age enclosure or 'Camp'. On its eastern extent, however, the hill also has two Neolithic long barrows, though these are out of sight of the Avebury complex.

Two of the more dramatic 'distant' monuments are the **Devil's Den** (SU 152697) (see plate 20.) some three miles east of Avebury, which seems to be the remains of a stone-chambered long barrow, and **Adam's Grave** (SU 112633), a dramatic long barrow, probably stone chambered, on Knap Hill, just over four miles south of Avebury. Neither are intervisible with the Avebury complex.

There is a scatter of long barrows on the downs to the south-west and south of Avebury. There were some to the north-east, too, but these have disappeared.

While the obvious importance of Avebury in Neolithic times must have generated a wide sphere of influence encouraging the building of ceremonial monuments within a broadly local region, it is probable that the more far-flung sites had their own local sacral environments, and did not directly relate to the intensive and intimate ceremonial landscape of the core Avebury complex.

It is to that inner ceremonial landscape we now turn fresh eyes in order to perceive its open secrets.

7

THE OPEN SECRETS: A WAY OF SEEING

The landscape of the Avebury complex is thought to look today much as it did in the later Neolithic period. While tree-cover may have been somewhat greater four thousand or so years ago, it is unlikely to have been substantially different to now, as considerable woodland clearance took place in the area during Neolithic times. Cereal crops were grown then as now, though the scale of the farming today is of course much greater. In all essentials, then, the general character of the natural landscape around Avebury seems likely to have been similar to present conditions. It is by no means a perfect survival of a Neolithic landscape, but it is one of the best there is.

Knowing this, I repeatedly visited Avebury over the many years in which my personal involvement with the study of ancient sites and landscapes developed. I felt that if we have a fair survival of a Neolithic landscape around Avebury, the evidence of symbolic landscapes, alignments and cosmological astronomy should be evident.

The problem that eventually presented itself was that after these years of visiting Avebury, I could not find such evidence. I was to learn that was because I still had not *seen* the place. When the process of learning to *see* finally took hold, it led to the perception of some of Avebury's open secrets, which really are visible and undisguised aspects of the place, yet have seemingly been largely unnoticed. In the following pages I describe both the 'open secrets' and, also, how that process unfolded for me, as I suspect that the process is as important as what it happened to reveal.

The lessons begin

On one particular visit to Avebury in the mid-1980s, I became very frustrated at my inability to make sense of the monuments, their relationship to one another and to the natural topography. To be truthful, I did not even pay much attention to the natural aspects of the landscape, tending to see each site with a separate 'frame' around it. I was beginning to fear that perhaps, after all, this extra-archaeological, broader, 'alternative' or 'geomantic' approach to the ancient world was something of a delusion. In a moment of desperation, I literally fell to my knees within the West Kennet Avenue and made a mental plea to the spirit of the place, to the *genius loci*, to help me *see*, if there was, indeed, anything to perceive in the sense I meant. As the moment of *angst* passed, I rose to my feet rather bashfully, pleased to note on glancing around that no one else had seen my bizarre action, and walked on. I did not experience a sudden flood of enlightenment, and no mercurial spectre of some all-wise elemental being materialised before me. As Avebury is the only henge monument with a pub in the middle of it, I did the sensible thing and went and had a pint of ale - perhaps recalling similar activities at the site in Neolithic times. Unknown to my waking self, however, the old Dreamtime consciousness was beginning to weave its spell.

Deciding to make a final, conscious effort to come to terms with the Avebury complex, my instinct was to have a closer look at the Kennet Avenue. I first of all inveigled an old friend, archaeologist John Barnatt, to supervise a theodolite survey of the Avenue stones, with a view to checking future alignment possibilities, for it was amazingly the case that a full modern survey of the entire Avenue did not exist. This was done. But one evening as Barnatt and I were walking thoughtfully down the Avenue, he asked that if there were alignments in British prehistory, as ley hunters contended, where were they here, at relatively well-preserved Avebury? I had to concede that I could see none.

Later, a group of friends and I conducted a thorough photographic survey of West Kennet Avenue. I was working on the possibility that the stone pairs of the avenue might align to more distant features. Some did, but the 'foresights' tended to be the beautiful tree-topped Bronze Age tumuli on the eastern skyline from the avenue. Alas, they had been built *after* the avenue. While it is possible that the Bronze Age mound builders had deliberately arranged this, it was a dubious argument to pursue, and in any case did not address the Neolithic purpose. I felt that I was on the wrong track. But was there a right one?

I cannot remember the exact time that the real breakthrough in perception commenced, but I do know I began to develop a dawning realisation that the key to unlocking the Avebury complex was held by Silbury Hill. Surely *it* was the focus of that Neolithic landscape? It is all too easy to have one's attention hi-jacked by the great henge, with its impressive earthworks, stones and village facilities. So I began to walk around the landscape, simply looking at Silbury Hill from various angles. I had the strangest sensation that it was somehow communicating with me: the Dreamtime consciousness was beginning to stir. I have written elsewhere that I began to feel that Silbury was some kind of teacher, and I was a student. That remains an accurate description of how the process that was beginning to take place felt.

The first lesson I learned was that I should not think of the complex solely in terms of a map, and of alignments as lines on a map. I realised that I often subliminally projected an overhead view of my surroundings, a map-image spread over the back of my mind, as it were. Even when driving I would carry a mental 'window' that had a route plan unfolding as I travelled. Here within the Avebury complex, to see the secret landscape I persisted in believing was there, I would simply have to look, to see as nearly as possible through the eyes of the Neolithic people who inhabited and used that ceremonial landscape. But look at what?

My waking self, a product of modern Western rationalism, struggled against the encroaching Dreamtime awareness. So whenever I visited the complex, I would invariably have to have a theory to test out. I do not feel embarrassed saying this, because everybody acts in a similar fashion. Dowsers seeking their energy patterns with angle rods or pendulums are doing the same thing. Pagans and latter-day Druids with their contemporary ideas of ancient worship do likewise. Artists wanting to produce their unique vision of a site do it with their paints and brushes. Ley hunters with their maps do it. Photographers looking for the crucial, dramatic picture do it (through the viewfinder of a camera), as do researchers using electronic monitoring equipment (with an LED array). Astronomers seeking celestial alignments do it (squinting through a theodolite). Whimsical ancient mystery writers do it, with purple pens. Archaeologists looking for evidence of death rituals or domestic rubbish heaps do it. So do those wanting contact with their concept of Gaia or the Goddess - yes, even the most 'New Age' people do it. We all project our prejudices, fancies and fantasies.

My first bright idea was that by looking at the appropriate times of the year I might find that the sun rises or sets over some significant feature of the landscape as viewed from the top of Silbury, or, conversely, might rise or set behind Silbury if viewed from positions marked by Neolithic sites in the ceremonial landscape. My cherished ideas never quite worked out (though some came close). My fond theories dissolved. Yet at every visit to Avebury, visits which became ever more frequent, and usually with the stoic accompaniment of my wife, something curious and important became noticeable: even though my pet notions would fall by the wayside, I would pick up some other observation, some *unexpected* insight. These were usually quite modest, though they gradually built into a bigger picture. I recall one glorious summer afternoon, for instance, while standing at the northwestern end of East Kennet Long Barrow, facing towards Silbury, I happened to glance to my right and see a few stones of West Kennet Avenue a mile or so away. The curve of the topography allowed just a laserbeam-width sighting of that part of the Avenue. Numerous such experiences taught me to respect the subtlety of the placement of the monuments within the natural topography of the Avebury complex. I came to understand that the monuments and their natural environment were indivisible: they were one.

Increasingly, I learned to visit without bringing along any intellectual agenda. Slowly, I was able to just *pay attention*. I was at last prepared *to be shown* whatever Silbury or the Avebury complex in general wanted to reveal. Zen in the art of archaeology.

Of course, this is a sort of animistic attitude, effectively bestowing some form of sentience on the monuments and landscape. As uncomfortable as this is for a Westerner, I realised that when I visited Avebury I had to do it. It was a *model* of consciousness that I learned to be able to switch on and off. One can only *see* certain things in certain mental frameworks: the eyes do not change, nor what happens in front of them, but what goes on behind them does. (Any given model of consciousness is not necessarily 'better' than another, it is just that one model might be more appropriate for a given problem or situation than another. I have seen people using a dreamy, non-analytical type of mentality when they damned well ought snap out of it and employ some crisp thinking. Equally, I have seen people using a 'hard-headed' approach to things that need more intuitive skill, more feeling than analysis. Our Western culture on the whole errs towards this former condition.)

To use the terminology employed in Part One of this book, what had happened was that I was learning to adopt a Dreamtime view of Avebury's ceremonial landscape. And that view had to be closer to the Neolithic perception than that provided by the standard contemporary mindset. The crucial factor was to make perceptions that had not been predetermined, that I had not planned, thought or known about beforehand; to avoid projecting a personal agenda. To be surprised. To be taught. So, basically, I just hung around the landscape waiting for something to happen. Various things usually did - I got cold, I got wet, my nose ran. Then one day I was standing on top of West Kennet Long Barrow, near the eastern end. Looking north, I pondered the same problem that had perplexed numerous other researchers before me: why was Silbury built where it was? It is in the lowest part of the Kennet valley, hard by the equally-high ridge of Waden Hill. (See plate 21.) Why go to the tremendous effort of building a 130-foot-high mound, and then virtually lose it in the landscape? Many first-time visitors remark on their sense of surprise at suddenly coming across Silbury. It virtually ambushes the unknowing motorist travelling west along the A4 road. Its main purpose could not have been some grandiose statement by a boastful Neolithic tribe. Yet it seems not to have been a giant burial mound either. So what was it about?

The first open secret

As I stood on the barrow, I again had that sense that Silbury was somehow communicating. I got just the faintest hint, a whisper as it were. As I strolled to the west end of the long barrow, it suddenly became obvious - Silbury had truly been communicating an open secret all the time. One just had to stand in the right place and *see*. From that Neolithically-designated spot, the western terminus of the West Kennet Long Barrow, the northern skyline, which is formed by Windmill Hill three miles away, intercepts the profile of Silbury Hill, about half-a-mile away, precisely at the point where a ledge or terrace is visible on its otherwise even, smooth slopes. It is a subtle feature that most people do not notice.

It will be recalled that Silbury was built as a stepped cone out of chalk blocks, and was then covered with earth. The steps were smoothed to the average 30° slope. The top step, however, seems to have been deliberately left as a ledge. R.J.C. Atkinson found that the inner angle of this feature had been re-cut, probably in late Saxon or Norman times, but it has always been an original feature of the hill. It runs all round

Silbury Hill viewed from the west end of West Kennet Long Barrow. The skyline is formed by Windmill Hill, and can be seen to cut the profile of Silbury at the position of the ledge on the mound's slope. This is a three mile long sightline involving three of the Avebury complex's key sites. (Author)

the mound, about 17 feet (5 m) below the flat summit. It is quite distinct on the northern and eastern slopes, but has become eroded and is only just discernable on the south and western sides (which face the prevailing weather). As I gazed at this skyline coincidence, the importance of that subtle feature of Silbury's morphology leapt into significance.

The suspicions of one or two archaeologists that West Kennet Long Barrow may have been extended westwards by the addition of an earthen "tail" also took on new importance. The original long barrow, the eastern half of the structure, was much older than Silbury, but if it is true that it was extended, it is quite possible that it was done at the time Silbury was being built. Whatever the case, the alignment only 'works' from a relatively small area around the western tip of the long barrow. It cannot be obtained from the eastern end. The viewing location was a specified spot in the ceremonial landscape.

So here was a three-mile-long alignment 'on the ground' - the western tip of West Kennet Long Barrow, Silbury Hill and the crest of Windmill Hill. But it was not just a map line, because it had a vertical dimension too - its accuracy was a product of both plan and elevation. It was not a map line - it was a *sight* line.

I immediately decided to complete a circuit of the major monuments surrounding Silbury, which is at the heart of the complex like the hub of a wheel. Would views from them also yield this skyline coincidence? Was there a pattern in this Neolithic landscape after all?

Other sightlines

Going anti-clockwise, the first stop was East Kennet Long Barrow, which virtually points at Silbury like a great earthen finger.

Standing at the north-western end of this rather inaccessible monument, facing Silbury it was suddenly apparent that the skyline intercepted the Silbury profile at virtually the height of the flat summit. As I set up a tripod to photographically record the sightline, my wife and I heard a curious crackling in the trees behind us. Only the two of us were there (we had walked along the spine of the wooded barrow and so we knew no one else was present). The sound was of twigs snapping in rapid succession across the lower slope of the barrow next to where we stood. The sound swung back and forth, first to the left, then crackling rapidly to the right. We felt as if we had walked into a Carlos Casteneda book! East Kennet Long Barrow is a curiously isolated place, and we suddenly felt a long way from human company! The photographs were quickly taken - with hair prickling on the back of my neck - and we beat a hasty retreat.

Next stop was the Sanctuary. A quick look confirmed that here again the skyline (formed by Oldbury Hill) dipped obligingly to intersect the top of Silbury Hill between its summit and ledge. The point where the skyline meets the northern (right-hand as viewed from the Sanctuary) side of the hill is now obscured by trees, but we have Stukeley's drawing (below) which confirms that the then bare horizon does cut behind Silbury just below the summit.

Next on the circuit was the henge itself. This is so big - where to stand? It is an oft-repeated fallacy that Silbury Hill is not visible from within the henge. It is, in fact, visible from several points within the northern part of the enclosure, particularly around the Cove area, and the horizon from here also dips beneath Silbury's summit. But it seemed to me that the key point had surely to be the centre of the southern inner circle where the Obelisk stone had stood. We know from records made by Stukeley that this was the largest stone in the entire henge as far as is known, considerably taller than any of the surviving stones and about eight feet across. It was fallen in Stukeley's day. Its position was marked by Keiller using an extra large concrete plinth (though much narrower than the original stone). Sure enough, viewed from this location, the very top of Silbury Hill can be seen 'wedged' between the sweeping northern slope of Waden Hill in the foreground and the far horizon, which dips remarkably as if going out of its way to meet the summit of Silbury. A more precise sightline could not be wished for. Actually, I could have already been aware of the visibility of Silbury from this spot had I paid more attention to Michael Dames *The Avebury Cycle* (one of two books by Dames we will come back to later), for he has a photograph there of the sightline. He did not, however, perceive the significance of the skyline coincidence.

There are also other special factors about this sightline. If one stands with one's back against the plinth, in what was presumably the centre position of the Obelisk's base, the view south-southwest towards Silbury is blocked by one of the inner south circle stones, known officially as Stone 102. Was the plinth correctly positioned in the

A proof copy of William Stukeley's picture of the Sanctuary. Note Stukeley's accurate rendering of the relationship of the skyline with Silbury Hill.

Stukeley's 1723 sketch of the fallen Obelisk stone.

centre of the Obelisk's socket? I asked archaeologist Stuart Piggott about this, as he had been Keiller's associate during the reconstruction work. It transpired that Piggott had not been present when the plinth was being placed, but it was his opinion that it could be assumed to mark the centre of the stone hole. I have also asked Peter Ucko if the electronic survey he and his colleagues carried out within the henge could help. I was informed that the ground had been so disturbed in the area that nothing could be ascertained for certain with the methods they employed. So the 'blocking' of the sightline by stone 102 is rather odd. Of course, it may have been put up later than the Obelisk, but it may be significant that the top half of the Obelisk would have reared much higher than Stone 102, and would always have been visible from the summit of Silbury. Also, there are pit marks next to the Obelisk position, now marked by concrete disks, that might have resulted from some timber structure. Whatever the situation, there is no doubt that when one stands touching either side of the plinth, let alone the broader Obelisk, the view to Silbury is unimpeded. And yet it can easily be missed, because only the very top, ledge-to-summit segment of Silbury is visible. In the summer, when the cereal crop on Silbury is high, the view is almost obscured by the crop, and sometimes can be completely blocked. It may have been the case that in Neolithic times when the crop obscured the view to Silbury from the Obelisk position, it was a signal, a ceremonial timing, for the harvest to begin. The sightline was thus *harvest-dependent*. This has important implications, as we shall see.

It is known from pollen analysis that cereals were grown on Waden Hill in the later Neolithic period, but I do not know if evidence has been collected on the part of Waden's slope involved with this sightline.

The final stop on the circuit was the Longstones Long Barrow at Beckhampton.

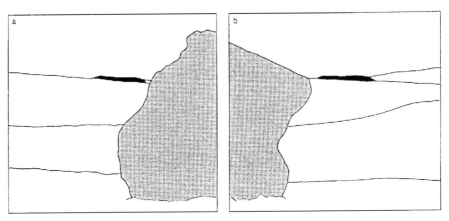

Looking past Stone 102 towards Silbury Hill (in silhouette) from the position of the Obelisk: (a) From the east side of the Obelisk marker plinth; (b) from the west side of the marker plinth. The bulk of Silbury Hill is concealed by the slope of Waden Hill, leaving only the stop segment visible. Note how the far horizon dips to 'meet' the top of Silbury. This sightline is effectively obscured just before harvest, when the cereal crop on Waden is at its tallest.

This required several visits, for the view to Silbury from the crest of the barrow is obscured by foliage, and winter is the only possible time for checking a sightline. Even then, it is difficult. Careful binocular work, however, has confirmed that the skyline cuts the edges of Silbury at about the height of the ledge.

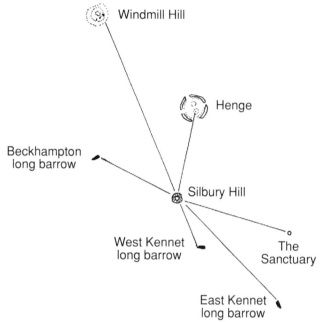

The Silbury skyline sightlines in the core Avebury complex.

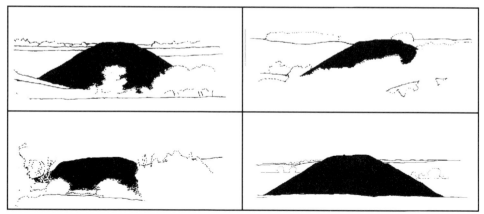

The relationship of Silbury Hill (in silhouette) with the horizon as viewed from (a) East Kennet Long Barrow; (b) the Sanctuary; (c) the Longstones Long Barrow, Beckhampton, and (d) West Kennet Long Barrow, where the skyline is formed by Windmill Hill. It can be seen that the skyline always intersects Silbury's profile between ledge and summit.

Sitting out

So at the end of this 'lesson', I knew there was something important about the top segment of Silbury Hill, between the ledge and the summit. What could it be? I fought against forming theories (perhaps to disguise the fact that I could not think of one anyhow!) and simply visited the great mound, keeping as mentally open as possible.

This meant on a number of occasions just sitting out on top of the platform-like summit at various times of day and year. One time I arrived well before dawn, and the hill was shrouded in a dense mist. But this was hugging the ground, and on the top of Silbury I found it was thin enough to see the sky overhead. I sat on the circular summit as if on a round grass island surrounded by a candy floss sea. As the sky grew lighter, everything was tinted the most delicate pastel colours. Suddenly, as if a voice spoke *inside* my ear, I heard the statement: 'In this Mystery shall we dwell' (I use a capital 'M' because that seems appropriate for the august 'tone' of the 'voice'). Even as I started and looked around I knew that the voice had been a mental one, but of exceptional clarity.

I would now suspect it as being one of Jaynes' bicameral 'voices', probably precipitated by the fact that I was in a strange location in disorientating conditions (I could not see a horizon for example, and my vision was confined to a circuit of grass with no background reference points), it was an odd time of day - when one normally has one's most intense dream periods, and I had been sitting for a prolonged period in a quiescent and perhaps even slightly entranced state. Not to mention the strong numinous power that Silbury Hill itself exerts. Irrespective of the mechanisms involved, however, I accepted the voice on its own merits. It had carried a sense, an 'aura', with it that it had emanated from Silbury itself, which I felt to be feminine. For the Western rationalist, it may seem bizarre to suggest that a mound of chalk and earth could have a gender, but it must be remembered I am speaking about a perception from within a particular model of consciousness. Using that perception, I felt that my 'teacher' had now *actually* spoken to me.

At other occasions on Silbury, I received mental impressions that immediately evaporated, like a dream one forgets as one is awakening. It was as if I was sometimes receiving information just below the threshold of waking consciousness.

The double sunrise

I had my next major lesson shortly after dawn on 9 May, 1987 - the Beltane period of the Celtic calendar. I was on top of Silbury and had watched a beautiful red sun rise majestically over the distant Marlborough Downs to the east. I watched the glorious orb ride higher into the sky, then turned to leave the hill. In that moment I suddenly *saw* what I had only looked at dozens of times previously: the eastern skyline as viewed from Silbury's summit was *double*. What I mean by this is that as one looks eastwards from Silbury's summit, the ridge of Waden Hill is seen several hundred yards/metres away, and beyond that, several kilometres distant, the skyline formed by the Marlborough Downs and intervening ridges.

It is striking, really remarkable, how closely the far horizon echoes the contours of Waden Hill. There is only a small visual separation of the two as viewed from the top of Silbury. I slithered down to the east-facing ledge, thus lowering my viewing position by several yards/metres (as one's eye-level is lowered, the furthest horizon always seems to drop down correspondingly). Viewed from the ledge, the visual separation between the distant skyline and the top of Waden Hill thus becomes even more minimal. At one point, the further horizon dips out of sight altogether behind the nearby bulk of Waden for a short distance. I thought it was likely that I had seen the sun rise out of this section of the horizon, but I could not be absolutely sure. If it had, I assumed that because of this 'double horizon' as viewed from Silbury, the sun would appear to rise once over the far skyline when viewed from Silbury's summit, and to rise a second time over the top of Waden Hill if the viewing position was moved down to the ledge. The dip the horizon makes behind Waden as viewed from the ledge would provide a 'window' to allow this 'double sunrise' to occur.

Looking NNE towards the henge from the summit of Silbury Hill. Note how the distant horizon (in silhouette) follows the line of Waden Hill. (Foreground)

The sun rises from the same part of the horizon at the Beltane May period as at the Lammas (Christian) or Lughnasadh (Celtic) period of early August. I knew I had to arrange to witness the actual moment of sunrise in one or other of those periods, but because of the pressures of my own schedule and the vagaries of the British weather, the opportunity to do that did not occur until 1 August, 1989. As coincidence would have it, I was in the Avebury area at that time because of a BBC radio show I was recording with two archaeologists, in which we and others were discussing various monuments on site. At our hotel in Marlborough on the last evening of July, I told my companions that I was going up to Silbury at dawn the following day. One of them, Christopher Chippindale, joined me. The dawn was crystal clear, and to my relief the double sunrise effect did occur. We saw the first gleam of the rising sun on the far skyline from the top of Silbury, and one or two minutes later, the sun 'rose' again over the top of Waden Hill when our viewing position was moved down to the ledge.

I later asked R.D.Y. Perrett, skilled in archaeoastronomical calculations, to check if the Lammas and Beltane sunrises could have occurred when Silbury was built, because the sun's rising position on any given day changes over long periods of time due to variations in the Earth's rotational axis. His preliminary calculations from limited topographical information indicated that these sunrises would have been

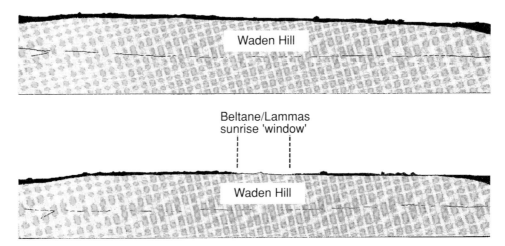

The eastwards view from Silbury across the top of Waden Hill to the distant horizon (in silhouette), (a) from Silbury's summit, and (b) from the ledge, indicating the approximate length of the far skyline that dips behind nearby Waden Hill. This vertical separation of viewing positions provided by Silbury allows sets of 'double sunrises' to occur within the 'window' indicated.

accommodated within the 'window' in 2600 BC, as would midsummer sunrise and the rising midwinter full moon at minor standstill, a key time in the moon's 18.6-year cycle.

These astronomical effects would have been of a ceremonial nature rather than any form of exact astronomical observation, because the window was wide enough to accommodate sunrises over a period of weeks. The fact that it happens in the early August period, though, is of particular interest because we have already noted that was when Silbury Hill first began to be constructed, and the sightline from the Obelisk is obscured by the intervening cereal crop at harvest time, which is Lammas. Was the double sunrise a celebratory effect conjured by the builders of Silbury Hill to commemorate the spring, the midsummer and the harvest? We will return to these speculations.

There is a further implication of this double horizon effect. The coincidence between the Waden Hill and Marlborough Downs skylines would have allowed the effects to have been observable only from the position in which Silbury Hill is placed, and at the height to which the mound is built; that is, its height is about the minimum at which the skyline separation could have been effected. This suggests the possibility that the north-south location of the Hill may have been governed by this. By similar reasoning, its east-west positioning could have been governed to a considerable extent by the Windmill Hill -West Kennet Long Barrow sight-line. Furthermore, if Silbury had been built any significant distance to the west of Waden Hill, Waden's bulk viewed from Silbury would have been visually diminished, and the double sunrise effect would have been impaired.

The double sunrise thus gave a rationale for the top segment of Silbury Hill, and the monument's height and position in the ceremonial landscape. Silbury Hill thus seems to be a physical embodiment of the land and sky within the Neolithic landscape; it is a result of the human observation of the interaction of the heavens with the Earth at that place.

The Silbury Glory

But Silbury had not finished delivering lessons yet. On the dawn after confirming the Lammas double sunrise, my wife and I climbed Silbury to obtain photographs of the sunrise effect. The job done, we turned to leave the summit only to confront a most startling spectacle. This had eluded me the previous morning due to the preoccupation with confirming the double sunrise effect, and, to be sure, to the fact that both Chippindale and I had our attention further caught by spotting a set of the mystery crop circles in a nearby field. But this morning, Charla and I were treated to a view of Silbury's vast shadow thrown onto the golden fields to the west. Out of the top of that shadow emerged a huge golden glow of light. As one moved, the glorious light effect also moved. It later transpired that this was a 'glory' caused by refraction in dewdrops on the crop in the fields. If one stands in a dew-laden field at sunrise, the refractive effect will create a glow around the shadow's head. What happens on Silbury is that a person's shadow is thrown across the top of the hill as far as the shoulders, but the head is engulfed in the monument's own shadow far below. Thus a hugely magnified 'glory' is created. (See plate 22.) This effect is maximised at the Lammas and Beltane period because then the shadow is thrown onto the optimum slope of ground to the west. The glory effect is most pronounced at the Beltane period, because the crops are still green and fresher with dew.

Further work

I have gone on to check the views from as many surviving Neolithic sites as possible around Avebury, but the list is not yet exhausted. I have checked some distant long barrows, such as Adam's Grave, the Oldbury Hill long barrows (SU 046693), and the Beckhampton Road Long Barrow (SU 066677), close to the A361 Devizes road. These sites have no intervisibility with Silbury Hill, or indeed, with the core complex at all. In geomantic or sacred geographical terms they are separate, or, at least, not directly connected.

Within the core region, Silbury seems to have been placed either to have the specific visual relationship to the other sites as described above, or to be totally invisible from them. There are no 'half-and-half' situations, with the one exception of the Horslip Long Barrow on the south-west slopes of Windmill Hill. It was built long before Silbury was constructed, and points towards West Kennet Long Barrow, which may have been contemporary with it. Standing on Horslip, another intriguing sightline is experienced that seems hard to dismiss as coincidence: the *eastern*, original and entrance end of West Kennet Long Barrow is seen to just 'touch' the western slope of Silbury Hill. It is difficult to believe that the builders of Silbury were not as deliberately responsible for this precision as they almost certainly were for the other sightlines described above.

Looking southwards towards West Kennet Long Barrow (in silhouette) from Horslip Long Barrow on the lower slopes of Windmill Hill. It can be seen that the east end of West Kennet just 'touches' the slope of Silbury Hill (stippled). It seems as if the builders of the great mound respected the Horslip-West Kennet sightline with some precision.

It seems to me that careful study of these visual relationships - and there are probably more yet to be *seen* - would tell much about the chronological organisation of the sites within the Avebury complex. Clearly, Silbury was one of the last statements of the Neolithic builders there, and it seems they wedded it to the sacred geography of the existing ceremonial landscape with consummate skill, making adjustments to existing sites where necessary to make their scheme perfect.

Silbury Hill was a symbol that united land, sky, seasons and major ceremonial sites in the Avebury complex. But though a rationale can now be given for the summit-ledge segment that seems to figure so prominently in the sightlines, it does not explain the entirety of the concept held by the late Neolithic users of the place. Further *seeing* of the Avebury landscape will doubtlessly tell more, for as we now know, its secrets are open ones. Sometimes, however, the best way to keep a secret is to keep it open!

8

DREAMSTONES AND OTHER SPECULATIONS

The Avebury complex was clearly a symbolic landscape. It was also doubtlessly a mythologised one, but we do not know what the symbols related to nor what the mythic consciousness was of the Neolithic inhabitants of that landscape. It is ironically true that we know more about the mythologised lands of Australian Aborigines than we do about this small region of ancient English landscape.

The 'open secrets' that we have been describing are visual facts - anyone can now go and check them out for themselves and, who knows, may *see* more of them in the process. I hope so. But when we come to attempt to understand the meaning of the sacred geography around Avebury we can only speculate, and we can only do that by considering every clue, however subtle. In these closing pages I briefly summarise some of my own and other people's speculations. They *are* speculations - not all of them will be correct, and even if one or two do eventually turn out to be going in the right direction, they will only hold fragments of the truth. But, again, it is perhaps the process that is the really important aspect of the exercise.

Dreamstones

Visitors who spend any time at Avebury, particularly if they walk around the henge and West Kennet Avenue at various times of day and at different seasons, catching all casts of light, will be forcibly struck by the shapes and forms of some of the stones. A lion's head here, a horse's head there; a face staring skywards; a weathered and venerable face peering out; a mother and child. We can see a few of them in the photographs in this book. (See plate 23.) There are also gnarled stones that provide convincing representations of various parts of the body, particularly the female genitalia. (In doing this, however, one must beware of certain stones that were found broken by Keiller and his team, and were cemented back together making some bizarre shapes!)

The sceptic will say that these forms are merely the result of weathering and would not have been present when the Neolithic builders erected them. There can be no doubt that four-and-a-half thousand years of standing in all weathers will definitely have affected the appearance of the stones to some extent, but the shapes discernible in some of them are so integral that they would always have been evident. Further-

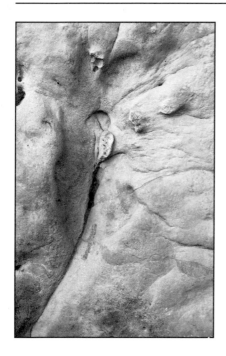

This stone from the southern inner ring of the henge contains forms strikingly evocative of vulvic symbolism. (Author)

more, the weathering theory can be turned back on itself, for it could be that some stones were more distinctly zoomorphic or anthropomorphic in appearance when freshly erected and which weathering has subsequently softened and distorted.

Of course, one has to be careful. I sometimes receive photographs of the Avebury stones which some enthusiast has marked in pen for me so I do not miss seeing the host of faces or figures that person perceives them as containing. While I would by no means automatically dismiss all of these, most clearly result from what could be described as a megalithic version of the Inkblot or Rorshach Test - a mental projection onto accidental, ambiguous shapes. Such shapes are called simulacra - unintentional, natural forms that people simply read other things into, like faces in clouds, castles in embers. But while images in the Avebury stones are simulacra in the sense that they have not been formed by human design, some may have been *recognised* by human intent.

If we can see these shapes now, could not the megalithic builders have seen them too, and perhaps more readily than we can? Perhaps certain stones were selected specifically for their imaging effects; there could be a whole pantheon of Neolithic gods standing grey at Avebury if we would but *see* them. It is appropriate to recall the discussion in Part One about the nature of the consciousness possessed by prehistoric peoples. We noted that in dream consciousness exterior objects can become invested with dream, and therefore mythic, attributes. The Avebury stones may have their subtle, suggestive shapes because they were selected by people observing them in

22. The 'Silbury Glory'. See text. (Author)

a

b

c

23. *Four examples of 'dreamstones' at Avebury. (a) This detail from one of the author's paintings show three zoomorphic or anthropomorphic stones from the Avebury complex. No 'artistic licence' has been taken - these stones do look like this in appropriate lighting conditions. (b) This interesting stone also stands in the Avenue. Is it a Hag stone - the Earth Goddess in one of her three aspects? Alone of the Avenue stones, it stands at right angles to the course of the Avenue. Michael Dames has also claimed that it stands on a midsummer sunrise line linking Falkner's Ring with Silbury Hill. (Author) (c) This henge stone bears a likeness to a lion's head. (Author)*

24. *The slopes of Silbury Hill and the Great Pyramid echo one another's lines of latitude.*
An accidental coincidence? (Author)

25. The course of the River Kennet below the Swallowhead spring.
Although it is supposed to be dry only over the winter months, the river was
already without water when this photograph was taken in September, 1991. (Author)

that kind of way, and, reciprocally, perhaps they were used to engender imagery in the minds of the users of the site. Truly dreamstones.

In addition to suggestive human and animal forms in the old stones of Avebury, it is noteworthy that some of the surviving stones, particularly in the southern inner ring of the henge, have various notch formations on their top edges. There happens to be a midwinter sunset viewable from the Obelisk position in which the sun sinks behind a distinct notch in the top of Stone 105. While this is probably fortuitous, it might be worth checking the astronomical possibilities of Avebury's notched stones.

One of the several cleft-topped or notched stones in Avebury henge. (Author)

West Kennet Avenue

Whether or not the avenue incorporated one or two sites *en route*, we know it ultimately linked the henge and the Sanctuary. But what was it for? For processions? If so, in which direction did the processions proceed? I often ask people this question on site, and it works out that a shade more people think the processions would have been towards the henge. But, in truth, there is no way of us knowing. Perhaps it was two-way! And if there were processions, we cannot be sure that the people necessarily processed between the rows of stones, for Ucko and his colleagues have found from their geomagnetic surveys that the ground along the *outside* edges of the rows is as worn as that inside. We could even speculate that the Avenue was not for the use of people at all - perhaps it was a Spirit Way.

When he was reconstructing the Avenue, Keiller noticed that two basic stone shapes had been used there - tall, pillar-like thin stones, and broader, diamond-shaped ones. They had generally been placed opposite one another. Keiller suggested that perhaps the pillar stones were symbolic of the male, and the diamond stones of the female.

An example of opposed pillar and diamond stones in West Kennet Avenue. (Author)

Finally, I mention in passing that I have noted on the inside face of Stone 26B (on the west side of the avenue about halfway along the reconstructed section) what may possibly be a form of cup-and-ring marking.

Bronze Age continuity?

During the description of the Avebury complex presented earlier, it was occasionally noted that Neolithic sites had been re-used or obviously respected by the later Bronze Age peoples. The main features these later people left on the Avebury landscape were their round barrows or tumuli. That they were consciously adding to the existing Neolithic ritual landscape is suggested by a simple visual test: standing within the henge or West Kennet Avenue, and looking to the southeast and east, round barrows (often capped by trees) are prominent features on the exact visible skyline. The implication is that they were deliberately sited in order to be seen on the horizon from the old Neolithic ceremonial centre.

Possible hints of a more sophisticated form of such Bronze Age placing came to me while I was conducting my 'sitting out' sessions on Silbury Hill. I noticed that the midwinter sun as viewed from there set behind what appeared to be the remains of a round barrow. More dramatically, while scanning the horizon to the southwest of Silbury through binoculars, I saw a small group of round barrows (at, I think, SU 079678) whose arrangement from that angle happens to form a 'gunsight' notch where a distant hill slope intercepts an intervening ridge. (Such points on the skyline are always worth special checking for prehistoric sightlines). I have not yet checked for any astronomical significance, but it is vaguely possible that these 'gunsight mounds' mark sunset around early February (Imbolc in the Celtic calendar). And air photographs show that now ploughed-out round barrows once clustered on the northern slopes of Waden Hill; these would have been powerful skyline features viewed from Silbury's summit.

The 'gunsight' formed by Bronze Age round barrows as viewed from the summit of Silbury.

Stukeley's meridian

It has already been noted that Stukeley came to think that the arrangement of henge and avenues at Avebury marked out a huge landscape snake or serpent. (I have information in my possession that Stukeley may have had an extraordinary experience at Avebury, which he coded with the term *incessus*, which led him to this belief; but until I have completed considerable research, I am not in position to publish further on it or discuss the authenticity of the information.) He also referred to a 'meridian' which was a line he projected through Silbury Hill and the Cove within the henge. It seems he found a now disappeared stone circle or long barrow on a southern extension of this line, several hundred yards to the southwest of West Kennet Long Barrow at approximately SU 098671.

Light phenomena

I have written extensively elsewhere of curious light phenomena that I have dubbed 'earth lights' (see bibliography) and referred to them in Part One. These seem to be produced by processes in the earth, perhaps sometimes in conjunction with atmospheric conditions. They particularly haunt fault zones, areas of mineral deposits, bodies of inland water, especially reservoirs, high-tension cables, and isolated projections in the landscape such as TV transmitter masts, rocky outcrops, lone buildings, and so on. They seem to be of the same family (though probably not precisely the same phenomena) as ball lightning and earthquake lights, and possess various characteristics that suggest electromagnetic properties. They possess some exotic characteristics as well, however, that seem currently beyond the frame of contemporary geophysics.

We saw in Part One that such lights are known to a great many ancient and indigenous peoples around the world, from Australian Aborigines and Malaysian villagers to Amerindians or Chinese Buddhists. Such people variously identify the lights as 'spirits', 'shamans fighting', 'fire creatures', 'devils', 'expressions of the Dharma' - even as the spectral heads of women who have died in childbirth! European folklore also refers to them in various guises - 'fairies', 'dragons', 'corpse candles' and 'treasure lights'. They have been repeatedly witnessed in modern times, photographed on many occasions, and a number of prehistoric sites have had light phenomena reliably reported at them. Despite all this, earth lights are not yet understood and, most strangely, remain culturally unperceived. They slip through the crack formed between, on the one hand, sceptics who do not believe there is anything unknown happening in our skies, and, on the other, 'ufologists' who are convinced we are being visited by aliens in spaceships. These two basic groups detest one another, and a truth is lost somewhere between their positions. Earth lights are apparently not considered suitable subject matter for TV documentaries, which must be the ultimate sign of their cultural invisibility!

The Avebury complex has produced a number of accounts of strange light phenomena in recent years. In 1987, I collected the report of a lifelong inhabitant of Avebury. Several years earlier, she had been walking her dog late in the evening when she saw a light 'like the moon' softly descend within the southwestern arc of the great circle within the henge. It touched the ground and 'went out' without a sound. She checked the place the next morning, and there were no marks or burns on the short grass where the light had extinguished itself. In July 1988, a woman saw what was described as 'a hollow pencil-shaped tube (not a beam) of light' glowing between a cloud and Silbury Hill. This lasted for about two minutes. While I was at Avebury in 1989 conducting research on the 'open secrets' described in this book, there were local reports of orange lightballs seen over a field immediately to the north of Silbury Hill prior to the appearance of crop circle formations there, which I was able to visit and photograph. Also in 1989, a witness situated next to the footpath which leads up to West Kennet Long Barrow from the A4 road, saw at night a ball of light some 30 - 40 feet (10-13 m) across descending over the field just to the south of Silbury Hill and the A4. It was orange in colour and brightest at its edges. It slowly touched down onto the field and gave a 'little bounce' then disappeared. The next day, circular crop marks were discovered in the field.

Obviously, the 'crop circle mystery' is, or has become, associated with light phenomena. Much care has to be taken with this crop circle effect, though, as it is becoming increasingly clear that a great many corn circles have been hoaxed over the last decade or so. This is particularly true of the complex shapes that have been variously described as 'pictograms' and 'insectograms'. Nevertheless, it is possible that a core of markings of the simple circle and ringed-circle variety do relate to an unusual geophysical phenomenon.

One researcher who has studied crop circle formations for many years is Terence Meaden, and he suggests that they are caused by a rare form of descending vortex created by the shape of the topography and certain wind patterns. Such a vortex, like all violent spiral motions in the air, such as tornados, can become ionised and thus electrically charged, causing it to glow. Meaden has noted that the area around Avebury seems a focus for light phenomena and, in recent times, crop circles. He suggests that both these phenomena were observed by the Neolithic peoples and thus the region was considered a holy area, resulting in the concentration of the monuments there. Meaden puts this forward as a strong likelihood, but in fact it is a questionable speculation, especially regarding the Neolithic occurrence of crop circles. It is in any case not original: a more modest suggestion that a particular stone circle (Castlerigg in Cumbria, north-west England) was erected because of strange light phenomena witnessed there was put forward by T. Sington as early as 1919, and I have made similar but broader observations during the 1980s.

As a footnote to this entry on Avebury lights, I should mention the experiences of two artists. Ancient sites artist and researcher, John Palmer, told me about a most curious experience he had many years ago. He had spent a day exploring the monuments of the Avebury complex and when evening fell he decided to retire for the night inside one of the side chambers in West Kennet Long Barrow. He unrolled his sleeping bag, settled down and fell asleep. After what he took to be some hours later, he was awoken by a light moving about out in the central passageway. Thinking that it may be a farmer or some local official with a flashlight checking if anyone was in the monument, Palmer scrambled out of the chamber to quickly assure the person that he was doing no harm. But as he got out into the passageway, he could no longer see the light nor any person. A little confused, he walked to the entrance. The landscape outside was flooded in moonlight, but as he looked around, Palmer realised that it was no longer familiar to him - it was not the same one he had left when he had entered the barrow. Palmer did absolutely the correct thing - instead of starting to wander around in a panic, he simply went back to his sleeping bag and forced himself back to sleep. When he awoke in the morning, everything was as it should be. After the discussion in Part One, we can now recognise that Palmer had seen the Interworld.

In *The Ley Hunter* journal, Monica Sjöö, a well-known painter and writer on Earth Goddess themes, reported a dream she experienced one autumn night in 1984 while sleeping close to Silbury Hill. In the dream she saw a 'pulsating, light-radiating "shape" that appeared organic and moving'. The powerful 'atmosphere' or numinosity of the dream was still with her when she awoke, and its deep impression on her provided the source for a series of artworks. The dream took place well before there was any public discussion of light phenomena around Avebury.

Stone symbolism

The Neolithic inhabitants of Avebury may have found oolitic limestone to be a sacred substance. It has been found in drystone walling at West Kennet Long Barrow and Adam's Grave, and pieces have been recovered from other long barrows in the region and from the Windmill Hill enclosure. Grains of oolite were also used as filler in pottery found at Windmill Hill and West Kennet. What is intriguing is that this stone is not local to the area. Its source has been identified as the Bath-Atworth area many miles to the west. The use of the stone was thus seemingly a deliberate act and must have had some symbolic importance. This is a known phenomenon in other ncient cultures: there are symbolic types of stone in Australian Aboriginal traditions for example, and the ancient Egyptians distinguished between limestone, to them symbolic of the mundane world, and granite, symbolic of spirit.

Shamanic lines?

I have a 'gut feeling' that the relationship between Windmill Hill and West Kennet Long Barrow was pivotal in the early Neolithic Avebury landscape, and was known about and in a curious way strengthened during the later Neolithic phase, which included the building of Silbury Hill. I base this hunch first of all on the intervisibility between the sites. When looking between the two places I experience a sense of inter-communication I cannot express in words. The embellishment of Silbury on that line of intervisibility merely highlights it.

Secondly, there seems to be a relationship between the pottery found in the barrow and that found at Windmill Hill: pottery from primary contexts at both places are comparable.

Third, there are the bones. Aubrey Burl suggests that some of the bones found at Windmill Hill were for magico-religious purposes, and had been taken out of sites like West Kennet. Skulls, particularly, seem to have been favoured for ritual usage. This immediately calls to mind Jaynes' ideas of bicameral auditory hallucinations (Part One), in which he proposes that hallucinated voices of the ancestors were presented to the waking consciousness of the people concerned as if emanating from revered skulls. I feel it is also possible that Windmill Hill and West Kennet may have been conceived as being connected by a 'spirit path', which the strong sense of intervisibility and the exchange of bones symbolised. Out-of-body trance 'journeys' (Part One) by Neolithic shamans between the two sites may have taken place during ritual activities. Silent, line-of-sight 'spirit flight', unmarked but symbolised.

Windmill Hill was the centre of ritual activity for the early Neolithic phase of the landscape, but there is a sense from the findings of archaeologists, and they sense it themselves, that over the millenium or so between the earlier and later Neolithic usage of the ceremonial landscape, beliefs and rituals changed to some degree. If West Kennet Long Barrow really was sealed off when the henge and Silbury were being built, and lengthened so as to more precisely fit a a clearly-marked sightline connection with Windmill Hill, we are presumably seeing a development of earlier rites, even if 'under new management'. The former function of the barrow was closed down, but its link with Windmill Hill was remembered, re-established and strengthened for the new order. In that new order, Silbury was the focal point. It was the focus for the Sanctuary, East Kennet Long Barrow and the (then) new henge, as we have seen. Horslip barrow, belonging irrevocably, it would seem, to the old Windmill Hill-centred order, had its link with West Kennet respected by Silbury Hill but was not incorporated into the new scheme.

If this flight of fancy is in any way true, then it may have been that the platform provided by Silbury Hill's summit was where the Neolithic priests, priestesses or shamans did their 'sitting out', with the spirit flight sightlines linking the ritual centres of the ceremonial landscape. Sitting alone and silent on Silbury's summit today (which, I ought to point out, is now not allowed due to the erosion of the monument caused by tourists) still carries a weird but powerful sense of connection with the immediately surrounding sites.

Silbury Hill

However all that might be, there is no getting away from Silbury as being the key geographical element in the final phases of Avebury's Neolithic ceremonial landscape. 'Silbury is that marvaillous hill...,' wrote Stukeley, 'every way between the downs we are of a sudden saluted by its vast circumference.' What was its symbolism to its builders? How did they mythologise it? Naturally, we can never know for certain, but by taking a slightly meandering course through various speculations, leading us from the legend of golden king to the presence of a goddess, we can make a few educated guesses.

Silbury, folklore tells us, contains a king, Sil or Zel, buried in a golden coffin, or on horseback, with the king in golden armour. Some researchers have taken the view that the name 'Sil' together with the image of a golden personage relates to the sun. One such was Moses B. Cotsworth, who at the turn of the century interpreted Silbury Hill as a great calendrical device. In his *Rational Almanck* of 1900, he wrote:

> The 30° slope of Sylbury not only enabled the Druid astronomers to sight the visible daily elevation between the equinoxes and the winter solstice, but also as the midday sun rose from the spring equinoctial footing to its midsummer soltstice height, it would be graded up the slopes to its turning point on the top north edge and down again to the autumnal equinox as autumn approached. In that way the four seasons of the year could be clearly indicated and comparative records kept by notching the daily and monthly points upon logs laid up the north meridian slope, as was done by the old clog almanacks which were used over Northern Europe ages before printed almanacks were invented.

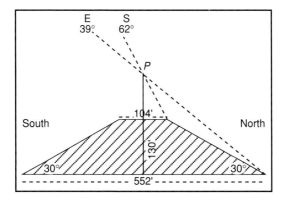

Moses Cotsworth's diagram of his Silbury-as-gnomon idea.

To Cotsworth, therefore, Silbury was a kind of gigantic sundial. Amongst other interesting observations, he noted that the ledge on Silbury coincides with the May shadow or sighting point. This prompts me to think about our 'open secret' of the 'double sunrise' at Beltane, early May: as the May Day sun rises, Waden Hill presumably throws a shadow onto Silbury Hill that cuts the slope at the height of the ledge?

For his Neolithic sundial scheme to have worked, Cotsworth calculated that there would have to have been a pole about 95 feet tall on top of the giant mound. He ascertained that in his day, at least, it was possible to obtain locally a straight fir-tree that would meet those requirements. In addition, there had to be an observation point, a backsight, some distance to the north of Silbury Hill. He did some superficial searching for this, and found a loosened stone at about the correct position. In 1970, Andrew Davidson, making an analysis of Cotsworth's claims (see bibliography), also found three pieces of a single stone at the appropriate spot due north of Silbury. Davidson made some useful additional observations surrounding Cotsworth's findings, including the note that graduated 'shadow-staffs' were used by mendicant friars and other travellers as late as the eighteenth century.

The 30° angle of Silbury's slopes has prompted the observation by other researchers of a coincidence between this giant conical monument and the Great Pyramid in Egypt. (See plate 24.) The angle of slope of the Great Pyramid is between 51° and 52°. Silbury's location is between the 51° and 52° lines of latitude. Conversely, Silbury's 30° angle of slope echoes the Great Pyramid's line of latitude at 30° north. I have noted that the coincidence does not end there, however. In his *Beyond Stonehenge*, Gerald Hawkins of the Smithsonian Institution, the man who conducted much astronomical work 'decoding' Stonehenge, gives an anecdote regarding a task he was set by the Tennessee Valley Authority. They wanted a *working astronomical* reproduction of Stonehenge in a recreation area they were planning. Stonehenge is but 20 miles south of Avebury. 'I was intrigued,' wrote Hawkins. 'Stonehenge, 51°.2' north, required a rectangle of stones [the "Station Stones"] for the sun-moon lines. Farther north or south the figure becomes distorted to a pushed-over parallelogram. Only one other latitude, as far as I could determine, gave a distinctive shape, and that was 30°, the latitude of the chosen TVA site.' It is also the latitude, we have noted, of the Great Pyramid. These latitudinal lines of the Earth's globe clearly have special properties when the astronomically-based symbolic form of a sacred site is considered, it seems. Further, it has been claimed that the gauge of Silbury's shadow, in other words its movement over the ground as the sun journeys overhead, is the same as that of the Great Pyramid.

The implication of all this is, of course, that the builders of Silbury knew the dimensions of the Earth. Then again, it could all be just an accidental coincidence. But what a remarkable one, if so!

There are other associations that can be derived from the name 'Silbury', as Patrick Eyres (bibliography) points out. *Bury* means hill. *Sele*, also Sil, Seille, Seal, *Seale* and

Sael, all pronounced 'Sil', was the ancient Harvest Festival, deriving from Old Norse *Saell*, happy, and Old Teutonic, *Saeli*, blessed. Other associations include *Silie*, the Generous Season, and *Sul*, the British goddess worshipped on hilltops above springs, hence *Sulis* at the Celtic, and originally Neolithic, hot springs at modern Bath, the Roman *Aquae Sulis*. The Romans linked Sulis with their Minerva, hence the Sulis-Minerva composite deity at Bath. What is of note here, of course, is that we now know the sacred oolite limestone (above) came from this very area. Perhaps we get here a hint of the essence behind the stone symbolism around the Avebury complex?

So - harvest and goddess. Does Silbury Hill relate to these themes? We shall see that it does, and the sun remains a factor throughout.

First, the harvest. We have already seen that the construction of the first mound of Silbury Hill commenced at what is now called Lammas (Loaf Mass), the late July - early August harvest period, which, even in the early Church could extend from the Sunday before 1 August to the Sunday after. We have further learned that the double sunrise and 'Silbury Glory' spread over the crops celebrates this period, and was, indeed, confirmed at Lammas in 1989. In addition, it has been noted that the henge (Obelisk) sightline to Silbury's top segment is harvest-dependent - when the crops on the northern slope of Waden Hill are at their highest, Silbury's visibility becomes obscured (and ancient cereals would have been taller than modern strains, which have been developed for mechanical harvesting).

Hilltops and Lammas were associated in Ireland, as elsewhere in Europe. People gathered at Lammas, the Celtic Lughnasadh, we noted in Part One, on the Paps of Anu, for instance. Michael Dames, who has written two intriguing books on Silbury Hill and the Avebury complex (see bibliography), remarks in *The Silbury Treasure* that virtually all the known Irish Lammas assembly sites were on hilltops that were 'isolated hillocks, often conical in shape, and sometimes flat-topped.' Of 195 known Lammas assemblies, only 17 enjoyed Christian sponsorship, such was their known, deep-rooted pagan nature. In Scotland, 'Lammas Towers' were built. 'Each community agreed to build a tower in some conspicuous place, near the centre of their district, which was to serve as the place of their rendezvous on Lammas Day,' James Anderson recorded in 1792. 'This tower was usually built of sods; for the most part, about four feet diameter at the bottom, and tapering to a point at the top which was seldom above 7 or 8 feet from the ground. In building it, a hole was left in the centre for a flag staff...' Each tower was located by a well of pure water. In England, the Lammas assembly died out earlier than in Ireland or Scotland, though Stukeley noted that an Eastertide assembly was maintained in his day at Silbury Hill, and included bull-baiting, races around the base of the mound, bonfires and general festivities.

Dames has argued persuasively that Silbury Hill was a great, monumental Neolithic version of the Lammas Towers. It was a harvest hill. We have seen that all the circumstantial evidence, the only evidence that survives, supports this notion. Further, Dames has maintained, Silbury was an effigy of the Great Goddess, the All Mother, Mother Earth, who was, acknowledged in the traditional corn dollies made from the last sheaves of harvested corn. Although in my opinion Dames went too far in pressing some of his claims, and became besotted by the idea of the goddess to the point of seeing her in just about everything, he has nevertheless made a convincing case in parts.

This case cannot be properly summarised here and I will not attempt to do so, but accounts as recent as 1942 show that people in Ireland still recalled the seating of a girl in a chair on the summit of the hill selected for a Lammas assembly, and that in former times an effigy of a woman was set up there. Dames remarks that such an effigy can only be interpreted as the Earth Goddess, a figure Anne Ross identifies with Bride, Ana or Anu, 'more archaic than the gods'. In the Lammas assemblies at the Paps of Anu, therefore, we see humanity almost literally gathering at the bosom of the All Mother, for the hills, as we have discussed, were mythologised as the breasts of the Great Goddess. This reciprocity of landscape and body imagery was noted by G. Oeri, only in the reversed way: 'The human body participates in its environment. It is a landscape itself, permeable, mutable, with its valleys and ridges, cavities and peaks.' He might have added 'and its navel'.

At Lammas time, Silbury was the womb, the pregnant squatting goddess, giving birth. Dames likened the image produced by the mound and ditch of Silbury as viewed from the air to Neolithic and earlier carved figurines of the squatting goddess. Of course, Neolithic people did not have aircraft, so how could they sensibly have envisaged its form from the air? But the same question could be asked of the effigy mounds and desert drawings in the Americas that were desrcibed in Part One. There, I have suggested, the ability (or hallucinated ability) to fly over the land in out-of-body trance experience explains this aerial perspective. I suggest the very same answer may apply in the case of Silbury Hill, if the speculations on shamanic lines (above) within the complex have any validity.

The Lammas Towers were built near a well of water. So, too, was Silbury. Less than six hundred yards south of the monument is the Swallowhead spring, a source of the River Kennet, which dries up over the winter period, theoretically from Winter's Eve or Samhain (the end of October) to Imbolc or early February. (See plate 25.) The waters retire underground, as it were, but, without fail, the spring floods back into life to prepare the way for the new agricultural cycle. Stukeley recorded that the country people called Swallowhead 'by the old name of Cunnit and it is not a little famous among them'. The cunt, vulva, is the name thus echoed by 'Kennet', probably a word reaching to us from the Neolithic tongue itself. The word 'cunning' also probably derives from the same root, meaning, in its earlier sense, a possessor of knowledge, wise in magical skill.

Finally, let us return to the theme of the sun. Stukeley remarked that herbs growing around the Swallowhead spring were locally held in high regard for their healing virtue. In particular, Stukeley noted the presence there of 'apium' (*Apium Nodiflorum*). This herb was supposedly especially beneficial in treating eye infections. Folklorist John Goulstone (see bibliography) notes that Swallowhead was thus just one of the many holy springs around the countryside which reputedly cured eye afflictions, and suggests that this recurring feature of folk superstition was 'a faint echo of the cult of the Neolithic Great Goddess symbolised by the eye motif'. This prehistoric motif was sometimes a distinct eye symbol on various goddess depictions, and sometimes the image of a circle or concentric rings with radiating lines, which can be read as a sun symbol as much as an eye. Dames claimed to have found a sarsen stone with a hollow, an 'eye', in it on the bed of the Kennet where a sightline from the Sanctuary to the forecourt of West Kennet Long Barrow, the site of another 'eye stone' according to Dames, crosses. He also felt that one aspect of Silbury's symbology was as a great eye of the goddess in the landscape.

That the eye was also symbolic of the sun is shown in simple evidence such as that provided by the modest 'daisy', which means 'Day's Eye', in recognition of the little flower's symbolic likeness to a sun disk with surrounding rays.

Two Neolithic examples of goddess eyes from Spain. The provenance of the top one is unrecorded; the lower is from a pot found at the site of Los Millares. Note also figure C on page 15.

The goddess and the sun were, therefore, symbolically linked, a connection reinforced at Swallowhead, for the waters of the River Kennet flow towards the northeast, hence symbolically *towards the sunrise*. We can be sure this was regarded with special significance, for, as Goulstone notes, there are many known cases where water associated with the sun took on particular sanctity. An Anglo-Saxon charm, for instance, required 27 cups of water to be drawn by a maiden over a nine-day period from a stream running eastwards, and in Cerne Abbas, Dorset, there was a tradition that survived up until the last century of dipping a newborn baby into a spring as the first rays of sunlight struck the water. At Swallowhead, water, the lifeblood of the planet, flowed from the vulva of the Earth Mother towards her symbol, the sun. That lifeblood was withdrawn during the darkest months of the year, back into the secret, nurturing recesses of the Mother; a hydrological expression of the Persephone myth. Stukeley observed that vessels of Swallowhead water were taken to Silbury at the time of the Eastertide assembly.

It has been the habit of too many scholars, mainstream and 'alternative' alike, to associate the sun with the masculine, and the moon with the feminine (an error I have myself been guilty of at times.) Certain researchers, such as Nigel Pennick, have always warned against this gross generalisation, and Janet McCrickard's book, *The Eclipse of the Sun* (see bibliography) has now provided accessible chapter and verse to set the record straight on this matter, showing how widespread and ancient the association between the sun and the goddess actually was. From Australia, where, McCrickard tells us, the sun is feminine to virtually every Aboriginal tribe, to Eurasia. In the Baltic countries, the moon was always male, *Meness,* and the sun always female, *Saule* - perhaps the echo we get in *Sil* bury. In Norse and Teutonic mythology, the sun was likewise always feminine - *Sunna.* The Nordic invaders of Britain brought Sunna with them, and gave us our modern English 'sun'.

The sun was thus feminine in ancient Britain. 'But during the sixteenth and seventeenth centuries,' McCrickard informs, 'changes in the English language combined with Christian influence and revived interest in classical mythology to change the sex of the Sun.' In modern German, however, the Sun still retains her true gender - *die* Sonne, and the moon remains masculine - *der* Mond. The oldest Europeans, the Basques, still retain their feminine sun.

Some of the old names for the feminine sun, such as the Norse Sunna or the Welsh Olwen (Haul-en), also meant wheel - again a link with the 'eye' sun symbol, the circle with radiating lines.

So the sun figures everywhere in the mythologised image of Silbury - probably in the name itself, in one of its possible functions, and in its water and goddess connections. A twelfth-century English herbal treatise (British Library, Harl MS 1585 12a f.) actually identifies the Earth Goddess with the sun:

> Divine Goddess Earth, Mother of Nature, who generates all things, and brings forth ever anew the sun which you alone show to the folk upon the earth: Thou guardian of heaven and sea, and arbiter of all the gods... you are she who restores day and puts the darkness to flight... you send forth the glad daylight...

All the connections are directly experienced on Silbury Hill at a Beltane or Lammas/ Lughnasadh dawn; mythology becomes event with the celebratory, sacramental double sunrise flooding the eastern sky, and with Silbury itself - 'herself' in Dreamtime consciousness terms - casting its own mysterious golden light, its 'glory', like a blessing across the land, over the crops.

'In this Mystery shall we dwell.'

REFERENCES

PART ONE: THE DREAMTIME EARTH

Chapter 1. The Mythologised Land and its Sacred Geography
1. Lucien Lévy-Bruhl, *Primitive Mythology* (1935), University of Queensland Press edition, 1983.
2. James Cowan, *The Mysteries of the Dream-Time*, Prism Press, 1989.
3. Ibid.
4. Charles Mountford, *Winbaraku and the Myth of Jarapiri*, Rigby, 1968.
5. Cowan, 1989, op cit.
6. T.G.H. Strehlow, *Aranda Traditions*, Melbourne University Press, 1947. (Cited in Joseph Campbell, *The Way of the Animal Powers*, Vol.1, Part 2, Harper & Row, 1988.)
7. Mountford, op cit.
8. Ibid.
9. Lévy-Bruhl, op cit.
10. Ibid.
11. Vincent Scully, *The Earth, The Temple, and the Gods*, Yale University Press, 1962.
12. Ibid.
13. Ibid.
14. Ibid.
15. Ibid.
16. Erich Neumann, *The Great Mother* (1955), Bollingen Series edition, 1963.
17. O.G.S. Crawford, *The Eye Goddess*, Phoenix, 1957.
18. Cosimo Favaloro, 'Cretan Geomancy', in *The Ley Hunter* 105, 1988.
19. Mircea Eliade, *Shamanism - Archaic Techniques of Ecstasy* (1951), Bollingen Series edition, 1964.
20. Favaloro, op cit.
21. William R. Biers, *The Archaeology of Greece* (1980), Cornell University Press edition, 1987.
22. Anne Ross, 'Landscape and Ritual in the Pagan Celtic World', paper given at 'The Ley Hunter's Moot' 91, Wales, September, 1991. See also 'Moot 91 Report', *The Ley Hunter* 115, 1991.

23. Proinsias MacCana, 'Celtic Religion and Mythology', in *The Celts*, V. Kruta, O.H. Frey, B. Raferty and M. Szabo (eds.), Thames & Hudson, 1991.

24. Ross, op cit.

25. Anne Ross, *The Pagan Celts* (1970), Batsford edition, 1986.

26. Hugh Benson, 'Church Orientations and Patronal Festivals', in *Antiquaries Journal*, Vol. 36. (Date not known)

27. Marco Bischof, 'Alpine Lightshows', in *The Ley Hunter* 113, 1990.

28. John Michell, *New Light on the Ancient Mystery of Glastonbury*, Gothic Image, 1990.

29. Ibid.

30. Joseph Campbell, *The Way of the Animal Powers*, Vol.1, Part 2, Harper & Row, 1988.

31. Gary Urton, *At the Crossroads of the Earth and the Sky*, University of Texas Press, 1981.

32. Anne Ross 1991, op cit.

33. Scully, op cit.

Chapter 2. Dreaming the Earth

1. Eliade, 1951/1964, op cit.

2. J.F. Thackeray, 'On Concepts Expressed in Southern African Rock Art', in *Antiquity*, Vol. 64, No. 242, March, 1990.

3. Sheila Savill, *Pears Encyclopaedia of Myths and Legends - Northern Europe, Southern and Central Africa*, BCA edition, 1977.

4. Alan Watts, Myths and Ritual in Christianity (1954), Thames & Hudson edition, 1983.

5. Ibid.

6. G.S. Kirk, *The Nature of Greek Myths*, Pelican, 1974.

7. V.W. Turner, in *International Encyclopaedia of the Social Sciences*, 10, 1968. (Cited in Kirk, ibid.)

8. Lévy-Bruhl, op cit.

9. Richard Strassman, 'The Pineal Gland: Current Evidence for its Role in Consciousness', in *Psychedelic Monographs and Essays*, Vol. 5, PM&E Publishing Group, 1990.

10. Serena Roney-Dougal, *Where Science and Magic Meet*, Element, 1991.

11. Lévy-Bruhl, op cit.

12. A.P. Elkin, *The Secret Life of the Australian Aborigines*, cited in Lévy-Bruhl, ibid.

13. Cowan, 1989, op cit.

14. Jung & Kerényi, op cit.

15. Cowan, 1989, op cit.

16. Ibid.

17. Paul Devereux, *Earth Memory*, Quantum (Foulsham), 1991.

18. Richard Katz, *Boiling Energy*, Harvard University Press, 1982.

19. A.P. Elkin, op cit.

20. Paul Wirz, *Die Marind-anim von Holländisch-Sud-Neu-Guinea*, cited in Lévy-Bruhl, op cit.

21. Philip O'Connor, *Britain in the Sixties: Vagrancy*, Penguin, 1963.
22. Julian Jaynes, *The Origin of Consciousness in the Breakdown of the Bicameral Mind*, Houghton Mifflin, 1976.
23. Ibid.
24. Quoted in ibid.
25. In *Earthmind*, by Paul Devereux and John Steele, David Kubrin; Harper & Row (USA), 1989. (Also Inner Traditions, USA, and Kyoikusha, Japan.)
26. Jaynes, op cit.
27. Quoted in ibid.
28. Gerald Hawkins, *Beyond Stonehenge*, Hutchinson, 1973.
29. Jaynes, op cit.
30. In *The Atlas of Archaeology*, K. Branigan (ed.), Macdonald, 1982.
31. Jaynes, op cit.
32. The Dragon Project Trust, Box 92, Penzance, Cornwall TR18 2XL, UK.
33. Paul Devereux, *Earth Lights Revelation*, Blandford Press, 1989.
34. Paul Devereux, *Places of Power*, Blandford Press, 1990.
35. Jim Swan, 'Sacred Places in Nature: One Tool in the Shaman's Medicine Bag', in *Shaman's Path*, Gary Doore (ed.), Shambhala, 1988.
36. Alberto Villoldo & Stanley Krippner, *Healing States*, Simon & Schuster, 1987.
37. Michael Harner, *The Way of the Shaman* (1980), Bantam edition, 1982.
38. Helmut Tributsch, *When the Snakes Awake*, MIT Press, 1982.
39. Roney-Dougal, op cit.
40. Strassman, op cit.
41. Alan Ereira, *The Heart of the World*, Jonathan Cape, 1990. See also *From the Heart of the World*, originally shown on BBC TV, 4 December, 1990.

Chapter 3. The Shamanic Landscape

1. Joan Halifax, *Shaman - The Wounded Healer*, Thames & Hudson, 1982.
2. Holger Kalweit, *Dreamtime and Inner Space* (1984), Shambhala edition, 1988.
3. Marlene Dobkin de Rios, *Hallucinogens: Cross-Cultural Perspectives* (1984), Prism Press edition, 1990.
4. Eliade, 1951/1964, op cit.
5. Ibid.
6. Ibid.
7. Paul Devereux, Shamanism and the Mystery Lines, Quantum (Foulsham), 1992.
8. R.K. Siegel & L.J. West (eds.), Hallucinations: Behaviour, Experience and Theory, John Wiley, 1975.
9. Geraldo Reichel-Dolmatoff, *Beyond the Milky Way: Hallucinatory Imagery of the Tukano Indians*, UCLA Latin American Center, 1978. See also 'Drug-induced optical sensations and their relationship to applied art among some Colombian Indians', in *Art in Society*, M. Greenhalgh & V. Megaw (eds.), Duckworth, 1978.

10. R.K. Siegel & M.J. Jarvik, 'Drug-induced Hallucinations in Animals and Man', in *Hallucinations*, 1975, op cit.
11. Quoted by Claude Naranjo in 'Psychological Aspects of the Yagé Experience in an Experimental Setting', in Hallucinogens and Shamanism, Michael Harner (ed.), Oxford University Press, 1973.
12. Richard Bradley, *The Dorset Cursus: The Archaeology of the Enigmatic*, Wessex Lecture III, Council for British Archaeology Group 12, 1986.
13. Paul Devereux in *Lines on the Landscape*, Nigel Pennick & Paul Devereux, Robert Hale, 1989.
14. S. Barrett and E.W. Gifford, 'Miwok Material Culture', in *Bulletin of the Public Museum of the City of Milwaukee* 4, 1933. (Cited in *Chaco Roads Project Phase I*, Chris Kincaid (ed.), U.S. Dept. of the Interior, Bureau of Land Management, 1983.
15. Paul Devereux, *The World's Secret Heritage*, Blandford Press, 1992.
16. The Navajo elder was Hosteen Beyal, who informed researcher Neil Judd in 1927. See Kendrick Frazier's *People of Chaco*, Norton, 1986.
17. Anthony F. Aveni (ed.), *The Lines of Nazca*, The American Philosophical Society, 1990.
18. Evan Hadingham, *Lines to the Mountain Gods*, Random House, 1987.
19. T. Zuidema, 1982, cited by H. Silverman in 'The Early Pilgrimage Center of Cahuachi and the Nazca Lines: Anthropological and Archaeological Perspectives', in *The Lines of Nazca*, 1990, op cit.
20. See David S. Whitley's contribution to J.D. Lewis-Williams' & T.A. Dowson's 'The Signs of All Times', in *Current Anthropology*, Vol. 29, No. 2, April, 1988.
21. Halifax, 1982, op cit.
22. Joseph Campbell, 1988, op cit.
23. Anne Biesele, cited by Campbell, ibid. See also Katz, 1982, op cit.
24. R. Gordon Wasson, 'The Hallucinogenic Fungi of Mexico' (1960), in *The Psychedelic Reader*, University Books, 1965.
25. Rogan Taylor, 'Who is Santa Claus?', in *The Sunday Times Magazine*, 21 December, 1980. Cited by Susan Blackmore in *Beyond the Body* (1982), Granada edition, 1983.
26. Weston La Barre, 'Anthropological Perspectives on Hallucinations and Hallucinogens', in *Hallucinations*, 1975, op cit.
27. Ibid.
28. Cited in Eliade, 1951/1964, op cit.
29. Ross, 1970/1986, op cit.
30. Gerald Weiss, 'Shamanism and Priesthood in Light of the Campa Ayahuasca Ceremony', in *Hallucinogens and Shamanism*, 1973, op cit.
31. Eliade, 1951/1964, op cit.
32. Ibid.
33. Ibid.
34. Ross, 1970/1986, op cit.
35. Eliade, 1951/1964, op cit.
36. Eric Partridge, *Origins* (1958), RKP edition, 1961.

37. A. Sihler and H. Scharf, cited in J.P. Mallory, *In Search of the Indo-Europeans*, Thames & Hudson, 1989.
38. Eliade, 1951/1964, op cit.
39. John Palmer, 'The Deathroads of Holland', in *The Ley Hunter* 109, 1989; 'Deathroad', in *The Ley Hunter* 113, 1990; 'Deathroads III', in *The Ley Hunter* 114, 1991.
40. Ulrich Magin, 'Geisterwegen - The Secret of Watkins' Leys?', in *The Ley Hunter* 116, 1992.
41. *Handwortbuch des deutschen Aberglaubens*, de Gruyters, Berlin, 1935. (The sources for the quoted entry, however, are dated to 1901 and 1908.)
42. Dermot MacManus, *The Middle Kingdom* (1959), Colin Smythe edition, 1973.
43. Cowan, 1989, op cit.
44. Alastair I. McIntosh, 'Beliefs about Out-of-the-Body Experiences Among the Elema, Gulf Kamea and Rigo Peoples of Papua New Guinea', in the *Journal for the Society of Psychical Research*, Vol. 50, No. 785, September, 1980.
45. Eliade, 1951/1964, op cit.
46. Nigel Pennick, *Practical Magic in the Northern Tradition*, Aquarian Press, 1989.
47. See p. 231 of *Lines on the Landscape*, 1989, op cit.
48. See Alan Ereira, *The Heart of the World*, 1990, op cit, and *From the Heart of the World* (TV documentary), 1990, op cit. There is a trust fund for the protection and survival of the Kogi: The Tairona Heritage Trust, 90 Summerlee Avenue, London N2 9QH.
49. Pennick, 1989, op cit.
50. See *Lines on the Landscape*, op cit, for example, or various items by Tom Graves, Nigel Pennick and Paul Devereux in *The Ley Hunter* 113, 1990.

Chapter 4. Interworld

1. Richard Heinberg, *Memories and Visions of Paradise*, Jeremy Tarcher, 1989.
2. Eliade, 1951/1964, op cit.
3. Ibid.
4. Campbell, 1988, op cit.
5. Cowan, 1989, op cit.
6. Henry Corbin, *Spiritual Body and Celestial Earth* (1976), I.B. Taurus edition, 1990.
7. Ibid.
8. Ibid.
9. Ibid.
10. Ibid.
11. Muhsin Fayz Kashani, *Kalimat maknuna*, ch. XXX, lith., Teheran, p. 69, cited in ibid.
12. Corbin, 1976/1990, op cit.
13. Ibid.
14. William Wordsworth, *Lines Composed a Few Miles Above Tintern Abbey, On Revisiting the Banks of the Wye During a Tour. July 13, 1798*.
15. William Wordsworth, *Ode - Intimations of Immortality From Recollections of Early Childhood, 1803-6*.

16. George William Russell (AE), *The Candle of Vision* (1918), in Raghavan & Nandini Iyer's compilation of Russell's mystical works, *The Descent of the Gods*, Colin Smythe, 1988.
17. Ibid.
18. Ibid.
19. Ibid.
20. Ibid.
21. Ibid.
22. In an interview with W.Y. Evans Wentz included anonymously in *The Fairy-Faith in Celtic Countries* (1911), Colin Smythe edition, 1977.
23. Aldous Huxley, 'The Doors of Perception' (1954), in *The Doors of Perception and Heaven and Hell*, Penguin edition, 1959.
24. Ibid.
25. Aldous Huxley, 'Heaven and Hell' (1956), in *The Doors of Perception and Heaven and Hell*, op cit.
26. Ibid.
27. Ibid.
28. Corbin, 1976/1990, op cit.
29. Cited by Campbell, 1988, op cit.
30. Campbell, 1988, op cit.
31. Corbin, 1976/1990, op cit.
32. Frederick Van Eeden, 'A Study of Dreams' (1913), in *Altered States of Consciousness*, Charles T. Tart (ed.), John Wiley, 1969.
33. Keith Hearne, *The Dream Machine*, Aquarian Press, 1990.
34. Celia Green put forward this idea in several works. A good account is given in Celia Green & Charles McCreery, *Apparitions* (1968), Institute of Psychophysical Research edition, 1989.
35. Stephen LaBerge, *Lucid Dreams*, Ballantine, 1985.
36. Susan Blackmore, *Beyond the Body* (1982), Granada edition, 1983.
37. Weston La Barre, 1975, op cit.
38. Susan Blackmore, personal communication, cited by Devereux in *Shamanism and the Mystery Lines*, op cit.
39. Corbin, 1976/1990, op cit.
40. Halifax, 1982, op cit.
41. Russell, *The Candle of Vision*, in Iyer, 1988, op cit.

PART TWO: A GUIDE TO THE OPEN SECRETS OF AVEBURY

Bibliography

Atkinson, R.J.C., *Silbury Hill*, BBC Publications, 1969.

Atkinson, R.J.C., 'Silbury Hill, 1969-70', in *Antiquity*, Vol. 44, 1970.

Barker, C.T., 'The Long Mounds of the Avebury Region', in *Wiltshire Archaeological and Natural History Magazine*, Vol. 70, 1985.

Bradley, Richard, 'The Bank Barrows and Related Monuments of Dorset in the Light of Recent Field Work', in *Dorset Natural History and Archaeological Society Proceedings*, 105, 1983.

Burl, Aubrey, *Prehistoric Avenue*, Yale University Press, 1979.

Dames, Michael, *The Silbury Treasure*, Thames & Hudson, 1976.

Dames, Michael, *The Avebury Cycle*, Thames & Hudson, 1977.

Davidson, Andrew, 'Silbury Hill', in *Glastonbury and Britain: A Study in Patterns* (1969, 1971), R.I.L.K.O. edition, 1990.

Devereux, Paul, *Earth Lights Revelation*, Blandford Press, 1989.

Devereux, Paul, 'Silbury's Secrets', in *The Ley Hunter*, 110, 1989.

Devereux, Paul, *Places of Power*, Blandford Press, 1990.

Devereux, Paul, *Earth Memory*, Quantum (Foulsham), 1991.

Devereux, Paul, 'Three-dimensional aspects of apparent relationships between selected natural and artificial features within the topography of the Avebury Complex', in *Antiquity*, Vol. 65, No. 249, December, 1991.

Eyres, Patrick, *Sumer Is Icumen In*, New Arcadians, 1982.

Goodchild, Eileen, 'Gender, Sun and Myth', in R.I.L.K.O. *Journal* 39, 1992.

Gordon, E.O., *Prehistoric London* (1914), Covenant edition, 1932.

Goulstone, John, *The Summer Solstice Games*, Private (ISBN: 0 9510556 07), 1985.

Grinsell, Leslie V., *Folklore of Prehistoric Sites in Britain*, David & Charles, 1976.

Hawkins, Gerald, *Beyond Stonehenge*, Hutchinson, 1973.

Keys, David, 'Huge "temple" found under Avebury circle', in *The Independent*, 22 November 1990.

Malone, Caroline, *The English Heritage Book of Avebury*, Batsford, 1989.

McCrickard, Janet, *Eclipse of the Sun*, Gothic Image, 1990.

Meaden, Terence, (ed.), *Circles from the Sky*, Souvenir Press, 1991.

Pennick, Nigel, *Practical Magic in the Northern Tradition*, Aquarian Press, 1989.

Piggott, S., *The West Kennet Long Barrow: Excavations 1955-6*, HMSO, 1962.

Saunders, Nick, 'Avebury Revisited', in *New Scientist*, 20 April, 1991.

Sjöö, Monica, 'Monica Sjöö's Silbury Dream', in *The Ley Hunter*, 112, 1990.

Thomas, Julian, & Whittle, Alasdair, 'Anatomy of a Tomb - West Kennet Revisited', in *Oxford Journal of Archaeology*, 5, 1986.

Thurnham, John, 'On Examination of a Chambered Long-Barrow at West Kennet, Wiltshire' (1860) in *Archaeologia* 38, Vol. XXXVIII.

Ucko, P.J., Hunter, M., Clark, A.J., & David, A., *Avebury Reconsidered: From the 1660s to the 1990s*, Unwin Hyman, 1990.

Vatcher, Faith de M., & Vatcher, Lance, *The Avebury Monuments*, HMSO, 1976.

Whittle, Alasdair, 'A late Neolithic complex at West Kennet, Wiltshire, England', in *Antiquity*, Vol. 65, No. 247, June 1991.

INDEX

dindshenchas 24
Dikte, Mnt. 17
divination 47
Diw 112
djang 10
Dobkin de Rios, Marlene 73, 89
Dodona 47, 103
Doodwegen (deathroads) 80, 81
Dorset Cursus 67
Dowson, T.A. 62
Downing Street 114
Dowth 102
Dragon Project Trust 49, 51
Dream Journey routes 8, 9, 10, 11-12, 37,
      48, 86
Druids 47, 76, 77
Dionysius 18

Earth Goddess (*see* Earth Mother)
earth lights (*see* light phenomena)
Earth Lights Revelation 49
Earth Mother 13-20 *passim*, 25, 30, 31, 32,
      46, 58, 78, 139, 157, 158, 161-164
Eclipse of the Sun, The 164
ecstasy (*see* altered states of
      consciousness)
Eden 91, 92, 101, 103
Eeden, Frederick Van 106
effigy mounds 60, 64, 73, 89, 162
Egypt 15, 44-45, 51, 112, 160
Elburz Mnts. 97
Eleusis 18-20
Eliade, Mircea 51, 55, 56, 57, 60, 77, 78, 80,
      83, 93, 94
Elkin, A.P. 37, 38
Elm 27, 28
Elysian Fields 91

Emain Macha (Navan Fort) 26, 27, 58
energy
      effects at sacred sites 49-53
      dowsing 89-90, 139
      lines 89-90
entoptic images 61-63, 73, 104, 109
Epidaurus 21, 22
Epimenides 17, 51
Epona 26
Eran-Vej 95, 96, 97, 98, 100, 106, 112
Erechtheus 21
Erechtheion, the 21
ergot 19, 48
Ereira, Alan 87, 88
Eskimos 75
Etruscans 29, 44, 50, 58
Evans, Sir Arthur 32
eye
      magic flight symbol 75
      goddess symbol 163
      sun symbol 163, 164
Eyres, Patrick 160

fairy paths 82
Father Christmas (*see* Santa Claus)
fault lines 50, 51, 155
Favaloro, Cosimo 16, 17
Fechner, G.T. 95
feng shui 82, 86
Finland 52
flight (*see* magical flight; out-of-body
      state)
Fly Agaric 48, 58, 59, 75, 84
flying buck 73-75, 93
flying ointments 74, 75
Forbidden City 79
Fox, George 50

Gothic Image Publications is a Glastonbury-based imprint dedicated to publishing books and pamphlets that offer a new and radical approach to our perception of the world in which we live.

As ideas about the nature of life change, we aim to make available those new perspectives which clarify our understanding of ourselves and the Earth we share.

Current publications include:

Devas, Fairies and Angels: A Modern Approach
William Bloom

Dowsing the Crop Circles
Edited by John Michell

Dragons: Their History and Symbolism
Janet Hoult

Eclipse of the Sun: An Investigation into Sun and Moon Myths
Janet Crickard

Euphonics: A Poet's Dictionary of Sounds
John Michell

The Glastonbury Festivals
Lynne Elstob and Anne Howe

Glastonbury: Maker of Myths
Frances Howard-Gordon

The Glastonbury Tor Maze
Geoffrey Ashe

The Green Lady and the King of Shadows
Moyra Caldecott

Hargreaves' New Illustrated Bestiary
Joyce Hargreaves

Meditation in a Changing World
William Bloom

Needles of Stone Revisited
Tom Graves

New Light on the Ancient Mystery of Glastonbury
John Michell

The Sacred Magician
William Bloom

Spiritual Dowsing
Sig Lonegren

Gothic Image Publications are available from all good bookshops or direct from:
Gothic Image Publications
7 High Street
Glastonbury
Somerset BA6 9DP
Telephone 0458 831453
Fax 0458 831666